I0439020

Groundwater Resources of the East Mountain Area, Bernalillo, Sandoval, Santa Fe, and Torrance Counties, New Mexico, 2005

By James R. Bartolino, Scott K. Anderholm, and Nathan C. Myers

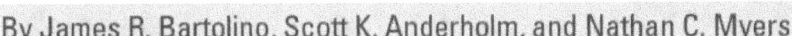

Prepared in cooperation with the New Mexico Office of the State Engineer

Scientific Investigations Report 2009–5204
Revised April 2011

U.S. Department of the Interior
U.S. Geological Survey

U.S. Department of the Interior
KEN SALAZAR, Secretary

U.S. Geological Survey
Marcia K. McNutt, Director

U.S. Geological Survey, Reston, Virginia: 2010

This and other USGS information products are available at http://store.usgs.gov/
U.S. Geological Survey
Box 25286, Denver Federal Center
Denver, CO 80225

To learn about the USGS and its information products visit http://www.usgs.gov/
1-888-ASK-USGS

Suggested citation:
Bartolino, J.R., Anderholm, S.K., and Myers, N.C., 2010, Groundwater resources of the
East Mountain area, Bernalillo, Sandoval, Santa Fe, and Torrance Counties, New Mexico, 2005:
U.S. Geological Survey Scientific Investigations Report 2009–5204, 88 p. (Revised April 2011)

Contents

Abstract 1

Introduction 2

    Purpose and Scope 2

    Location of Study Area 2

    Previous Studies 2

    Methods of Study 7

    Acknowledgments 10

Hydrologic Setting 10

    Climate 10

    Surface Water 12

    Hydrogeology 13

        Structural Features 13

            Sandia, Manzanita, and Manzano Mountains 13

            Estancia Basin 15

            The Barton Trough and Edgewood Embayment 15

            Española Basin 15

            San Pedro Synclinorium 15

            La Bajada and San Francisco Faults 15

            Hagan Structural Basin 15

            Tijeras Fault System 15

            Frost Fault Block-Monte Largo Horst-Tijeras Graben 15

            The Ortiz Porphyry Belt 16

Groundwater Resources 16

    Geologic Units and Water-Bearing Characteristics 16

        Precambrian Rocks 16

        Pennsylvanian Sandia and Madera Formations 17

            Potential Sources of Alkalinity and Dissolved Carbon 26

        Permian Abo and Yeso Formations 26

        Permian Glorieta and San Andres Formations 28

        Triassic Moenkopi Formation and Chinle Group 30

        Jurassic Entrada Sandstone, Wanakah Formation, and Morrison Formation 32

        Cretaceous Dakota Sandstone, Mancos Shale, and Mesaverde Group 34

        Cenozoic Geologic Units 38

    Groundwater Levels, Recharge, and Flow 39

        Recharge 41

        Volumetric Precipitation Estimates 42

        Deuterium and Oxygen-18 Ratios in Groundwater 42

Groundwater Areas...44
    Tijeras Canyon Groundwater Area 49
    Cedar Crest Groundwater Area..49
    Tijeras Graben Groundwater Area..51
    Estancia Basin Groundwater Area..52
    San Pedro Creek Groundwater Area..54
        Source of Water to San Pedro Creek...56
    Ortiz Porphyry Belt Groundwater Area 57
    Hagan Basin Groundwater Area 61
    Upper Sandia Mountains Groundwater Area 62
Effects of Development on Water Resources...62
    Water-Quantity Effects...62
    Water-Quality Effects...63
    Temporal Water-Level and Water-Quality Variations 64
Summary..67
Selected References..69
Appendix 1. Description of Map Units..82
Appendix 2. Selected Data for Wells and Springs in and Adjacent to
    the East Mountain Study Area [click here]...87
Appendix 3. Selected Groundwater-Quality Data for Wells and Springs
    in the East Mountain Study Area [click here]......................................88

Plate

[Click here]

Geohydrologic map of the East Mountain study area, central New Mexico.

Figures

1. Location of the East Mountain study area 3
2. Location of cities, towns, precipitation stations, Declared
   Underground Water Basins, and physiographic features in the East
   Mountain study area...4
3. Location of wells permitted by the New Mexico Office of the State
   Engineer..5
4. Names of U.S. Geological Survey 7.5-minute topographic quadrangle
   maps in the East Mountain study area and references for corresponding
   geologic maps...6

5. Example of a Piper diagram..9

6. Mean monthly precipitation at selected National Weather Service
   stations in or near the East Mountain study area...12

7. Palmer Drought Severity Index through 2005 for New Mexico Climate
   Division 6..13

8. Major structural features in the East Mountain study area..............................14

9. Piper diagram showing composition of water from the Precambrian
   hydrostratigraphic unit in the East Mountain study area..................................18

10. Map showing dissolved chloride concentration in groundwater and
    springs in the East Mountain study area...19

11. Map showing nitrate concentration in groundwater and springs in
    the East Mountain study area..20

12. Piper diagram showing composition of water from the Madera-Sandia
    hydrostratigraphic unit in the East Mountain study area..................................22

13. Map showing dissolved sulfate concentration in groundwater and
    springs in the East Mountain study area...23

14. Map showing pH of groundwater and springs in the East Mountain
    study area..24

15. Map showing dissolved fluoride concentration in groundwater and
    springs in the East Mountain study area...25

16. Piper diagram showing composition of water from the Abo-Yeso
    hydrostratigraphic unit in the East Mountain study area..................................28

17. Piper diagram showing composition of water from the San
    Andres-Glorieta hydrostratigraphic unit in the East Mountain study area......30

18. Piper diagram showing composition of water from the Chinle-Moenkopi
    hydrostratigraphic unit in the East Mountain study area..................................32

19. Piper diagram showing composition of water from the Jurassic
    hydrostratigraphic unit in the East Mountain study area..................................34

20. Map showing dissolved-solids concentration in groundwater and
    springs in the East Mountain study area...36

21. Piper diagram showing composition of water from the Cretaceous
    hydrostratigraphic unit in the East Mountain study area..................................37

22. Piper diagram showing composition of water from the Quaternary
    alluvium in the East Mountain study area...40

23. Selected watersheds used to estimate precipitation volumes in or
    near the East Mountain study area...43

24. Delta deuterium composition of groundwater and springs in the
    East Mountain study area..45

25. Graph showing relation between deuterium and oxygen-18
    composition in water from selected wells and springs in the
    East Mountain study area..46

26. Map of groundwater areas and selected wells with continuous
    groundwater-level or water-quality data..47

27. Water levels for selected wells in the Tijeras Canyon groundwater
area (350602106210401 and 350655106185601) 50
28. Water levels for a selected well in the Cedar Crest groundwater
area (350721106222101) 51
29. Water levels for selected wells in the Tijeras Graben groundwater
area (350531106224301, 350655106194501, and 350949106184501) 53
30. Water levels for a selected well in the Estancia Basin groundwater
area (350525106151701) 54
31. Water levels for selected wells in the San Pedro Creek groundwater
area (350930106210701, 350949106211801, 351011106220401, and 351014106202801) 55
32. Geohydrologic map of the San Pedro Creek area 58
33. Geohydrologic section of the San Pedro Creek area 60
34. Selected measurements of specific conductance and discharge
along San Pedro Creek between San Pedro Spring and Cottonwood Spring 61
35. Graph showing relation between nitrate concentration and dissolved
chloride concentration in water from selected wells in the East Mountain
study area 65
36. Graph showing seasonal variation in dissolved chloride concentration
in water from selected wells in the East Mountain study area 66
37. Graph showing seasonal variation in nitrate concentration in water
from selected wells in the East Mountain study area 66

Tables

1. U.S. Environmental Protection Agency drinking-water standards
for selected constituents 10
2. National Weather Service stations in or near the East
Mountain study area 11
3. Stratigraphic/geologic and hydrostratigraphic units of the East
Mountain study area 16
4. Statistical summary of selected water-quality data for water from
the Madera-Sandia hydrostratigraphic unit in the East Mountain
study area 21
5. Statistical summary of selected water-quality data for water from
the Abo-Yeso hydrostratigraphic unit in the East Mountain study area 27
6. Statistical summary of selected water-quality data for water from
the San Andres-Glorieta hydrostratigraphic unit in the East
Mountain study area 29
7. Statistical summary of selected water-quality data for water from
the Chinle-Moenkopi hydrostratigraphic unit in the East Mountain
study area 31
8. Statistical summary of selected water-quality data for water from
the Jurassic hydrostratigraphic unit in the East Mountain study area 33

9. Statistical summary of selected water-quality data for water from the Cretaceous hydrostratigraphic unit in the East Mountain study area 35

10. Statistical summary of selected water-quality data for water from the Quaternary alluvium in the East Mountain study area...39

11. Mean annual precipitation volumes (1961–90) for selected watersheds in or near the East Mountain study area...44

12. Summary of East Mountain groundwater areas and generalized defining characteristics 48

Conversion Factors and Datums

Multiply	By	To obtain
Length		
inch	2.54	centimeter (cm)
inch	25.4	millimeter (mm)
foot (ft)	0.3048	meter (m)
mile (mi)	1.609	kilometer (km)
Area		
acre	0.4047	hectare (ha)
square foot (ft^2)	0.09290	square meter (m^2)
square inch	6.452	square centimeter (cm^2)
square mile (mi^2)	2.590	square kilometer (km^2)
Volume		
gallon (gal)	3.785	liter (L)
cubic inch	16.39	cubic centimeter (cm^3)
cubic foot (ft^3)	0.02832	cubic meter (m^3)
acre-foot (acre-ft)	1,233	cubic meter (m^3)
Flow rate		
acre-foot per year (acre-ft/yr)	1,233	cubic meter per year (m^3/yr)
cubic foot per second (ft^3/s)	0.02832	cubic meter per second (m^3/s)
gallon per minute (gal/min)	0.06309	liter per second (L/s)
Mass		
ounce, avoirdupois (oz)	28.35	gram (g)
pound, avoirdupois (lb)	0.4536	kilogram (kg)
Specific capacity		
gallon per minute per foot [(gal/min)/ft)]	0.2070	liter per second per meter [(L/s)/m]
Hydraulic conductivity		
foot per day (ft/d)	0.3048	meter per day (m/d)
Hydraulic gradient		
foot per mile (ft/mi)	0.1894	meter per kilometer (m/km)
Transmissivity*		
foot squared per day (ft^2/d)	0.09290	meter squared per day (m^2/d)

Temperature in degrees Celsius (°C) may be converted to degrees Fahrenheit (°F) as follows:

$$°F=(1.8×°C)+32$$

Temperature in degrees Fahrenheit (°F) may be converted to degrees Celsius (°C) as follows:

$$°C=(°F-32)/1.8$$

Vertical coordinate information is referenced to the North American Vertical Datum of 1929 (NAVD 29).

Horizontal coordinate information is referenced to the North American Datum of 1927 (NAD 27) or 1983 (NAD 83) as indicated.

Altitude, as used in this report, refers to distance above the vertical datum.

*Transmissivity: The standard unit for transmissivity is cubic foot per day per square foot times foot of aquifer thickness $[(ft^3/d)/ft^2]ft$. In this report, the mathematically reduced form, foot squared per day (ft^2/d), is used for convenience.

Specific conductance is given in microsiemens per centimeter at 25 degrees Celsius (µS/cm at 25 °C).

Concentrations of chemical constituents in water are given either in milligrams per liter (mg/L) or micrograms per liter (µg/L).

Groundwater Resources of the East Mountain Area, Bernalillo, Sandoval, Santa Fe, and Torrance Counties, New Mexico, 2005

By James R. Bartolino, Scott K. Anderholm, and Nathan C. Myers

Abstract

The groundwater resources of about 400 square miles of the East Mountain area of Bernalillo, Sandoval, Santa Fe, and Torrance Counties in central New Mexico were evaluated by using groundwater levels and water-quality analyses, and updated geologic mapping. Substantial development in the study area (population increased by 11,000, or 50 percent, from 1990 through 2000) has raised concerns about the effects of growth on water resources. The last comprehensive examination of the water resources of the study area was done in 1980—this study examines a slightly different area and incorporates data collected in the intervening 25 years.

The East Mountain area is geologically and hydrologically complex–in addition to the geologic units, such features as the Sandia Mountains, Tijeras and Gutierrez Faults, Tijeras Graben, and the Estancia Basin affect the movement, availability, and water quality of the groundwater system.

The stratigraphic units were separated into eight hydrostratigraphic units, each having distinct hydraulic and chemical properties. Overall, the major hydrostratigraphic units are the Madera-Sandia and Abo-Yeso; however, other units are the primary source of supply in some areas.

Despite the eight previously defined hydrostratigraphic units, water-level contours were drawn on the generalized regional potentiometric map assuming all hydrostratigraphic units are connected and function as a single aquifer system. Groundwater originates as infiltration of precipitation in upland areas (Sandia, Manzano, and Manzanita Mountains, and the Ortiz Porphyry Belt) and moves downgradient into the Tijeras Graben, Tijeras Canyon, San Pedro synclinorium, and the Hagan, Estancia, and Española Basins.

The study area was divided into eight groundwater areas defined on the basis of geologic, hydrologic, and geochemical information-Tijeras Canyon, Cedar Crest, Tijeras Graben, Estancia Basin, San Pedro Creek, Ortiz Porphyry Belt, Hagan Basin, and Upper Sandia Mountains.

The source of water to springs discharging to San Pedro Creek was examined. The source of water to San Pedro Spring could be discharge from Quaternary alluvium or the Abo-Yeso or San Andres-Glorieta hydrostratigraphic units. Water at Rock Spring could be discharging from the Madera-Sandia or Abo-Yeso hydrostratigraphic units, or possibly both. The most probable source of water to Cottonwood Spring is groundwater flow in the alluvium forced to the surface by a buried constriction of consolidated rock or downdip/downgradient flow in the Abo-Yeso hydrostratigraphic unit west of the creek that discharges at the buried contact with alluvium in and near the channel. San Pedro Creek is one of two streams in the area with perennial reaches; thus, the source of water to springs that discharge to the creek and whether development can affect these flows are of concern. Streamflow and specific conductance of the water in San Pedro Creek vary downstream from San Pedro Spring in response to groundwater inflow and leakage from the stream.

Development and groundwater withdrawals in the area could affect the groundwater-flow system and water quality because groundwater withdrawals upset the natural equilibrium of the flow system and because infiltration and recharge of onsite wastewater has elevated concentrations of sodium, chloride, and nitrate relative to supply water. Annual water use in the East Mountain area was estimated to be 2,950 acre-feet in 2000 and consumptive use was estimated to be 1,475 acre-feet. Consumptive use of groundwater could affect the groundwater-flow system because this water is removed from the area as the result of evaporation and transpiration. Short-term water-level variations in some wells indicate water levels decrease during the summer months and increase in the winter months probably in response to varying seasonal pumping rates. Nitrate concentrations less than the assumed background of 2 milligrams per liter are found in many parts of the East Mountains area. Nitrate concentrations greater than 2 milligrams per liter are generally found along the major roads that had initial development and where home density is generally largest.

Long-term trends in water quality are difficult to determine in the area. The apparent lack of large, widespread, long-term increases in chloride and nitrate concentrations in water from wells in the area may be due to the length of time it takes for water from onsite wastewater systems to move to deeper parts of the aquifer where many wells are completed. Because groundwater quality at the water table would be affected by the composition of recharge from onsite wastewater-disposal systems initially, such effects may not have reached deeper parts of the aquifer where many wells are completed. The degree to which water mixes in the aquifer and the time it takes for water to move from the water table or point of recharge downward to well screens or pump intakes is unknown.

Introduction

The East Mountain area refers to an area east of Albuquerque, New Mexico, on the eastern slopes of the Sandia, Manzanita, and northern Manzano Mountains, and encompasses parts of Bernalillo, Sandoval, Santa Fe, and Torrance Counties (figs. 1 and 2). The area includes parts of the Sandia, Estancia, and Rio Grande Declared Underground Water Basins, in which appropriation and use of groundwater are under the jurisdiction of the New Mexico Office of the State Engineer (NMOSE). (In this report the area of Estancia Basin is taken as mostly that of the Estancia Declared Underground Water Basin.) As first characterized by Titus (1980), the East Mountain area is composed of several hydrogeologic areas, distinctive in subsurface geology, groundwater flow, and often, water quality. Water-bearing geologic units in the East Mountain area consist of limestone, sandstone, siltstone, and unconsolidated alluvium. Folding and faulting of these water-bearing units exists in some areas. In addition, highly varied water availability conditions, variable storage, fractured flow, and aquifer compartmentalization contribute to the complexity of the hydrogeology of the study area.

Recently, population has increased in the East Mountain area, particularly in the northwestern and eastern parts of the area, and more development is planned. Population in the study area at the 2000 census was about 33,000 people in 12,000 households; in 1990 22,000 people were in 8,000 households (U.S. Census Bureau, 2005). The population has continued to grow rapidly since the 2000 census. The locations of wells permitted by the NMOSE are shown in figure 3. The density of permitted wells varies throughout the East Mountain study area because of the variation in development and lot size, wells installed prior to declaration of the underground water basin by the NMOSE are not included, some permitted wells are not shown because of inaccurate location, and many areas of development are serviced by community water systems. With many new and planned residential developments, the growth trend is expected to continue and has raised questions about the sustainability of groundwater resources and possible effects on surface-water flows. Concerns about the availability and sustainability of groundwater resources, and possible effects of development on groundwater quality by residents and New Mexico State legislators resulted in a cooperative study by NMOSE and the U.S. Geological Survey (USGS). This report was prepared in cooperation with the NMOSE.

Purpose and Scope

This report documents current (2005) groundwater resources, water quality and composition, and trends in conditions in the East Mountain study area, and updates interpretations of hydrogeologic controls on groundwater flow. The geology and hydrogeology are described, including structural features and geologic units and the water-bearing characteristics, groundwater areas and movement, and effects of development on water resources. Existing data for the study area were compiled and are presented. Additional data collection activities during this investigation were focused on areas where few data existed or in newly developed areas. The well and spring data and the water-quality data are presented in appendixes 2 and 3 at the end of the report. Water-level contours are shown on a simplified geologic map (Williams and Cole, 2007) of the study area (plate).

Location of Study Area

The East Mountain study is about 400 square miles (mi^2) and lies in parts of Bernalillo, Sandoval, Santa Fe, and Torrance Counties in central New Mexico (fig. 1). The study area boundaries were selected to include surface-water drainages from the eastern Sandia Mountains, South Mountain, and the San Pedro Mountains, which are thought to be areas of groundwater recharge. The study area includes parts of the following USGS 7.5-minute quadrangles (1:24,000-scale): Placitas, Hagan, Golden, Sandia Crest, Sandia Park, San Pedro, Tijeras, Sedillo, and Edgewood (fig. 4).

Previous Studies

The study areas of previous hydrogeologic reports overlap parts of this study area. Though the geology was first described by Jules Marcou (a member of Lieutenant A.W. Whipple's 35th Parallel expedition) in 1853, the first hydrogeologic investigation was by Meinzer (1910 and 1911). Meinzer's groundwater study in the Estancia Valley, done in response to a drought, investigated the feasibility of using groundwater for irrigation and included the first depth-to-water map of the area. Much of the Estancia Valley was later included in Smith's (1957) report on the groundwater resources of Torrance County. Smith described the hydrogeologic framework of this area and included a water-level map and water-quality data. Kelley and Northrop (1975) did not address groundwater but mapped the area and presented the geologic framework of the East Mountain area. Titus (1980) made the first comprehensive study of the water resources of the East Mountain area; his report included a water-level map and water-quality data. In response to growth and resulting concerns about water availability and quality in the East Mountain area, Kues (1990) did a detailed study of three sites in eastern Bernalillo County as analogues to the entire area. White (1994, p. 2) studied the water resources

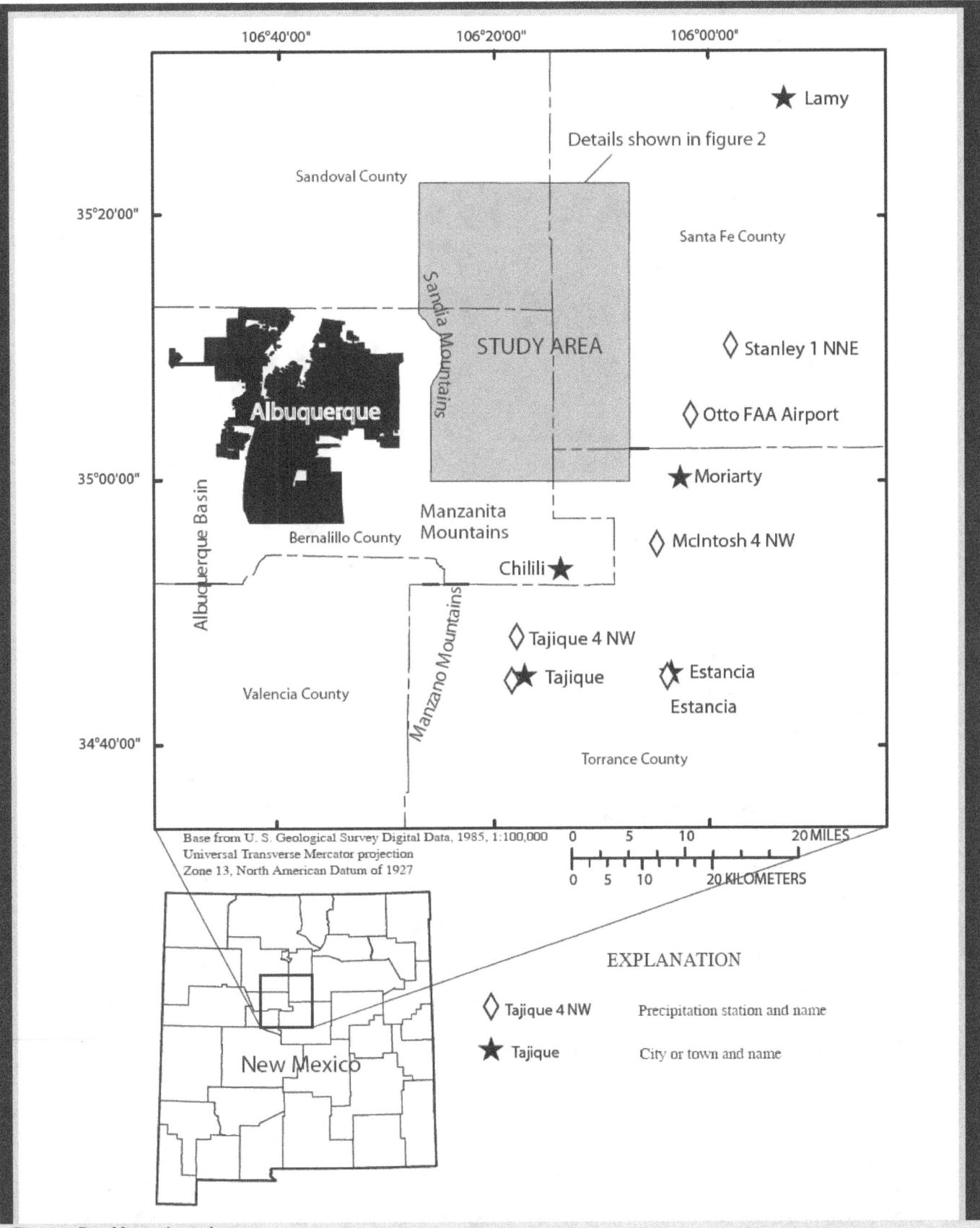

106°40'00"   106°20'00"   106°00'00"

★ Lamy

Details shown in figure 2

Sandoval County

Santa Fe County

35°20'00"

STUDY AREA

◇ Stanley 1 NNE

Sandia Mountains

◇ Otto FAA Airport

Albuquerque

★ Moriarty

35°00'00"

Albuquerque Basin

Manzanita Mountains

Bernalillo County

◇ McIntosh 4 NW

Chilili ★

◇ Tajique 4 NW

Manzano Mountains

◇★ Tajique

✦★ Estancia

Estancia

Valencia County

34°40'00"

Torrance County

Base from U. S. Geological Survey Digital Data, 1985, 1:100,000
Universal Transverse Mercator projection
Zone 13, North American Datum of 1927

0   5   10   20 MILES

0   5   10   20 KILOMETERS

New Mexico

EXPLANATION

◇ Tajique 4 NW   Precipitation station and name

★ Tajique   City or town and name

Figure 1. East Mountain study area.

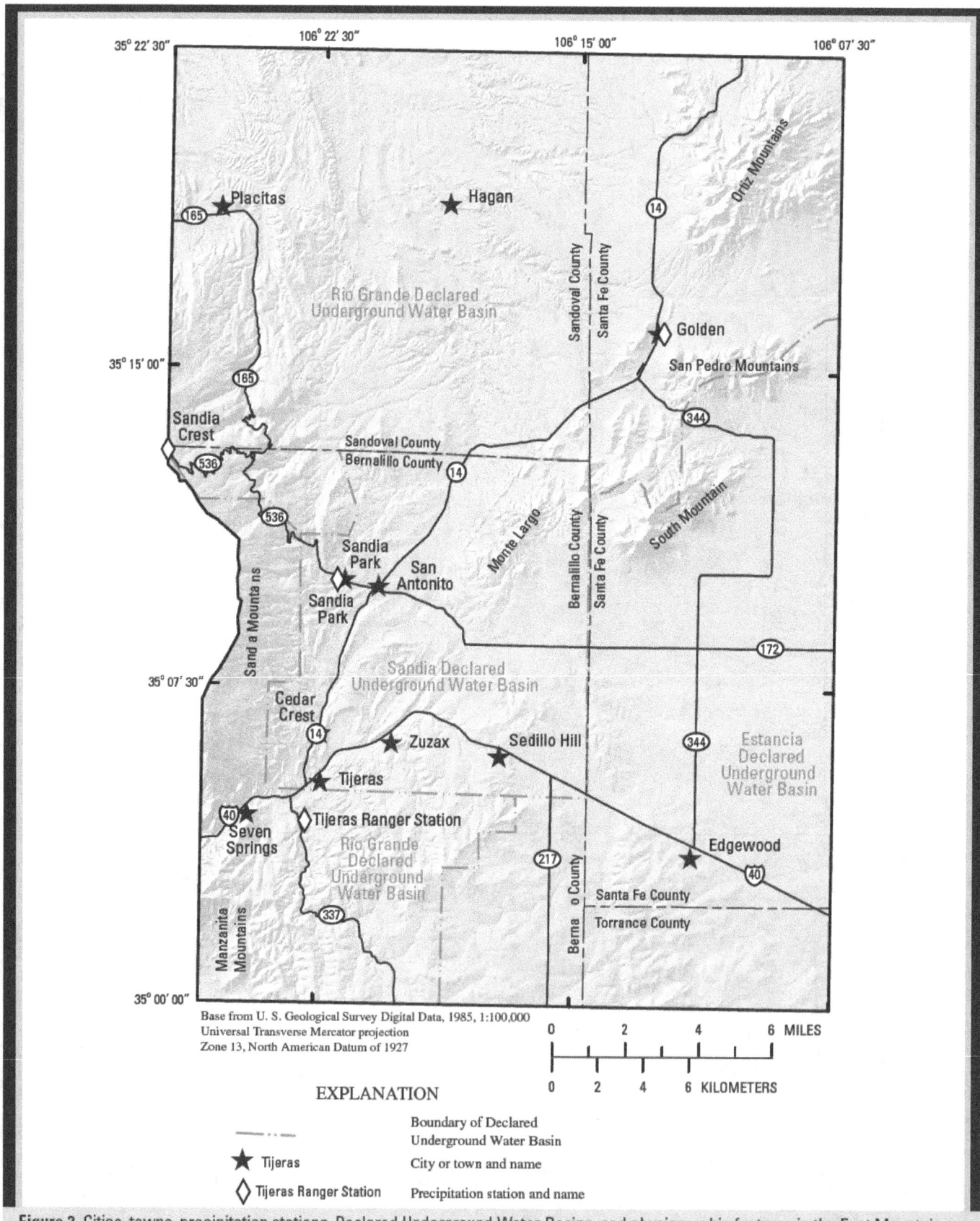

Figure 2. Cities, towns, precipitation stations, Declared Underground Water Basins, and physiographic features in the East Mountain study area.

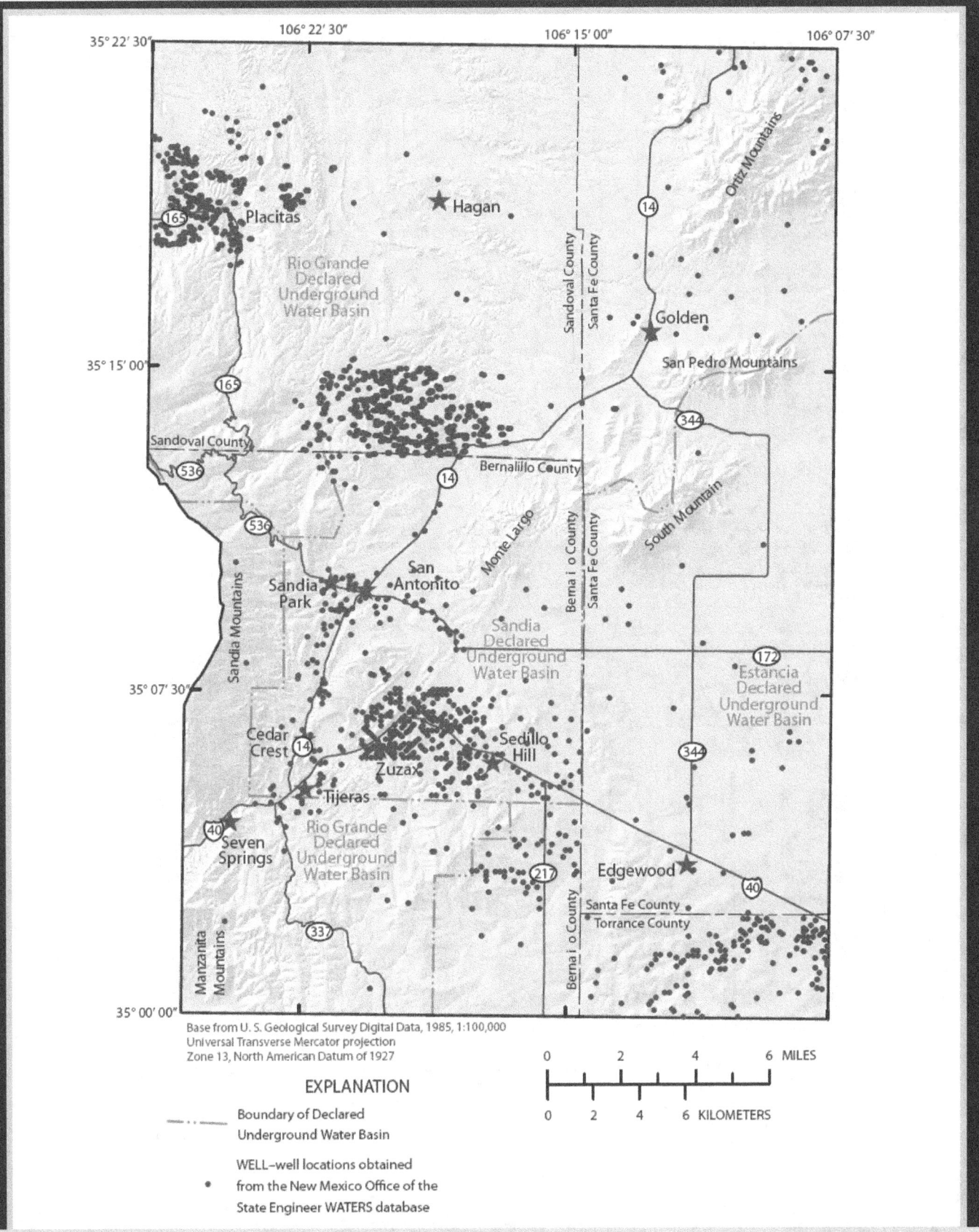

EXPLANATION

— ·· —   Boundary of Declared
          Underground Water Basin

          WELL–well locations obtained
•   from the New Mexico Office of the
          State Engineer WATERS database

Figure 3. Wells permitted by the New Mexico Office of the State Engineer.

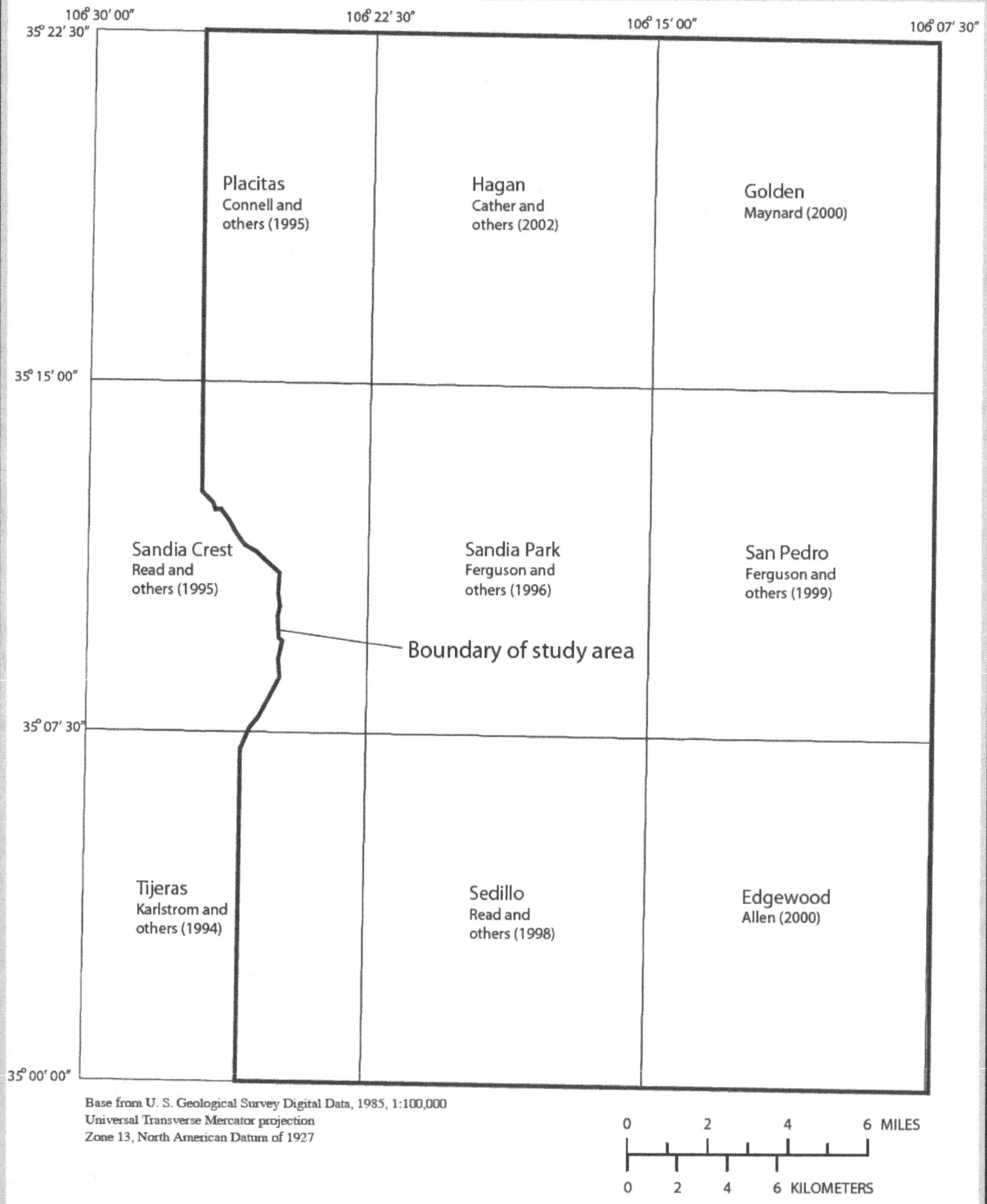

Figure 4. U.S. Geological Survey 7.5-minute topographic quadrangle maps (1:24,000-scale) in study area and references for corresponding geologic maps.

of the Estancia Basin with "an emphasis on groundwater conditions in irrigated areas." Kues and Garcia (1995), Rankin (1996), Rankin (2000), and Blanchard (2003) presented water-level and water-quality data collected in the East Mountain area. Blanchard and Kues (1999) discussed the hydrogeology and groundwater quality of the East Mountain area and susceptibility of groundwater to contamination by wastewater disposal. Rankin (1999) summarized hydrogeologic characteristics of the Madera Limestone and proposed a study plan to better characterize the aquifer. Johnson (2000) studied the geology and groundwater and surface-water resources of the Placitas development area. Blanchard (2004) discussed groundwater dating and changes in water levels and water quality in the East Mountain area. The New Mexico Bureau of Geology and Mineral Resources (NMGMR) prepared geologic maps of the nine 7.5-minute quadrangles of the study area shown in figure 4. These maps and other maps were simplified and compiled into a single 1:100,000 scale geologic map by Williams and Cole (2007). The East Mountain part of this map that includes the study area serves as the basis for much of the discussion of the geologic units and geologic structure of the area (plate).

Several consultants' reports also have addressed localized parts of the study area. These reports address available water supply typically related to a development request. The reports commonly contain information about groundwater levels, water quality, aquifer tests, and predicted groundwater development effects. Examples are Newcomer and Peery (1994) and Balleau Groundwater, Inc. (2000). Many other such reports were obtained from the NMOSE and are listed in the References section, though not cited in this report. Most of the aquifer-property data (aquifer-test results) presented in this report were compiled from consultant reports.

The New Mexico Legislature in 1987 passed legislation implementing a regional water-planning process. This program is administered by the New Mexico Interstate Stream Commission who divided the state into 16 water-planning regions. The plan for each region must document available supplies, project demand, and plan for future supplies. The East Mountain area falls into three of these water-planning regions: the Estancia Basin, Jemez y Sangre, and Middle Rio Grande regions. Of these plans, the Estancia Basin plan is most relevant to the East Mountain area because that plan addresses hydrologic conditions in the Madera Formation (Estancia Basin Planning Committee, 1999). The Jemez y Sangre plan concentrates on groundwater in the Santa Fe Group aquifer system. Whereas the Jemez y Sangre plan mentions the Galisteo Formation as a water-bearing unit in the Galisteo Creek drainage, the plan notes that data are sparse in this area, which limits further discussion (D.B. Stephens and Associates, 2003). The Middle Rio Grande plan emphasizes the Santa Fe Group aquifer system in the Albuquerque Basin; however, that plan incorporates Johnson's (2000) previously noted study of the water resources of the Placitas development area (Middle Rio Grande Water Assembly, 2004). Finally, though not part of the regional water-planning process, the East Mountain Area plan (Bernalillo County, 2006) described historical and existing physical and environmental conditions for the 321 mi^2 of easternmost Bernalillo County.

Methods of Study

Wells were located and recorded and groundwater levels measured in accordance with procedures described in USGS Office of Ground Water Technical Procedure Documents (U.S. Geological Survey, variously dated). Many of the wells visited by earlier investigators did not have a geologic unit assigned for the well completion. The geologic unit was determined on the basis of geologic maps (Michael Timmons, New Mexico Bureau of Geology, written commun., 2005) and available well information for this study. Wells were assigned a primary geologic unit in geologically complex areas that included several geologic formations, particularly in areas where Cretaceous and Jurassic rocks crop out at land surface. An effort was made to obtain well permits on file at the NMOSE for all wells used in this report; however, matching well permits to many of the wells included in this report was not possible because of ownership changes since the well was installed, because locations obtained from the NMOSE well permits did not match the locations determined in the field, or because of errors in extending the public land-survey system onto land grants. Determining the geologic unit for all wells was not always possible.

The public land-survey system does not include land grants and cannot be uniformly extended across the grants, so well identification in this report is by the 15-digit USGS site identification number as used in the USGS National Water Information System (NWIS). This number is based on the latitude and longitude of the well when originally inventoried; however, the site number may not reflect the most accurate location as determined by subsequent site visits, improved maps, or the advent of handheld global positioning system units. To prevent confusion, the site identification number is not changed as the location information improves, only the separate latitude and longitude fields in NWIS are updated. Thus the site identification number may not contain the most accurate location.

Transmissivities from aquifer tests reported in the literature, including consultants' reports, are given in this report. Reported transmissivities from these various sources may include multiple analyses of a single test, multiple tests of the same well, or averaged values for multiple wells. Coupled with occasional poor or changing well identification, well modification, rounding errors, and use of previously cited values, which values may apply to the same well is unclear. For this reason only ranges of transmissivity are cited for an approximate number of wells.

Inventory and documentation of wells that went dry or new wells that were drilled and did not contain water (dry holes) was attempted during this study with slight success. The files of the NMOSE were checked for applications for replacement of wells that had gone dry or locations of dry holes. Most homeowners seem to apply for a new well permit instead of a replacement well permit when a well goes dry because so few replacement well permits were in the files. Records of dry holes also were not evident in the files. An advertisement in the local East Mountain newspaper was placed requesting home owners to contact the USGS if their well had gone dry. Two individuals contacted the USGS indicating their wells had gone dry. Thus there is no discussion in this report of areas where wells have recently gone dry because the necessary information could not be obtained.

Water-quality samples collected for the study were collected, processed, measured for field propterties according to procedures described in the USGS National Field Manual for the Collection of Water-Quality Data (U.S. Geological Survey, variously dated), and analyzed for major cations, anions, nutrients, and trace elements. An equipment blank was collected during the water-quality sampling; all constituents were less than the detection limits, which indicated that sampling equipment and methods did not result in the introduction of constituents to the samples collected. Samples were analyzed by the USGS National Water-Quality Laboratory in Lakewood, Colorado (*http://nwql.usgs.gov/*).

Piper diagrams are used to show water composition in various aquifers, and are useful for examining differences in water quality of many samples. A water analysis is represented by three points on a Piper diagram, one point in each of two triangular diagrams and a point in a diamond-shaped field (fig. 5). The lower left triangle represents the composition of cations (calcium, sodium plus potassium, and magnesium) in the sample, the lower right triangle represents the composition of anions (chloride plus fluoride, bicarbonate plus carbonate, and sulfate) in the sample, and the diamond represents the overall composition of the sample. The point in the diamond-shaped field is the intersection of the rays projected from the points in the two triangles. The percentage of an individual cation is computed from the milliequivalent concentration of the ion divided by the sum of the individual cation milliequivalent concentrations. Percentages of individual anions are computed from the milliequivalent concentration of the ion divided by the sum of the individual anion milliequivalent concentrations. Two samples with a similar distribution of ions can plot at the same point on a diagram; however, the actual concentrations of ions can be much different for the two samples because the concentrations are normalized or plotted as percentages of the total cations or anions.

Occasionally, more than one sample (chemical analysis) was collected from a particular well. When more than one sample was collected from a well, data presented on the Piper diagrams, in summary statistics, and on the areal plots represent the most recent sample with an electrical balance of 10 percent or less. When only one sample was collected from a well and the absolute value of the electrical balance was greater than 10 percent, data were not plotted on the Piper diagram but were used to calculate summary statistics and shown on the areal plots. Electrical balance was computed by subtracting the sum of milliequivalents of cations from the sum of milliequivalents of anions and dividing by the average of the sum of milliequivalents of cations and anions.

Samples were analyzed for different constituents depending on the purpose for which the water samples were collected. Alkalinity and nitrate concentrations in many samples are listed under several constituent codes. To allow use of as many samples as possible on the Piper diagrams, summary statistics, and areal plots, representative alkalinity, dissolved-solids, nitrate, ammonia, and orthophosphate concentrations were determined for each sample. Alkalinity, for example, was determined in the field for filtered and unfiltered samples by the Gran (Gran, 1950 and 1952), incremental titration, or fixed endpoint techniques and in the lab by the fixed endpoint technique. A representative alkalinity was selected from the available values for each sample, on the basis of the following order of preference (first value is most preferred)—field alkalinity unfiltered sample, field alkalinity unfiltered sample incremental technique, field alkalinity unfiltered fixed endpoint technique, field alkalinity filtered sample incremental technique, and lab alkalinity fixed endpoint technique. In the second author's experience there is little difference in the alkalinity on filtered and unfiltered groundwater samples. Dissolved-solids concentrations were determined by using residue-on-evaporation values, if available; otherwise, the value derived from the sum of constituents was used. A representative nitrate concentration was determined by using the following order of preference—nitrite plus nitrate filtered sample, nitrite plus nitrate unfiltered sample, and nitrate filtered sample. In most cases, the nitrite concentration was less than 5 percent of the nitrite plus nitrate concentration. Representative ammonia concentrations were determined by using the concentrations in filtered samples first and concentrations in unfiltered samples if filtered ammonia concentrations were not measured. Representative concentrations of orthophosphate were determined by using orthophosphate concentrations in filtered samples first and phosphorous concentrations in unfiltered samples if filtered orthophosphate concentrations were not measured.

The U.S. Environmental Protection Agency (USEPA) has established standards for public drinking water (U.S. Environmental Protection Agency, 2005). Maximum contaminant levels (MCL) are enforceable drinking-water standards that are health based. Secondary maximum contaminant levels (SMCL) are nonenforceable drinking-water standards based on aesthetic factors such as taste or smell but do not affect the health of individuals consuming the water. These standards were used to evaluate water quality in the study area. Selected constituents and relevant standards discussed in this report are listed in table 1.

Determining the concentrations of ions in groundwater in the area prior to any human effects (background concentrations) is difficult because the extent of human effect on water quality in the study area is not known. Sodium, chloride, and nitrate concentrations are elevated in wastewater discharging from homes relative to supply water (Cantor and Knox, 1985). These constituents also are found at elevated concentrations in the soil zone in parts of the arid west as the result of evaporation and transpiration of precipitation in the soil zone (Walvoord and others, 2003). Background ion

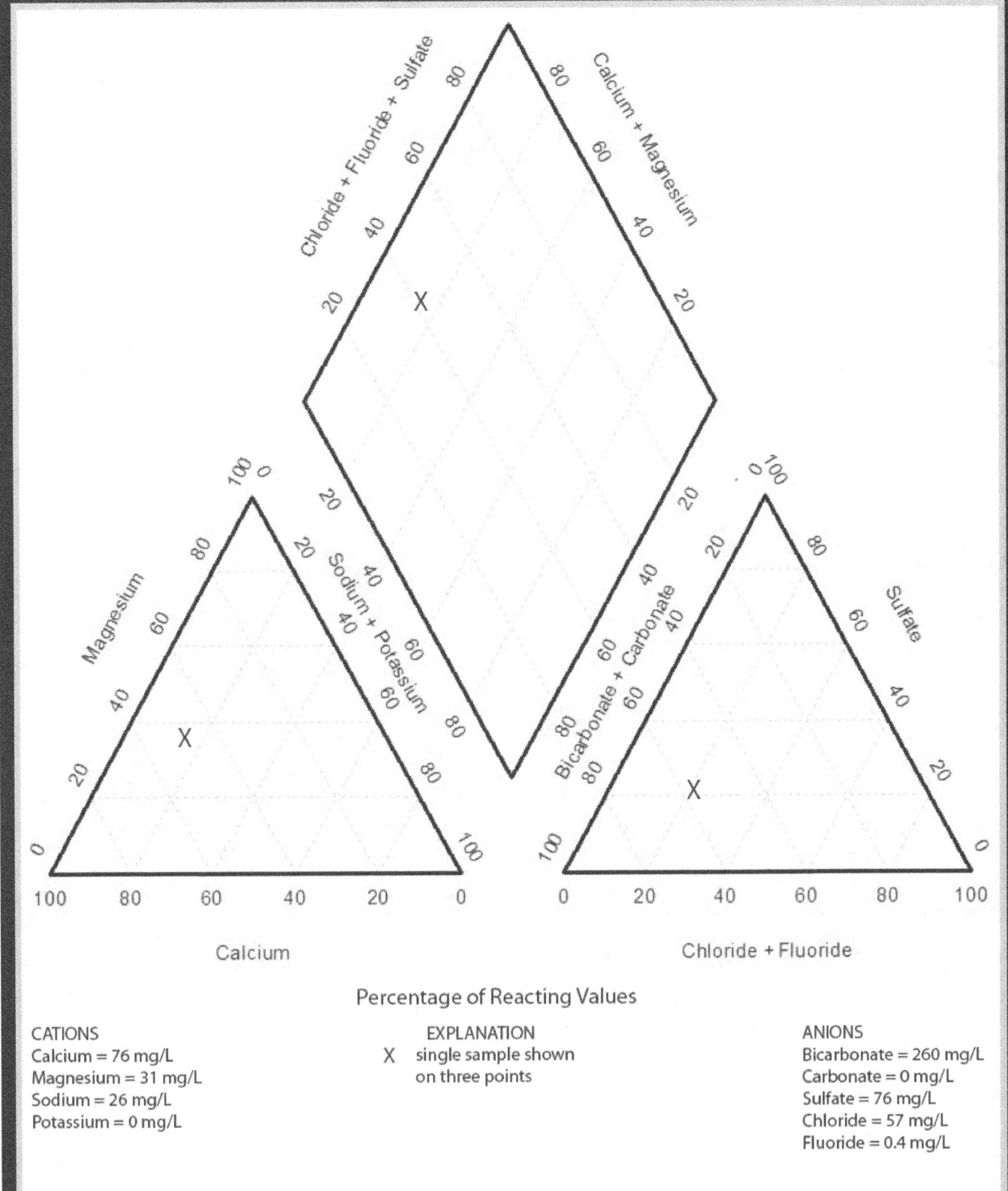

Percentage of Reacting Values

CATIONS
Calcium = 76 mg/L
Magnesium = 31 mg/L
Sodium = 26 mg/L
Potassium = 0 mg/L

EXPLANATION
X   single sample shown
     on three points

ANIONS
Bicarbonate = 260 mg/L
Carbonate = 0 mg/L
Sulfate = 76 mg/L
Chloride = 57 mg/L
Fluoride = 0.4 mg/L

Figure 5. Example of a Piper diagram.

Table 1. U.S. Environmental Protection Agency drinking-water standards for selected constituents.

[(U.S. Environmental Protection Agency, 2005); MCL, Maximum contaminant level; SMCL, Secondary maximum contaminant level; —, not applicable; mg/L, milligrams per liter; µg/L, micrograms per liter]

Constituent	MCL	SMCL
pH	—	6.5-8.5 pH units
Chloride	—	250 mg/L
Fluoride	4.0 mg/L	2.0 mg/L
Sulfate	—	250 mg/L
Total dissolved solids	—	500 mg/L
Nitrate	10 mg/L	—
Iron	—	300 µg/L
Manganese	—	50 µg/L

concentrations are probably a function of the location, source, and composition of recharge and the mineralogy of the aquifer. Occasionally, large variations in concentrations of constituents in the same aquifer over small distances were used to evaluate background concentrations and possible effects from development in specific areas in the study area. Background nitrate concentrations in the East Mountain area were assumed to be equal to or less than 2 milligrams per liter (mg/L) on the basis of a review of nitrate concentrations in groundwater throughout the United States (Mueller and Helsel, 1996, p. 14–15). Although concentrations of nitrate greater than 2 mg/L could be due to variations in the composition of natural recharge, concentrations greater than 2 mg/L were assumed to indicate the effects of development. All nitrate concentrations in this paper are reported in milligrams per liter as nitrogen (N) unless otherwise noted. Alkalinity values are reported in milligrams per liter as calcium carbonate ($CaCO_3$) unless otherwise noted.

Acknowledgments

The authors thank the well owners who allowed us to sample or measure water levels in their wells. Richard Costales of Cambell Corporation allowed access to San Pedro Spring and San Pedro Creek. John Jones of Entranosa Water Cooperative allowed access to wells and assisted in sampling of Entranosa Water Cooperative wells. Background information and land access was provided by Dave Wentworth, Howard and Mary Bernstein, and Reese Jones of San Pedro Creek Estates. The authors would like to recognize the Bernalillo County Public Works division for their interest in managing the water resources and long term hydrologic and water-quality data collection effort in the East Mountain area. Much of the data used in this report was collected as part of the long term Bernalillo County Public Works division/ USGS cooperative project to evaluate the hydrogeology of the East Mountain area. Technical discussions with Jack Frost, Andy Core, and Tom Morrison of the New Mexico Office of the State Engineer, John Hawley of Hawley Geomatters, Daniel McGregor of Bernalillo County Public Works division, and Paul Davis of Enviro Logic, Inc. contributed to a better understanding of the conditions in the study area. Bill Miller of the New Mexico Office of the State Engineer provided assistance in obtaining pertinent information and reports from the files and library of the Office of the State Engineer. Paul Bauer and Michael Timmons of the New Mexico Bureau of Geology provided preliminary geologic maps of the study area that were useful in assigning geologic units to wells and during interpretation of water levels and water quality. Ron Godby, Sue Beffort Wilson, and Kathy McCoy of the New Mexico Legislature provided support in response to their constituents' concerns. Helpful reviews were provided by Daniel McGregor of the Bernalillo County Public Works division and Scott Christensen of the U.S. Geological Survey. Stephanie Moore of the USGS provided field and technical assistance.

Hydrologic Setting

The East Mountain study area is part of the Basin and Range physiographic province (Fenneman, 1931). The Basin and Range province includes a large part of the western United States and is characterized by alluvial basins bounded by parallel mountainous areas. In much of this area, drainage from the mountains is to the enclosed basins.

Climate

Western, higher elevation parts of the study area lie in the subhumid/humid climate area. The remainder lies in the semiarid climate area (based on modified Thornwaite climate types by Tuan, Everard, and Widdison [1969]).

The National Weather Service (NWS) has many weather stations within 20 mi of the study area with at least 10 years of record (figs. 1 and 2), though only three (Estancia, Golden, and Stanley 1NNE) were active through 2005 (table 2). Currently (2005) no Natural Resources Conservation Service snow courses or SNOTEL (snowpack telemetry) sites are in or near the study area. The USGS established seven precipitation sites in eastern Bernalillo County, in the winter of 2000-01, four of which are in the boundaries of the study area. Data from these sites for 2001–03 are summarized in Blanchard (2004).

Mean annual temperatures at NWS stations in and near the study area range from 37.4°F at the Sandia Crest station to 50.6°F at the Estancia station (Western Regional Climate Center, 2006). The coldest month in the area is January, when average low temperatures range from 13.1°F at the Sandia Crest station to 19.2°F at the Tajique station. The warmest month is July, when average high temperatures range from 66.3°F at the Sandia Crest station to 88.5°F at the Estancia station.

Table 2. National Weather Service stations in or near the East Mountain study area.

[data from Western Regional Climate Center (2006). —, in operation through 2005; FAA, Federal Aviation Administration; ***, unknown location]

Station name (figs. 1 and 2)	Station number	Elevation (feet above NGVD29)	Latitude	Longitude	Dates in operation	
					Starting date	Ending date
Estancia	293060	6,120	34° 45' N	106° 04' W	January 1, 1914	—
Golden	293592	6,700	35° 16' N	106° 13' W	January 1, 1948	—
McIntosh 4 NW	295583	6,250	34° 55' N	106° 05' W	May 1, 1937	August 31, 1976
Otto FAA Airport	296492	6,230	35° 05' N	106° 01' W	May 1, 1941	October 31, 1954
Sandia Park	298011	7,019	35° 10' N	106° 22' W	January 1, 1939	December 31, 2001
Sandia Crest	298015	10,680	35° 13' N	106° 27' W	February 16, 1953	April 30, 1979
Stanley 1 NNE	298518	6,380	35° 10' N	105° 58' W	January 1, 1914	—
Tajique	298648	6,710	34° 45' N	106° 17' W	January 1, 1915	April 30, 1979
Tajique 4 NW	298650	6,990	34° 48' N	106° 18' W	February 1, 1914	October 31, 1970
Tijeras Ranger Station	298018	6,310	35° 04' N	106° 23' W	June 1, 1962	December 31, 1974
Willard (near)	299754	***	***	***	January 1, 1914	March 31, 1923

Moisture in storms is derived mainly from the Gulf of Mexico (Tuan, Everard, and Widdison, 1969). July and August are typically the wettest months when 29 to 41 percent of annual precipitation falls at weather stations in the study area (fig. 6) (Western Regional Climate Center, 2006). Mean annual precipitation ranges from 9.9 inches at the Otto FAA Airport station to 23 inches at Sandia Crest. Precipitation in the area comes from local thunderstorms that are due to orographic or convective uplift in the summer months and from frontal storms that are due to interaction of large masses of air in the winter months (Bullard and Wells, 1992). Because thunderstorms can be localized and brief, precipitation can be extremely variable from year to year and place to place in the study area.

Annual precipitation in the East Mountain area increases with elevation and much of this variation in precipitation is winter snowfall (Blanchard, 2004, p. 2–11). Mean annual precipitation for the period 1954-74 was 22.72 inches at the Sandia Crest station (10,680 feet (ft) above National Geodetic Vertical Datum of 1929 (NGVD29), 18.69 inches at the Sandia Park station (7,019 ft above NGVD29), and 14.58 inches at the Sandia Ranger Station (6,310 ft above NGVD29) (Blanchard, 2004). Mean precipitation from November 1 to April 30 was 10.46 inches at the Sandia Crest station and 7.06 inches at the Sandia Park station for the period 1954–74 (Blanchard, 2004). Much of the precipitation at these two sites during these months is snow. About 85 percent of the difference in mean annual precipitation between these two stations is from November 1 through April 30 and indicates the higher elevations probably receive more precipitation generally in the form of snow than lower areas.

Water-level hydrographs shown later in this report include monthly precipitation at the Estancia weather station.

The Estancia station was selected for several reasons. As shown in table 2, of the Weather Service stations with at least 10 years of record in and near the study area, only three were active past 2001—Estancia, Golden, and Stanley 1NNE. Of these three stations, the Estancia and Stanley stations have longest period of record. Though Stanley 1NNE is higher and closer to the study area than Estancia, Stanley 1NNE is missing precipitation data for 1941–54.

The East Mountain area was experiencing drought conditions during much of the time from January 1995 through December 2005. The October 20, 2006, drought report by the New Mexico Drought Monitoring Work Group stated that "Drought conditions have continued to improve over New Mexico with much of the state in drought-free status." One measure used to quantify drought is the Palmer Drought Severity Index (PDSI), a measure of long-term drought that uses precipitation, temperature, soil moisture, and other factors. The PDSI uses zero as normal, drought is represented as negative numbers, and excess precipitation is represented by positive numbers. The National Climate Data Center calculates the PDSI (and other drought indices) for states by climate division; the East Mountain area is in New Mexico climate division 6 (U.S Department of Commerce, 2006). The PDSI for division 6 from January 1900 through December 2005 is shown in figure 7. Of the 132 months from January 1995 through December 2005, 67 had PDSI values less than -0.5, indicating drier than normal conditions, 61 experienced mild to extreme drought conditions (less than -1), and 45 months experienced incipient wet spell to very wet conditions (greater than 0.5). The range of PDSI values is 3.38 (May 2005) to -5.79 (September 2003) from January 1995 through December 2005. The average PDSI value for these 132 months is -0.83 indicating drier than normal or average

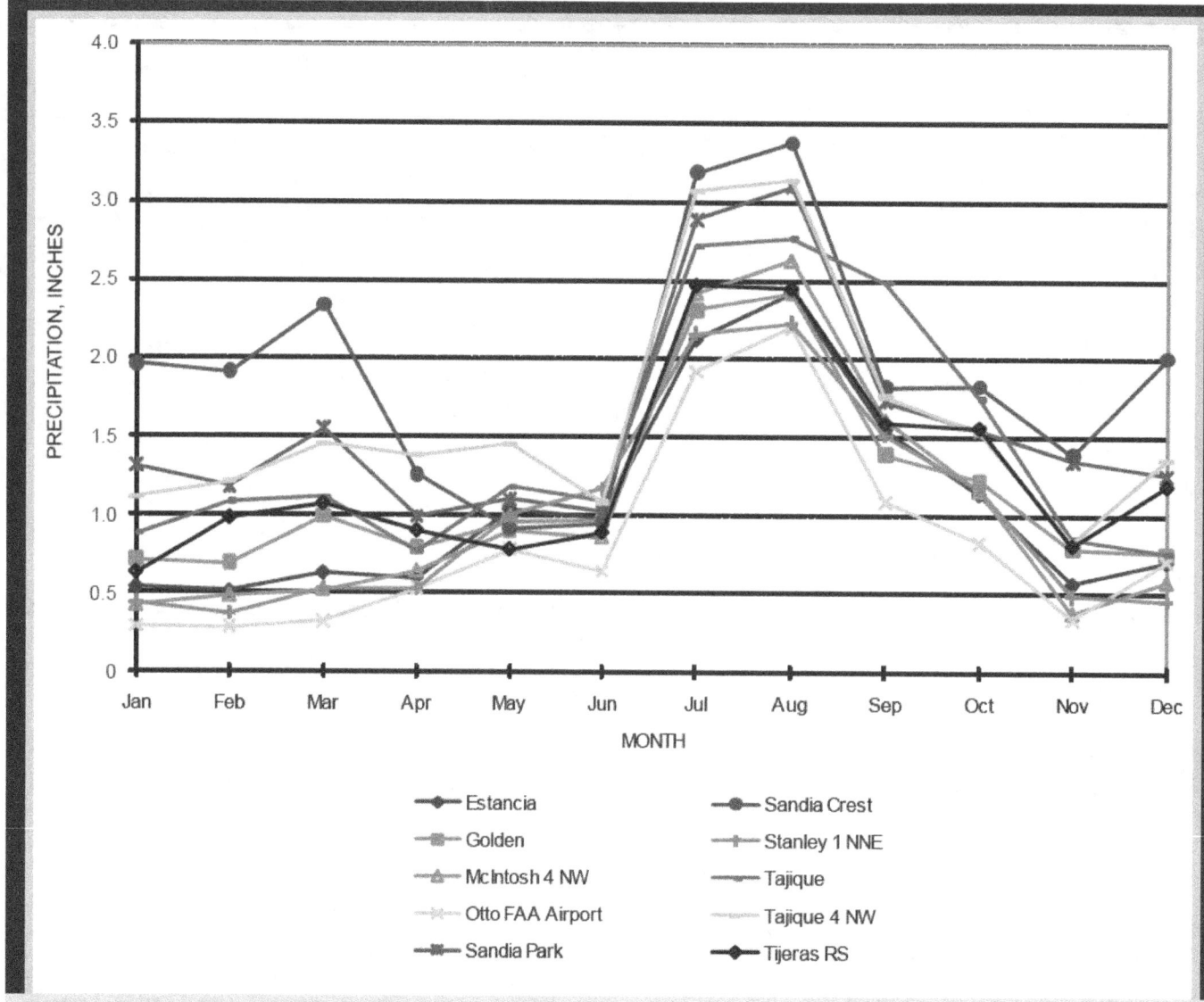

Figure 6. Mean monthly precipitation at selected National Weather Service stations in or near the East Mountain study area (data from Western Regional Climate Center, 2006).

conditions. Although drought can be defined in many different ways (meteorological, hydrological, or agricultural), the well-known droughts of the 1930s and 1942–56 are shown in figure 7 for comparison to the 1995 to 2005 drought. The drought conditions in 1995 to 2005 were not as prolonged and extreme as the drought in the 1940s and 50s; however, a large die-off of pinon trees happened in the East Mountain area from 2000 to 2005 because of pine beetles and the stress the trees were experiencing from lack of moisture.

Surface Water

Surface water in the study area flows to either the Rio Grande or Estancia Basin (plate). Drainage to the Rio Grande is primarily through two arroyos: Tijeras Arroyo on the south end of the Sandia Mountains and Arroyo Tonque on the north end of the Sandias. A small part of the study area on the north end of the Sandia Mountains drains to the Rio Grande through the ephemeral Las Huertas Creek. Surface water in most of the eastern part of the study area flows into the Estancia Basin, which is topographically closed. Though many ephemeral streams are in the study area, few have perennial reaches.

Many springs, especially along the lower flanks of the Sandia Mountains (plate), and seeps discharge to stream channels. Perennial flow in these channels does not generally extend more than several hundred feet downstream from the springs because the water infiltrates into the channel. During the spring particularly in years of greater than normal snowpack, discharge from many of these springs increases

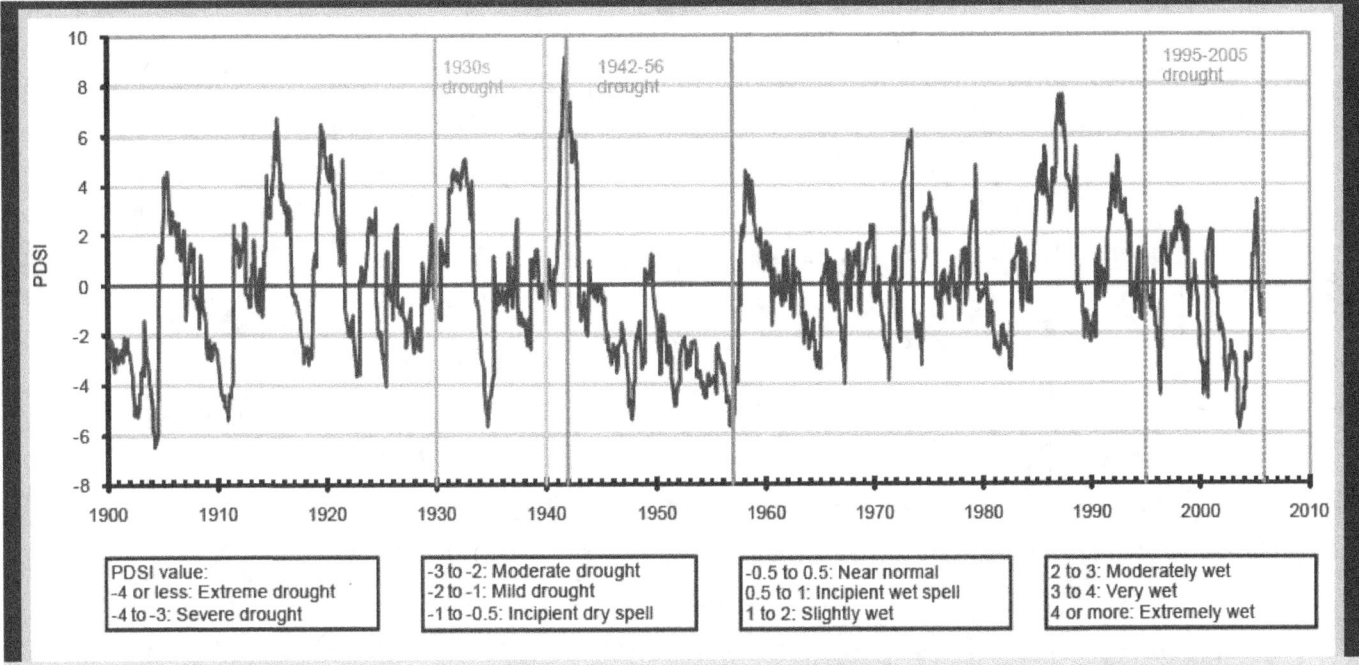

Figure 7. Palmer Drought Severity Index (PDSI) through 2005 for New Mexico Climate Division 6 (data from U.S. Department of Commerce, 2006).

substantially for several months resulting in flow in the stream channels several miles downstream of the springs. Flow in ephemeral channels results from runoff from intense summer thunderstorms; however, these flow events generally do not last for more than several hours after the thunderstorms have passed.

Hydrogeology

The East Mountain study area is geologically and hydrologically complex (plate; fig. 8). Geologic units and structural features such as the Sandia Mountains, Tijeras and Gutierrez Faults, Tijeras Graben, and the Estancia Basin affect the movement, availability, and water quality of the groundwater system. For this reason, a detailed discussion of the geology and structural features of the area is presented.

Structural Features

Major structural features such as the Sandia Mountains and the Estancia Basin affect groundwater movement; other structural features in the study area such as major faults, folds, and igneous intrusions also have profound effects. Major structural features that affect groundwater are shown in figure 8 and are discussed in the following section.

Sandia, Manzanita, and Manzano Mountains

The Sandia and Manzano Mountains (fig. 1) are commonly considered to be separate physiographic entities, but were formed by a single, major, east-tilted fault block that includes the Los Piños Mountains to the south (outside of the study area). This fault block is about 72 mi long and as much as 9 mi wide. Rocks of Precambrian age are exposed along the western fault-line scarp, and the dip slope to the east is formed mainly on strata of Pennsylvanian age that dips about 15 degrees. There may be a maximum of 25,500 ft of structural relief between the top of the Sandia Mountains and the deepest part of the Albuquerque Basin. The maximum structural relief is about 9,800 ft on the east between the Sandia Mountains and the northern part of the Estancia Basin and about 6,900 ft between the Manzano Mountains and the Estancia Basin to the east. The Manzano Mountains are south of the study area; however, Smith (1957) and White (1994) concluded that the mountains provide much of the recharge to the Estancia Basin.

The Manzanita Mountains separate the Sandia and Manzano Mountains. A "broad dissected plateau" (Kelley and Northrop, 1975, p. 84), the Manzanitas dip slightly to the east and are broadly folded into synclines and anticlines. The Manzanitas extend about 15 mi from the Tijeras Fault south to about the Bernalillo-Torrance county line, and from the Albuquerque Basin to about 15 mi east where the Manzanitas merge with the Estancia Basin (Kelley and Northrop, 1975). Titus (1980) included the Manzanita Mountains as part of the Manzano Mountains.

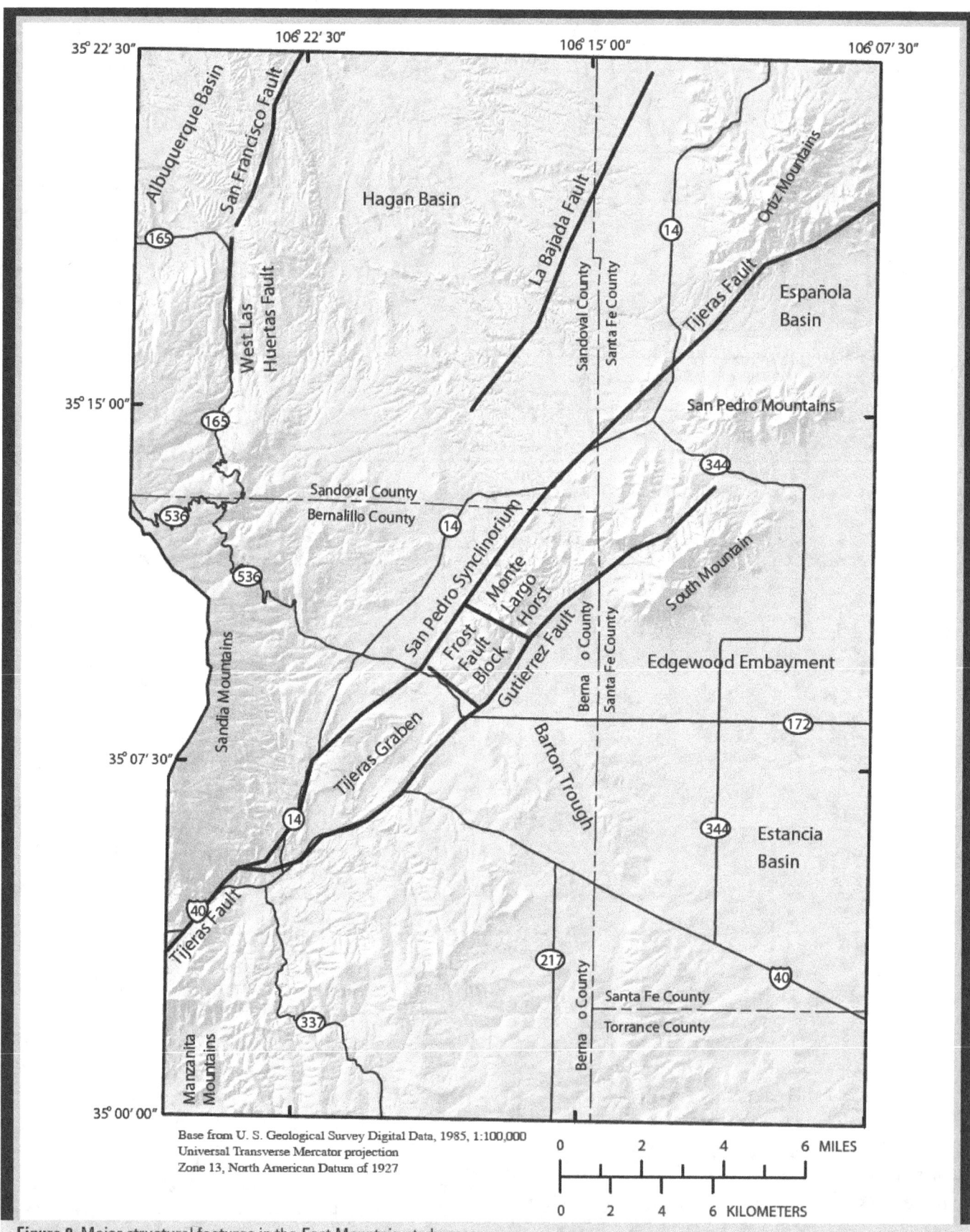

35° 22′ 30″

106° 22′ 30″   106° 15′ 00″   106° 07′ 30″

Albuquerque Basin

San Francisco Fault

Hagan Basin

La Bajada Fault

Ortiz Mountains

Tijeras Fault

Española Basin

165

West Las Huertas Fault

Sandoval County

Santa Fe County

35° 15′ 00″

165

San Pedro Mountains

536

Sandoval County

344

Bernalillo County

14

San Pedro Synclinorium

Monte Largo Horst

South Mountain

536

Frost Fault Block

Gutierrez Fault

Edgewood Embayment

Sandia Mountains

Berna o County

Santa Fe County

35° 07′ 30″

Tijeras Graben

Barton Trough

172

14

344

Estancia Basin

40

Tijeras Fault

217

40

337

Santa Fe County

Berna o County

Torrance County

Manzanita Mountains

35° 00′ 00″

Base from U. S. Geological Survey Digital Data, 1985, 1:100,000
Universal Transverse Mercator projection
Zone 13, North American Datum of 1927

0   2   4   6 MILES

0   2   4   6 KILOMETERS

Figure 8. Major structural features in the East Mountain study area.

Estancia Basin

The Estancia Basin is a large (about 2,400 mi²) internally drained basin (Shafike and Flanigan, 1999). The northwestern part of the Estancia Basin, which is included in the East Mountain study area, is bounded by the dip slope of the Sandia Mountains, the San Pedro Mountains, and the Espanola Basin (fig. 8). The flat laying Permian and Pennsylvanian sedimentary rocks in the basin are overlain by Quaternary alluvium that ranges from 400 ft near the center of the basin to a few feet thick along the basin margins (Shafike and Flanigan, 1999). The Estancia Basin south and east of the East Mountain study area contains large areas of irrigated agriculture (25,915 acres in 1995–96, Shafike and Flanigan, 1999). Many of the irrigation wells in the Estancia Basin withdraw water from the Quaternary alluvium, although some also withdraw water from the underlying Permian and Pennsylvanian rocks (White, 1994, p. 14).

The Barton Trough and Edgewood Embayment

The Barton Trough and Edgewood Embayment, described and named by Titus (1980, p. 9), are structural features with topographic expression on the west side of the Estancia Basin (fig. 8). The Barton Trough is a "6-mi-long north-trending valley containing the community of Barton." This block-faulted valley "was formed by uplift on the east of a barrier ridge of Madera limestone." The Edgewood Embayment "is a 10-mi-wide semicircular indentation into the lower east slopes" of the Manzano Mountains (Titus, 1980). The town of Edgewood is on the south side of the embayment. The embayment is defined by the contact of valley-fill alluvium with the Madera Formation to the south and west, with the Abo Formation to the north (around South Mountain), and with the Gutierrez Fault to the northwest.

Española Basin

The Española Basin is part of the Rio Grande Rift and is immediately north and east of the Albuquerque Basin, and north of the Estancia Basin (fig. 8). A potentiometric map of Santa Fe County using 1980–89 water-level data by Lewis and West (1995) suggests a groundwater divide that about coincides with the Espanola/Estancia Basin boundary. Because of scant well coverage, more water-level data are needed to better define the groundwater divide in the area.

San Pedro Synclinorium

The San Pedro synclinorium is a southwest plunging, northeast trending syncline separating the Monte Largo Horst from the Sandia Mountains (fig. 8). Originally defined as a syncline by Kelley and Northrop (1975), the syncline was reclassified as a synclinorium on the geologic map of Ferguson and others (1996).

La Bajada and San Francisco Faults

The La Bajada Fault generally is parallel to the Tijeras Fault near the Monte Largo Horst and forms the eastern boundary of the Hagan Basin (fig. 8) and, in conjunction with the San Francisco Fault, forms the eastern boundary of the Santo Domingo subbasin of the Albuquerque Basin. The San Francisco Fault generally forms the western boundary of the Hagan Basin (Personius and others, 1999).

Hagan Structural Basin

The Hagan Basin is bounded on the east and northeast by the La Bajada Fault, southwest by the Madera Formation of the Sandia Mountains, and on the west by the Sandia Mountains and San Francisco Fault (Kelley and Northrop, 1975; Pazzaglia and others, 1999a). Because the San Francisco Fault is poorly exposed at the northern extent, but appears to extend south to near Cochiti Pueblo, the northwestern margin of the Hagan Basin is not well defined (Personius and others, 1999). Thus, the Hagan Basin is often classified as part of the Santo Domingo subbasin of the Albuquerque Basin, despite generally east-dipping Santa Fe Group deposits.

Tijeras Fault System

The 60-mi-long Tijeras Fault System extends from Albuquerque to Santa Fe through Tijeras Canyon, Golden, and Lamy (Kelson and others, 1999) (fig. 8). Movement along this fault system is primarily strike slip with an unknown amount of lateral displacement. The two major components of the fault system are the Tijeras and Gutierrez Faults in the study area. The northeast-trending Tijeras Fault originates in the Albuquerque Basin to the west, runs through Tijeras Canyon along Interstate 40 and then about parallel to New Mexico Highway 14. The fault forms the west edge of the Tijeras Graben and Monte Largo Horst. The 15-mi-long Gutierrez Fault splays east from the Tijeras Fault in the southwest part of the study area and continues northeast forming the east edge of the Monte Largo Horst before ending south of the San Pedro Mountains (Kelley and Northrop, 1975).

Frost Fault Block-Monte Largo Horst-Tijeras Graben

Though the Tijeras and Gutierrez Faults are responsible for much of the complexity of the hydrogeologic system of the study area, in the about 2-mi-wide zone between the two faults is the Frost Fault Block (fig. 8), a geologically complex area containing outcrops of most of the geologic units in the study area. The Frost Fault Block consists of two main structural units—the downthrown Tijeras Graben to the southwest and the upthrown Monte Largo Horst to the northeast. The boundary between the two is perpendicular to the faults about midway across the Madera Formation outcrop. The Tijeras Graben, from east to west, is composed of a syncline, an anticline, and a syncline. A north facing cross section would show sedimentary rocks deformed to resemble a broad, flattened W. The sedimentary rocks of Cretaceous age in the Tijeras Graben overlie older rocks that are major aquifers used in most of the East Mountain area. The northeastern part of the Frost Fault Block, the Monte Largo Horst, is granite of Precambrian age, from which all younger sedimentary rocks have been eroded (Kelley and Northrop, 1975)

The role of the Tijeras and Gutierrez Faults in the groundwater system of the study area is problematic. The strike-slip and dip-slip faults that surround the Tijeras Graben may act as conduits, barriers, or have no effect on flow. The Tijeras Graben also could act as a barrier to groundwater flow eastward off the Sandia Mountains.

The Ortiz Porphyry Belt

The generally north-trending Ortiz Porphyry Belt is composed of igneous intrusive rocks of mid-Tertiary age that are expressed topographically (Kelley and Northrop, 1975; Woodward, 1982) (fig. 8). In the study area the porphyry belt includes the Ortiz Mountains, San Pedro Mountains, and South Mountain areas, and in the central part of these mountain areas the intrusive rocks have been exposed by erosion.

Groundwater Resources

Geologic Units and Water-Bearing Characteristics

The major water-bearing geologic units in the East Mountain area are sedimentary rocks of Paleozoic and Mesozoic age, and the primary unit is the Pennsylvanian Madera Formation. The differing hydraulic and chemical properties of the various water-bearing units are due to the dissimilar conditions under which the rock units were deposited and the subsequent alteration by geologic processes; thus, any discussion of the groundwater system of the area should start with characteristics of geologic units. However, in the East Mountain area most of these geologic units are hydraulically connected to one or more of the adjacent stratigraphic units and are often difficult to differentiate in well logs. Consequently, previous workers have combined these hydraulically connected stratigraphic units with similar properties into hydrostratigraphic units—this usage is followed in this report. When discussing stratigraphic units, the formal stratigraphic name or term "geologic unit" is used, such as Madera Formation, Mancos Shale, or Precambrian geologic unit. When referring to hydrostratigraphic units, either a combined stratigraphic name is used, such as Madera-Sandia hydrostratigraphic unit, or a geologic-time modifier, such as Cretaceous

hydrostratigraphic unit. Table 3 shows the stratigraphic/geologic and hydrostratigraphic units of the East Mountain area.

Precambrian Rocks

Precambrian rocks in and near the study area are igneous and metamorphic and include the intrusive rocks and metamorphic rocks (plate). Though a primary source of water for wells and springs in Tijeras Canyon west of the study area, in the study area few wells are completed in Precambrian rocks because of depth below land surface and general lack of permeability. Wells completed in Precambrian rocks are clustered in Tijeras Canyon where Precambrian rocks are exposed at the surface (plate). Wells and springs on Monte Largo produce water not from Precambrian metamorphic rock but from the surrounding sedimentary geologic units. The Precambrian rocks are grouped into the Precambrian hydrostratigraphic unit.

The Precambrian rocks in the East Mountain area have little porosity and permeability unless fractured. A search of previous work, including consultants' reports, found aquifer tests for 13 wells completed in the various Precambrian rocks

Table 3. Stratigraphic/geologic and hydrostratigraphic units of the East Mountain study area.

[Connell and others (1999) and Lucas and others (1999)]

Era	Period	Rock unit	Hydrostratigraphic unit
Cenozoic	Quaternary	Alluvium	
	Tertiary	Santa Fe Group	Cenozoic
		Espinaso Formation	
		Galisteo Formation	
		Diamond Tail Formation	
Mesozoic	Cretaceous	Mesaverde Group	Cretaceous
		Mancos Shale	
		Dakota Formation	
	Jurassic	Morrison Formation	Jurassic
		Wanakah Formation	
		Entrada Sandstone	
	Triassic	Chinle Group	Chinle-Moenkopi
		Moenkopi Formation	
Paleozoic	Permian	San Andres Formation	San Andres-Glorieta
		Glorieta Formation	
		Yeso Formation	Abo-Yeso
		Abo Formation	
	Pennsylvanian	Madera Formation	Madera-Sandia
		Sandia Formation	
Precambrian		Precambrian rocks	Precambrian

with reported transmissivities ranging from 0.9 to 500 ft squared per day (ft²/day) (Wells and others, 1980; Molzen-Corbin, 1991; Clay Kilmer and Associates, Ltd., 1994, 1995; Cravens, 1996; Cravens and Pease, 1996; Pease and Cravens, 1998).

Water-quality analyses are available for samples from three wells in the study area completed in the Precambrian hydrostratigraphic unit. Dissolved-solids concentrations in these samples ranged from 351 to 1,060 mg/L (appendix 3). In the two samples plotted on the Piper diagram, calcium was the dominant cation whereas sulfate was the dominant anion in one sample and chloride was the dominant anion in the other (fig. 9). The sulfate concentration in one sample and the chloride concentration in another were greater than 250 mg/L, which is greater than the USEPA SMCL for each constituent. Figures 10 and 11 show the chloride and nitrate concentrations, respectively, of water samples from wells and springs in the study area. Nitrate concentrations were 1.4, 1.6, and 14 mg/L in samples from the Precambrian hydrostratigraphic unit (appendix 3); the USEPA MCL is 10 mg/L. High nitrate concentrations have been detected in water from wells completed in the Precambrian hydrostratigraphic unit in the Tijeras Canyon area (Caprio, 1960; Titus, 1980, p. 38; Mc Quillan and others, 1988; Kues, 1990, p. 43–45; Blanchard and Kues, 1999). These high nitrate concentrations have been attributed to domestic wastewater recharging the aquifers in this area (Blanchard and Kues, 1999, p. 26). The sample from the well with 14 mg/L of nitrate also had a chloride concentration greater than 250 mg/L; this well is along Interstate 40 near Tijeras Canyon.

Pennsylvanian Sandia and Madera Formations

With the exception of minor amounts of sandstone (Read and others, 1999) and limestone of Mississippian age (Kelley and Northrop, 1975), the oldest unmetamorphosed sedimentary unit in the study area is the Sandia Formation of Pennsylvanian age. This geologic unit is typically an interbedded, slope-forming sequence of brown claystone, gray limestone, and olive-brown and gray sandstone, and sometimes a basal conglomerate (Kelley and Northrop, 1975; Titus, 1980; Williams and Cole, 2007). The average thickness of the Sandia Formation is about 190 ft; however, the thickness may range from less than 49 to about 300 ft, and this variation is probably due to pre-Sandia erosional relief on the Precambrian rocks. The Sandia Formation overlies Precambrian rocks except in a few places where Mississippian limestone of the Arroyo Peñasco Group is present. The Sandia Formation is not a major source of water to wells and springs in the study area, though several springs in Tijeras Canyon apparently discharge exclusively from the Sandia Formation (Titus, 1980).

The Madera Formation, often in conjunction with adjoining geologic units, is the primary water-bearing unit in the study area, especially in the area south of Interstate 40, east of the Gutierrez Fault, and in the San Pedro synclinorium. The

formation is exposed at the surface throughout much of the East Mountain study area (plate). Though previous geologists have raised the Madera to group status, recent mapping of the study area has classified the Madera as a formation, with an informal upper arkosic limestone member and a lower gray limestone member, primarily because of gradational contacts and other problems that make field identification difficult (Karlstrom and others, 1994; Connell and others, 1995a; Read and others, 1995; Ferguson and others, 1996; Read and others, 1998; Ferguson and others, 1999; Allen, 2000; Maynard, 2000; Cather and others, 2002). Total thickness of the Madera Formation is about 1,200 ft in the study area (Ferguson and others, 1996); however, the total thickness may be as much as 5,700 ft thick in the Estancia Basin to the southeast (Broadhead, 1997).

The lower gray limestone member is typically a massively bedded, ledge-forming limestone with thin interbedded shales. Near the lower contact with the Sandia Formation, the shales are particularly abundant. This member is generally equivalent to the Los Moyos Limestone of Myers (1973) (Karlstrom and others, 1994; Read and others, 1998).

About half of the upper arkosic limestone member is composed of a massive, thin bedded, gray, greenish-gray, olive-gray, and brown limestone. Interbedded among the limestone are variegated sandstones and mudstones. The sandstones are typically coarse to medium grained and often contain granules or pebbles. This member is generally equivalent to the Wild Cow Formation of Myers (1973) (Karlstrom and others, 1994; Read and others, 1998).

Massive limestones have very low primary porosity and are typically a good aquifer only where fractured and (or) dissolved by solution. The Madera Formation produces an appreciable quantity of water to wells and springs in areas that have such porosity enhancement or interbedded shale. The sandstones in the lower member do not appear to yield much water to wells or springs (Titus, 1980).

Because the Madera and Sandia Formations are in hydraulic connection and are often difficult to differentiate in well logs, previous hydrologists have often combined these formations into a single hydrostratigraphic unit. Thus, in keeping with common usage for the East Mountain area, these formations are combined into the Madera-Sandia hydrostratigraphic unit in this report.

A search of previous work, including consultants' reports, found aquifer tests for about 40 wells completed in the Madera Formation. Reported transmissivities ranged from 0.2 to 1.3×10^6 ft²/day (Trauger, 1974; Summers, 1978; Patterson, 1979; Jenkins, 1980; Geohydrology Associates, Inc., 1986, 1989; Hall Engineering Co., 1987; Molzen-Corbin, 1991; Watson and Shomaker, 1991; Turner Environmental Consultants, 1990; Newcomer and Peery, 1994; Cravens, 1995; Clay Kilmer and Associates, Ltd.,1997b; Drakos, Lazarus, and Hodgins, 1999; Turner Environmental Consultants, 1999b; Balleau Groundwater Inc., 2000; Corbin Consulting Inc., 2001). Aquifer tests for about eight additional wells completed in the combined Madera Formation and

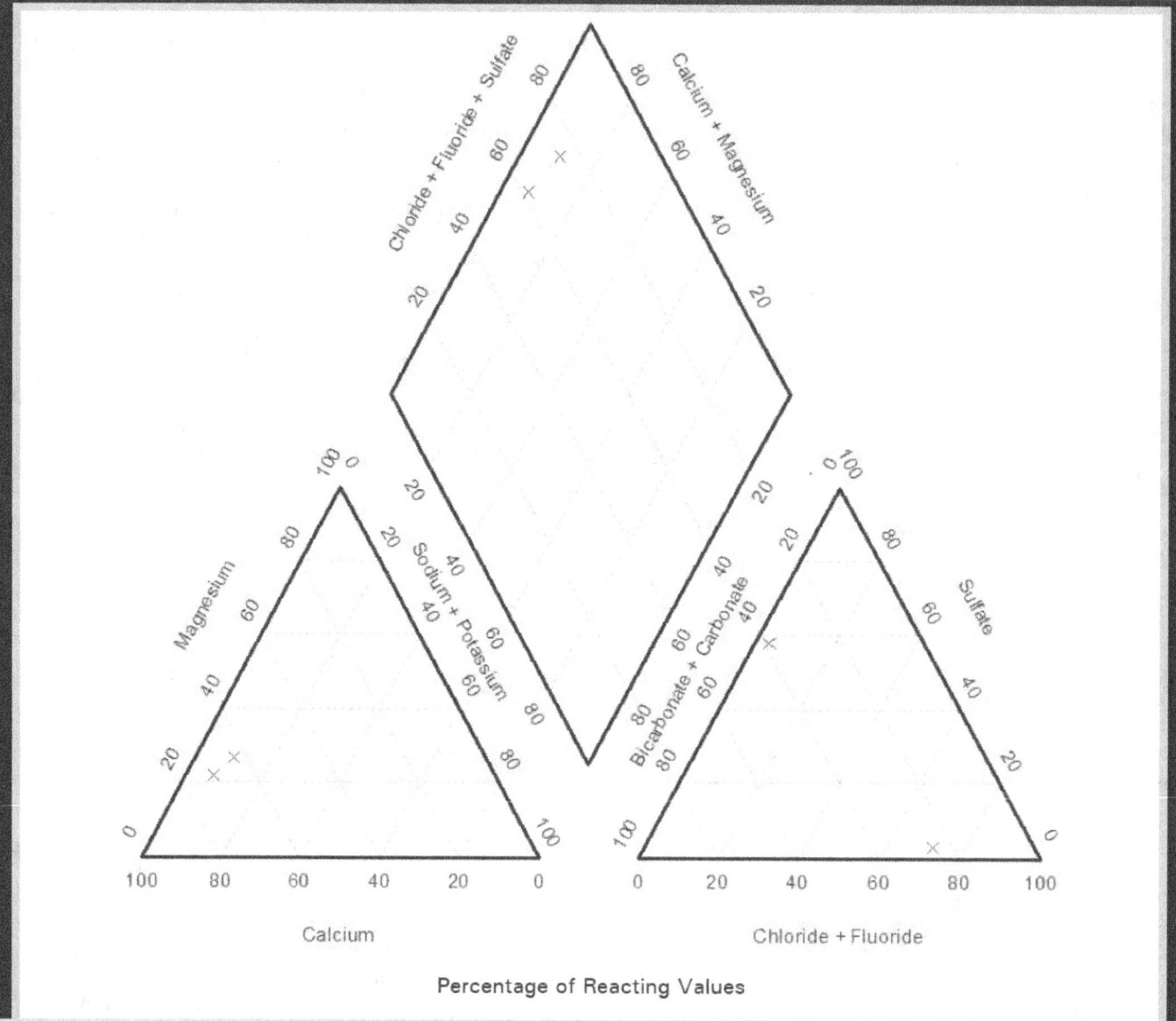

Figure 9. Composition of water from the Precambrian hydrostratigraphic unit in the East Mountain study area.

overlying Abo Formation reported transmissivities ranging from 152 to 40,000 ft²/day (Jenkins, 1980; Geohydrology Associates, Inc., 1989; Drakos, Lazarus, and Hodgins, 1999; Balleau Groundwater Inc., 2000). The groundwater-flow model of Shafike and Flanigan (1999) divided the Madera-Sandia hydrostratigraphic unit into three areal zones with differing hydraulic properties: a silty zone with transmissivities ranging from 30–300 ft²/day, a low zone with transmissivities ranging from 500–1,000 ft²/day, and a high zone with transmissivities ranging from 15,000–30,000 ft²/day. John Shomaker and Associates (1997) reported that in the Estancia Underground Water Basin the transmissivity of the Madera Group ranged from 401 to 1.3×10⁶ ft²/day, with an average of 150,040 ft²/day.

Transmissivities of the Madera-Sandia hydrostratigraphic units are generally much larger than transmissivities for other hydrostratigraphic units in the East Mountain area. In some areas near Edgewood, cavernous zones have been found in drill holes. Although measured transmissivities of the Madera-Sandia are high, wells in the area have been drilled below the zone of saturation and the wells produced little or no water indicating very low transmissivities. Titus (1980, p. 33–35) indicated many dry holes have been drilled in the Madera-Sandia hydrostratigraphic unit in the area west and north of the Barton trough. Titus indicates productive wells in the Madera-Sandia generally intercepted solution channels or shale beds interbedded with the limestone.

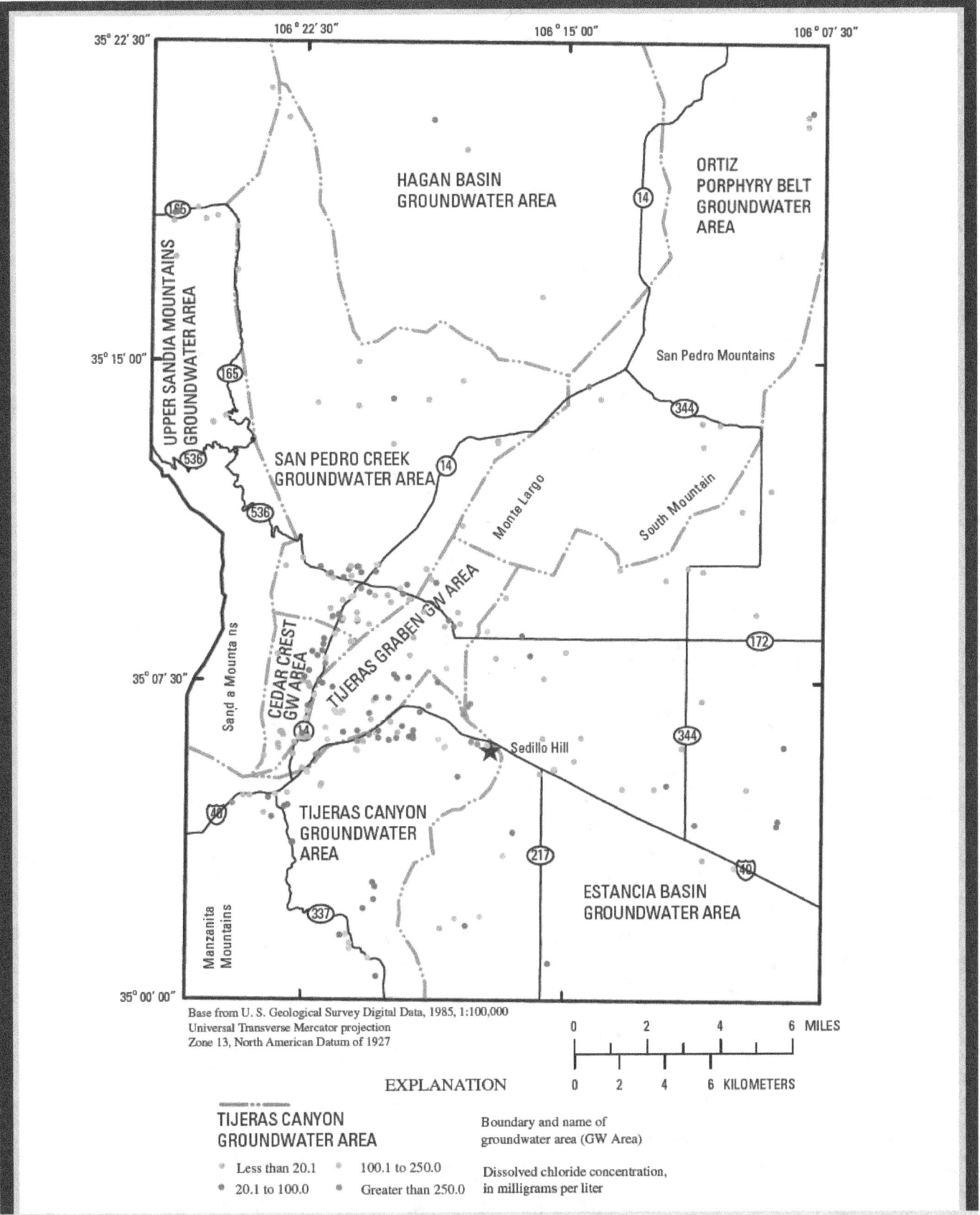

Figure 10. Dissolved chloride concentration in groundwater and springs in the East Mountain study area.

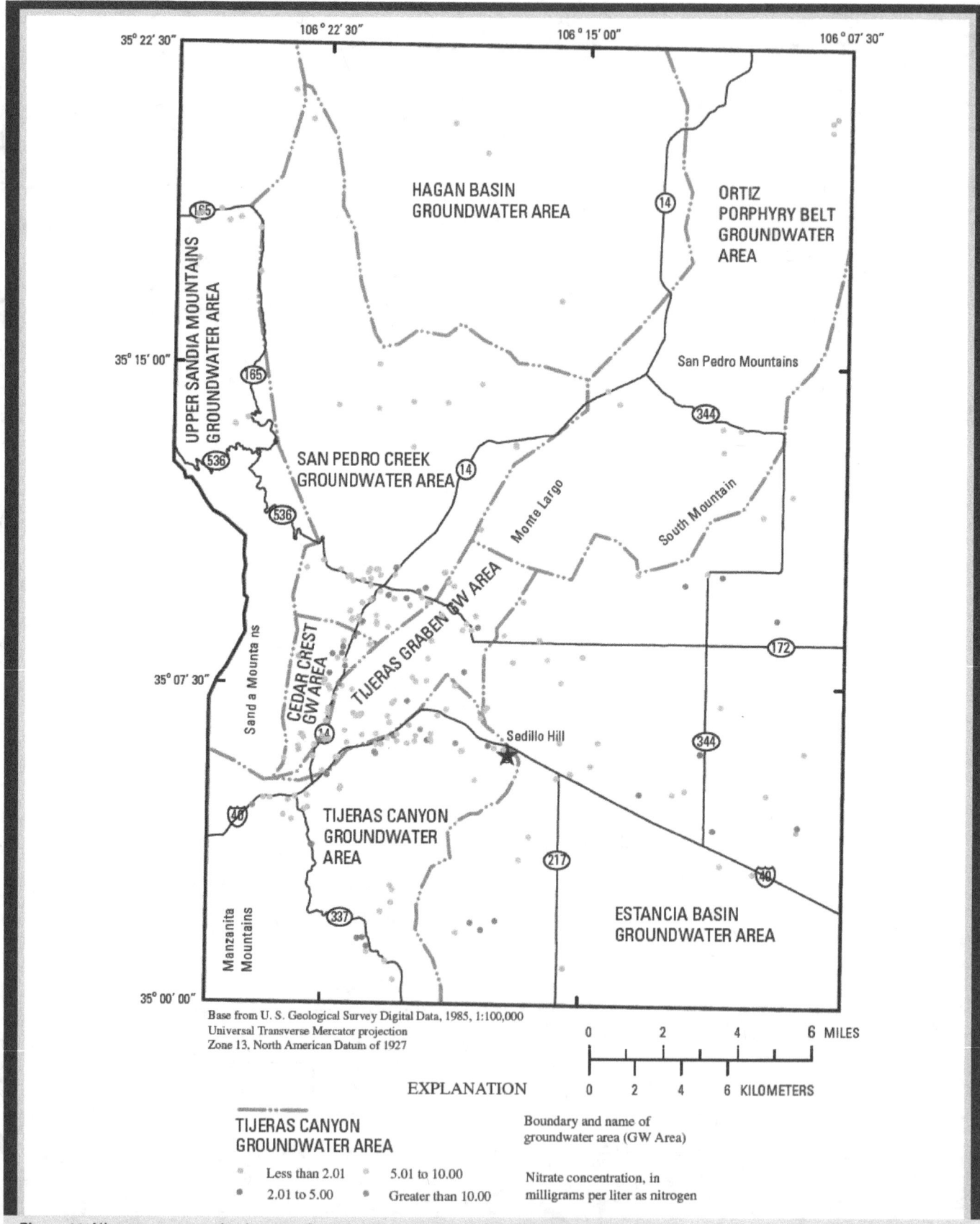

Figure 11. Nitrate concentration in groundwater and springs in the East Mountain study area.

Dissolved-solids concentrations in samples from wells completed in the Madera-Sandia hydrostratigraphic unit range from 192 to 1,820 mg/L (table 4). The median dissolved-solids concentration in 81 samples was 473 mg/L and in 38 samples dissolved-solids concentrations were greater than the SMCL of 500 mg/L. Calcium and bicarbonate are the dominant ions in most samples (fig. 12). Percentages of sodium plus potassium were greater than 60 in several samples indicating small calcium and magnesium concentrations. Alkalinity values in these samples are typically high. In many samples the percentage of chloride increased as the percentage of bicarbonate decreased. Some of these samples contain more than 60 percent chloride plus fluoride and

chloride concentrations seem high relative to those chloride concentrations in samples from other wells in the study area. Chloride concentrations were greater than the SMCL of 250 mg/L in six samples, and in three samples, sulfate concentrations were greater than the SMCL of 250 mg/L (table 4). Most of the samples with chloride and (or) sulfate concentrations greater than 250 mg/L were collected from wells near Interstate 40 in the Sedillo Hill area (figs. 10 and 13). Nitrate concentrations ranged from less than 0.02 to 16 mg/L; only one sample had a nitrate concentration greater than the MCL of 10 mg/L. Nitrate concentrations in 27 of the 82 samples were greater than the assumed background of 2 mg/L (table 4). Water from many of the wells with

Table 4. Statistical summary of selected water-quality data for water from the Madera-Sandia hydrostratigraphic unit in the East Mountain study area.

[µS/cm, microsiemens per centimeter at 25 degrees Celsius; mg/L, milligrams per liter; Na, sodium; $CaCO_3$, calcium carbonate; SiO_2, silicon dioxide; N, nitrogen; P, phosphorus; µg/L, micrograms per liter; --, not applicable; MCL, U.S. Environmental Protection Agency maximum contaminant level; SMCL, U.S. Environmental Protection Agency secondary maximum contaminant level; 9 (5), 9 samples exceed MCL and 5 samples exceed SMCL; ≤ less than or equal to]

Property or constituent	Number of samples	Number of samples less than detection limit	Number of samples greater than MCL or SMCL	Minimum	25th percentile	50th percentile	75th percentile	Maximum
pH (standard units)	80	--	1	6.1	7.1	7.3	7.6	8.5
Specific conductance (µS/cm)	86	--	--	228	622.25	801.5	1,120	3,020
Temperature (degrees Celsius)	73	--	--	3.5	12.7	14.7	16	20.1
Calcium (mg/L)	84	0	--	1.7	70.9	98.5	150	340
Magnesiuim (mg/L)	84	0	--	0.3	14.6	23.5	32.9	140
Potassium (mg/L)	74	0	--	0.1	1.6	2.1	2.8	7.6
Sodium plus potassium (mg/L as Na)	86	0	--	1.6	16	33	76	360
Sodium (mg/L)	75	0	--	1.6	17	32	73	360
Alkalinity (mg/L as $CaCO_3$)	87	0	--	137	240	276	341	910
Chloride (mg/L)	89	0	6	1.8	16	31	107.5	780
Fluoride (mg/L)	80	0	9 (5)	0.1	0.225	0.4	0.775	11
Silica (mg/L as SiO_2)	79	0	--	9.2	14	16	18.7	29
Sulfate (mg/L)	87	0	3	6.8	32	52.3	83	640
Dissolved solids (mg/L)	81	0	38	192	351	473	649	1,820
Nitrate (mg/L as N)	82	8	1	≤ 0.02	0.195	1.23	3.13	16
Ammonia (mg/L as N)	61	30	--	≤ 0.01	≤ 0.015	0.02	0.04	0.07
Orthophosphate (mg/L as P)	67	24	--	≤ 0.004	≤ 0.01	0.01	0.02	0.04
Boron (µg/L)	70	0	--	13	44.5	61.5	129.25	410
Iron (µg/L)	69	30	2	≤ 3	≤ 4	10	20	42,700
Manganese (µg/L)	60	32	3	≤ 0.1	≤ 1	≤ 2	6.25	518

nitrate concentrations greater than 5 mg/L also had chloride concentrations greater than 100 mg/L (figs. 10 and 11). These wells were typically in the Interstate 40/Sedillo Hill area. The reason for the high chloride, sulfate, and nitrate concentrations in samples from wells in the Interstate 40/Sedillo Hill area is unknown though high chloride and nitrate concentrations are found in several samples from this area. A large variation in pH (less than 7.0 to greater than 7.8) in water from the Madera-Sandia hydrostratigraphic unit was observed (table 4), and in the Interstate 40/Sedillo Hill area a large variation in pH over short distances was observed (fig. 14). The USEPA has established a SMCL for pH of 6.5 to 8.5; water from only one well was outside this range with a pH of 6.1. This sample

also had an alkalinity of 910 mg/L, which is fairly high. Titus (1980) noted fluoride concentrations greater than the MCL of 4 mg/L in some samples from wells completed in the Madera Formation. Concentrations were greater than 4 mg/L (MCL) in samples from five wells and were greater than 2 mg/L (SMCL) in a total of nine wells (table 4). In most of these samples, the pH values (greater than 7.8) and alkalinity concentrations (greater than 500 mg/L as $CaCO_3$) were high, and calcium concentrations were low (less than 50 mg/L). These samples were generally from wells in the Barton Trough area (fig. 15). Iron and manganese concentrations are typically less than 10 micrograms per liter (µg/L) in water from the Madera-Sandia hydrostratigraphic unit, although two samples exceeded the

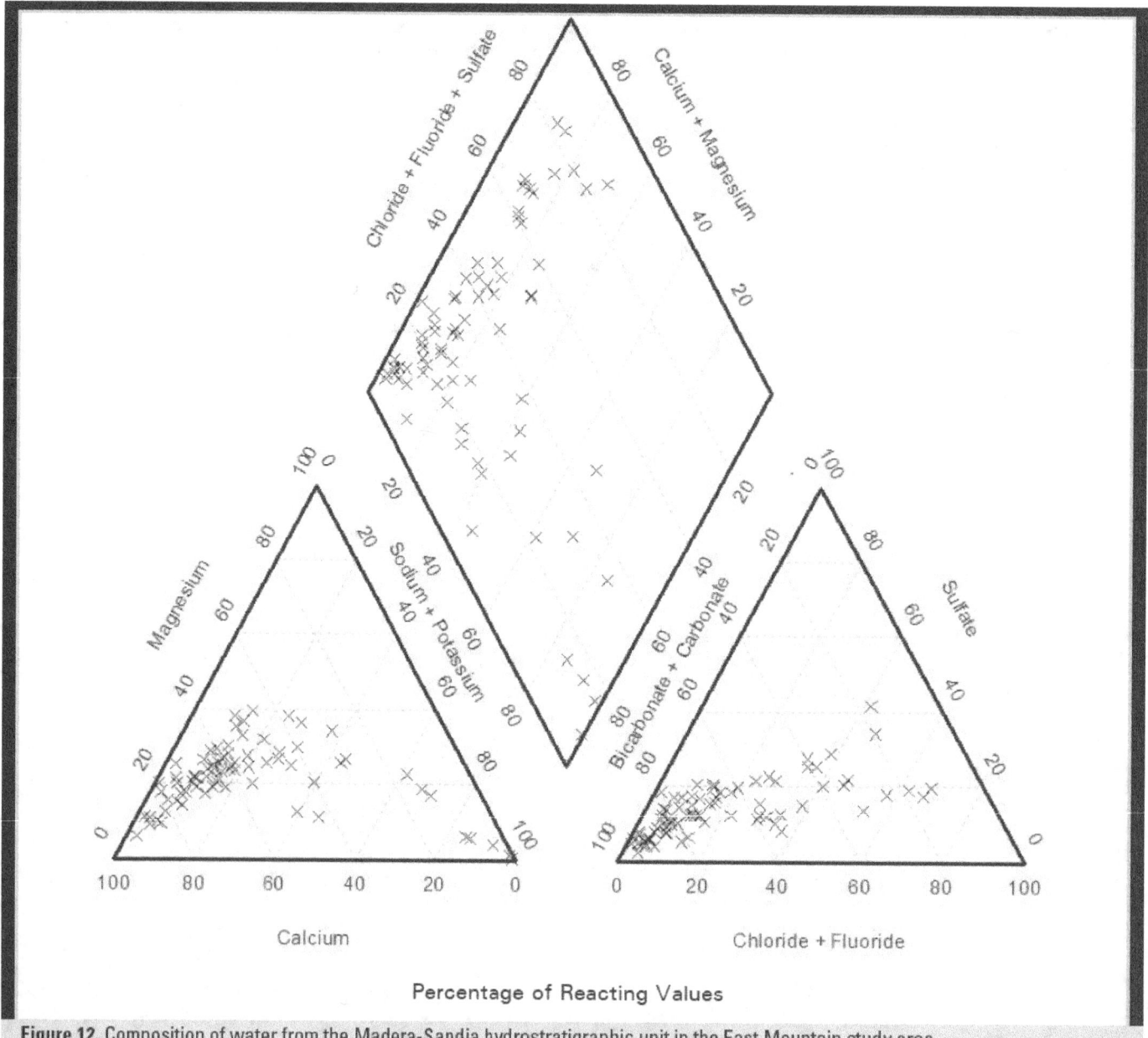

Figure 12. Composition of water from the Madera-Sandia hydrostratigraphic unit in the East Mountain study area.

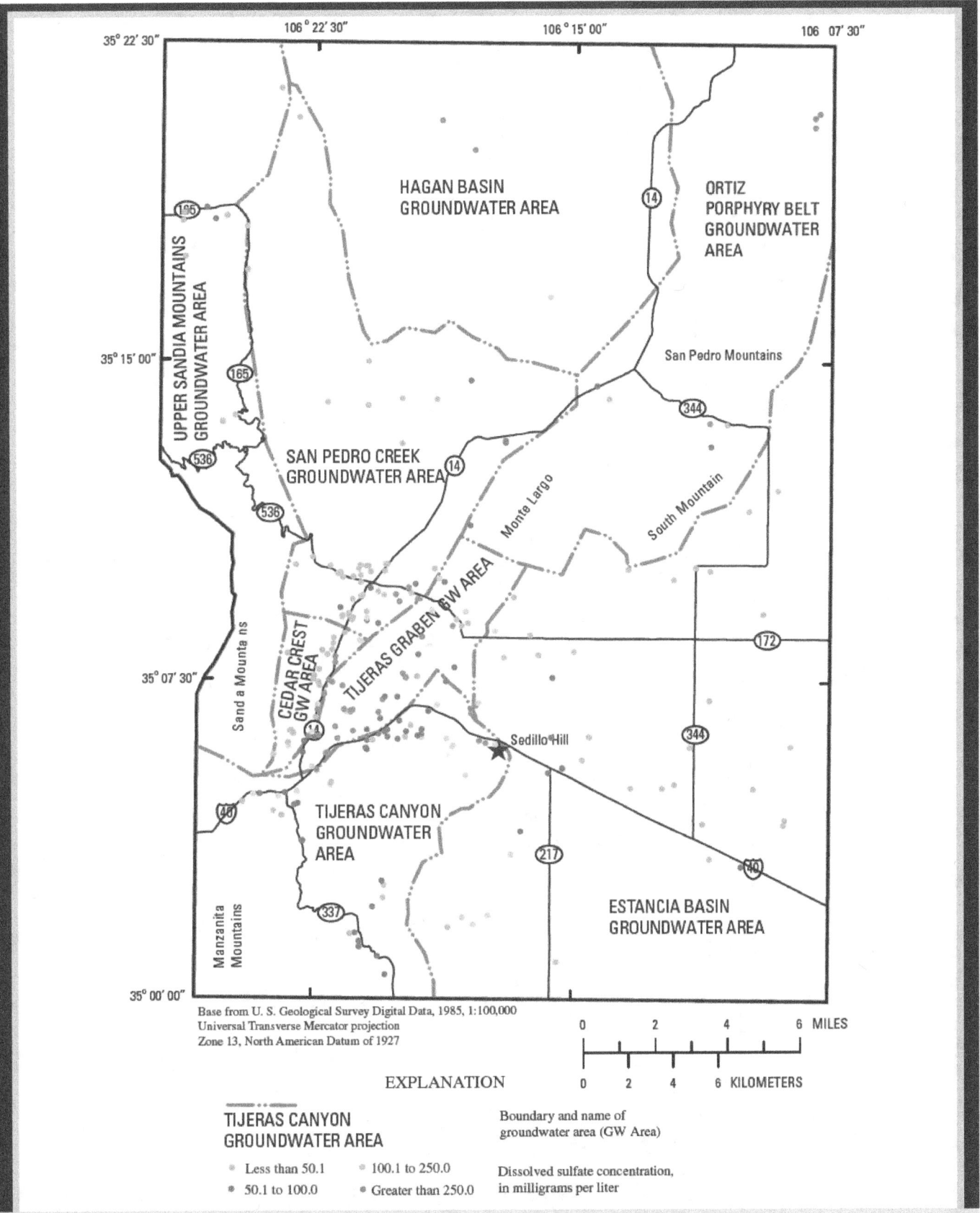

Figure 13. Dissolved sulfate concentration in groundwater and springs in the East Mountain study area.

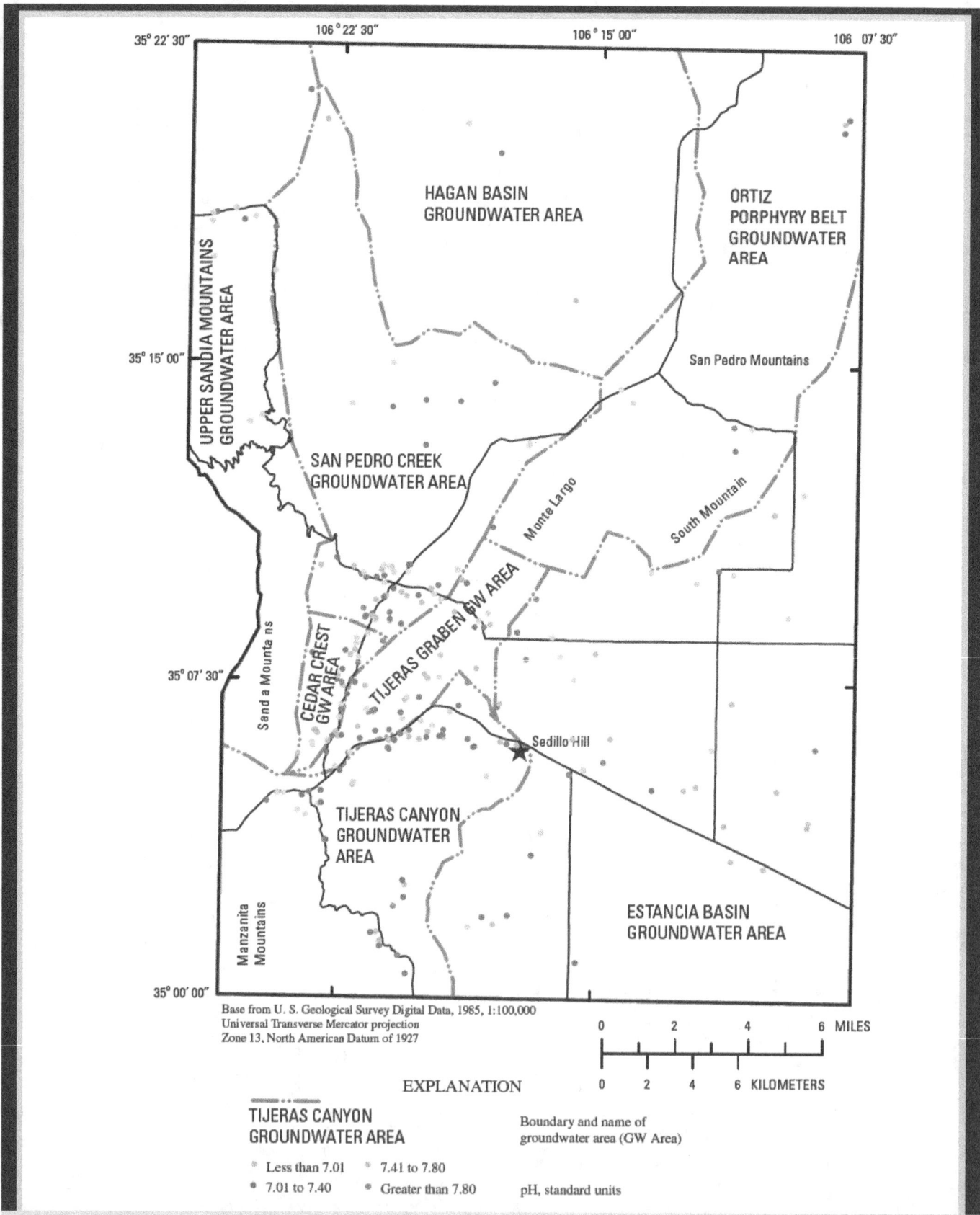

Figure 14. pH of groundwater and springs in the East Mountain study area.

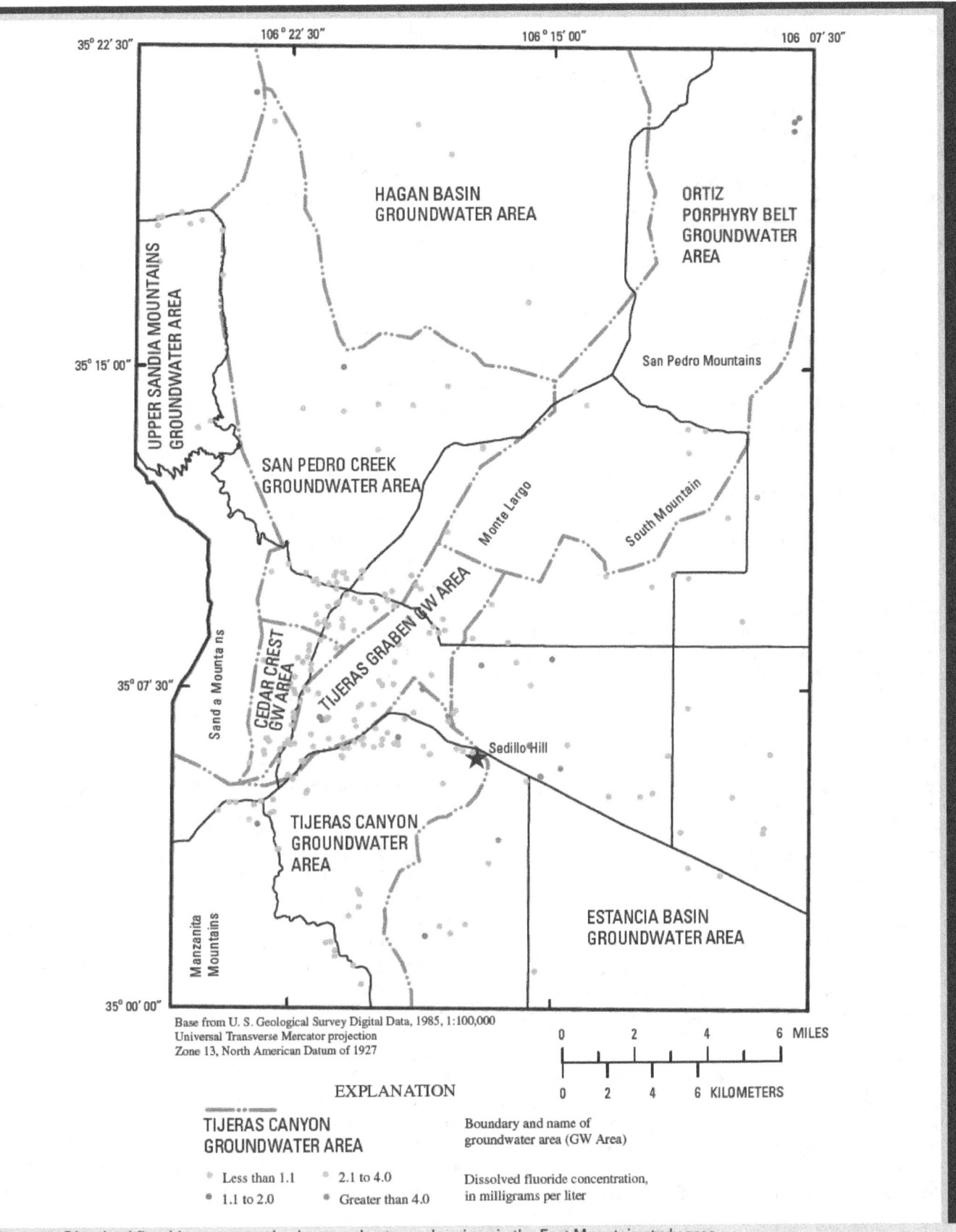

Figure 15. Dissolved fluoride concentration in groundwater and springs in the East Mountain study area.

USEPA SMCL for iron (300 µg/L) and three samples exceeded the SMCL for manganese (50 µg/L) (table 4).

Potential Sources of Alkalinity and Dissolved Carbon

Alkalinity greater than 500 mg/L in groundwater from several areas in the study area and caverns in the Madera Formation indicates dissolution of limestone by groundwater. This dissolution requires a source of carbon dioxide greater than that provided by atmospheric sources. South and east of the study area, carbon dioxide was produced commercially from the Estancia Basin south of Moriarity in 1934–42, and Titus (1980) reported water wells that produce carbon dioxide in the general area between Chililli and Tajique. At least seven geologic processes may be responsible for substantial amounts of carbon dioxide, three processes are most likely for carbon dioxide formation in the study area (Wycherley and others, 1999). These three processes are (1) metamorphism of carbonate rocks, (2) dissolution of carbonate rocks by hot, acidized groundwater, or (3) heating of kerogen-rich, petroleum source rocks. Processes one and two could happen as the result of Tertiary intrusions of carbonate rocks in the South Mountain and Ortiz and San Pedro Mountains. The third process also is a possibility—Broadhead (1997) identified the Sandia and Madera Formations as petroleum source rocks in the Estancia Basin.

Broadhead's (1997) study of the petroleum potential of the Estancia Basin identified the Pennsylvanian rocks as the only verified petroleum source rocks in the basin on the basis of three observations: the gray to black shales contain sufficient total organic carbon, the rocks are progressively more thermally mature with increasing proximity to the Rio Grande Rift, and the rocks contain oil-prone kerogen facies. Broadhead's study area encompassed this study area with the exception of four townships near Placitas. His maps of kerogen facies and maximum thermal maturity indicated that the Pennsylvanian strata in this study area are thermally mature and are entirely of the oil-prone kerogen facies. Isolated "hot spots" either from intrusions or variations in the geothermal gradient could provide the necessary heat to generate carbon dioxide in specific areas of the Pennsylvanian strata.

Although few samples in the study area have been analyzed for organic carbon, there seems to be a correlation between organic carbon concentrations and alkalinity. Although this correlation may suggest a petroleum source, the carbon dioxide may still be a result of metamorphism of carbonate rocks or the organic carbon in the shales. Broadhead (1997) stated that the source of carbon dioxide in the Estancia Basin is "enigmatic," and the data discussed in his report do not favor a single mechanism. Another possible source of organic carbon and high alkalinity is human activity, although the large areal distribution and a known source argue against this. Carbon-13 isotopic analyses of groundwater in areas of high alkalinity or total organic-carbon concentrations could provide a unique isotopic signature that would allow identification of the source.

Permian Abo and Yeso Formations

Throughout the study area the Abo and Yeso Formations of Permian age form a single sequence about 1,175-ft thick, of reddish-brown to light orange sandstone and mudstone. Recent geologic maps of the study area generally do not differentiate between the two geologic units, although Titus (1980) separated the Yeso Formation into two members. The areas where the Abo and Yeso Formations are commonly used as an aquifer are in the Tijeras Graben, adjacent to the Tijeras Fault System, and in the San Pedro synclinorium. The Abo and Yeso Formations also underlie Quaternary alluvium of the Estancia Basin east of South Mountain (Broadhead, 1997). The Abo and Yeso Formations are grouped into the Abo-Yeso hydrostratigraphic unit in this report (table 3).

A search of previous work, including consultants' reports, found aquifer tests for about 16 wells completed in the Abo and Yeso Formations. Transmissivities ranged from 5.9 to 5,500 ft²/day (Metric Corp., 1985; Geohydrology Associates, Inc., 1989; Molzen-Corbin, 1991; Newcomer and Peery, 1994; Drakos, Lazarus, and Hodgins, 1999; Balleau Groundwater Inc., 2000). As noted in the "Pennsylvanian Sandia and Madera Formations" section, about eight additional wells completed in the combined Madera and overlying Abo Formation were tested with reported transmissivities in these wells ranging from 152 to 40,000 ft²/day. The groundwater-flow model of Shafike and Flanigan (1999) assigned the combined Abo and Yeso Formations a transmissivity range of 50–300 ft²/day.

Dissolved-solids concentrations in samples collected from wells completed in the Abo-Yeso hydrostratigraphic unit ranged from 208 to 2,060 mg/L (table 5). The median dissolved-solids concentration in 32 samples was 414.5 mg/L, and concentrations in 11 samples were greater than the SMCL of 500 mg/L. Calcium and bicarbonate are the dominant ions in most of the samples and several contain greater than 30 percent chloride or sulfate, which is higher than in other samples from the Abo-Yeso hydrostratigraphic unit (fig. 16). Though samples with a high percentage of chloride or sulfate are from wells scattered throughout the area, many are from wells adjacent to Jurassic rocks, possibly indicating localized recharge with high chloride concentrations or movement of water from Jurassic rocks that have high sulfate concentrations into the Abo-Yeso hydrostratigraphic unit. In general, chloride and sulfate concentrations are less than 100 mg/L; however, chloride and sulfate concentrations in about 25 percent of the samples are greater than 100 mg/L (table 5). Chloride concentrations in four samples were greater than the SMCL of 250 mg/L and sulfate concentrations in three samples were greater than the SMCL of 250 mg/L. Nitrate concentrations ranged from less than 0.05 to 19 mg/L. The median nitrate concentration was 0.66 mg/L, and only one sample exceeded the USEPA MCL of 10 mg/L. Nitrate concentrations were greater than the assumed background concentration (2 mg/L) in 11 of the 35 samples. Nitrate concentrations in samples from the Abo-Yeso hydrostratigraphic unit vary considerably. In several of the samples with chloride concentrations

greater than 250 mg/L, nitrate concentrations were higher than 5 mg/L, and in many of the samples with chloride concentrations greater than 100 mg/L, nitrate concentrations were greater than 2 mg/L (figs. 10 and 11). This combination of high chloride and nitrate concentrations may indicate effects from onsite wastewater-disposal systems (septic tanks and leach fields). Iron and manganese concentrations generally were less than 10 µg/L.

Table 5. Statistical summary of selected water-quality data for water from the Abo-Yeso hydrostratigraphic unit in the East Mountain study area.

[µS/cm, microsiemens per centimeter at 25 degrees Celsius; mg/L, milligrams per liter; Na, sodium; CaCO₃, calcium carbonate; SiO₂, silicon dioxide; N, nitrogen; P, phosphorus; µg/L, micrograms per liter; --, not applicable; MCL, U.S. Environmental Protection Agency maximum contaminant level; SMCL, U.S. Environmental Protection Agency secondary maximum contaminant level; ≤, less than or equal to]

Property or constituent	Number of samples	Number of samples less than detection limit	Number of samples greater than MCL or SMCL	Minimum	25th percentile	50th percentile	75th percentile	Maximum
pH (standard units)	36	--	0	6.8	7.225	7.4	7.575	7.8
Specific conductance (µS/cm)	39	--	--	426	540	709	1,000	3,110
Temperature (degrees Celsius)	28	--	--	9	13	13.85	14.925	23.5
Calcium (mg/L)	28	0	--	23	74	92.15	137.5	288
Magnesiuim (mg/L)	28	0	--	7.3	14.75	26.8	41.25	113
Potassium (mg/L)	26	0	--	0.7	1.1225	1.65	2.83	5.3
Sodium plus potassium (mg/L as Na)	33	0	--	5.6	16.4	29	56.7	241.8
Sodium (mg/L)	27	0	--	5.2	18	30	57	240
Alkalinity (mg/L as CaCO₃)	39	0	--	112	230	257	280	341
Chloride (mg/L)	37	0	4	3.2	6.95	20	96	382
Fluoride (mg/L)	28	0	1	0.1	0.2	0.3	0.4	2.4
Silica (mg/L as SiO₂)	27	0	--	13.2	18	20	23	27
Sulfate (mg/L)	34	0	3	14	27.075	44.5	100	792
Dissolved solids (mg/L)	32	0	11	208	302.5	414.5	594.75	2,060
Nitrate (mg/L as N)	35	2	1	≤0.05	0.18	0.66	3.6	19
Ammonia (mg/L as N)	23	14	--	≤0.01	≤0.01	≤0.01	0.02	0.04
Orthophosphate (mg/L as P)	26	8	--	≤0.003	≤0.01	0.015	0.02	0.2
Boron (µg/L)	22	0	--	10	36.75	63	100	190
Iron (µg/L)	23	15	0	≤3	≤3	≤8	10	100
Manganese (µg/L)	21	14	0	≤0.2	≤1	≤2	6.85	32

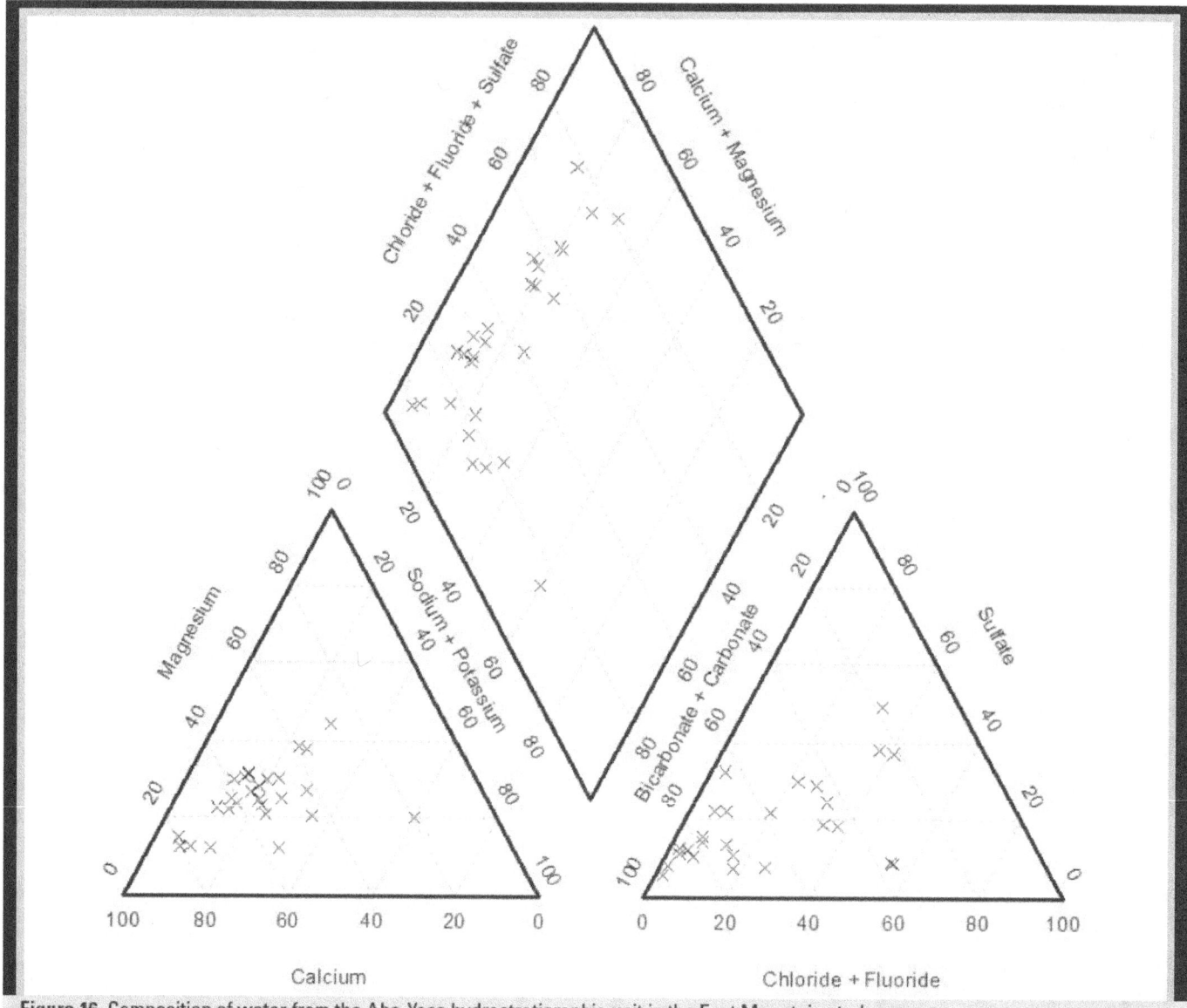

Figure 16. Composition of water from the Abo-Yeso hydrostratigraphic unit in the East Mountain study area.

Permian Glorieta and San Andres Formations

The Glorieta and San Andres Formations of Permian age intertongue in the study area and generally have not been differentiated on geologic maps or in previous reports. This relation has led to many changes in stratigraphic rank and relative position of the two geologic units, but in current (2005) geologic maps of the study area, both are ranked as formations (which includes usage of the term Glorieta Sandstone). Combined thickness is about 180 ft, where present (Williams and Cole, 2007).

The Glorieta Formation is a white, massive, plane- or cross-bedded, typically medium grained quartz sandstone. The San Andres Formation is a light gray to brown, thin- to medium-bedded limestone. Basally, at the Yeso Formation

contact, the Glorieta also may be pink and conglomeritic (Ferguson and others, 1996).

The San Andres-Glorieta seems to be a productive hydrostratigraphic unit and provides adequate water to wells and springs, although only a few wells in the study area (in the Tijeras Graben and west of the Tijeras Fault) are completed in the San Andres-Glorieta. Primary porosity of the hydrostratigraphic unit is fairly low except where fractured; some fractures in the San Andres limestone have been enlarged by dissolution (Titus, 1980). A search of previous work, including consultants' reports, found aquifer tests for about six wells completed in the combined Glorieta and San Andres Formations. Transmissivities ranged from 5,000 to 1.0×10^6 ft^2/day (Geohydrology Associates, Inc., 1985; Molzen-Corbin, 1991; Newcomer and Peery, 1994;

Balleau Groundwater Inc., 1997; Shomaker, 1987e). The groundwater-flow model of Shafike and Flanigan (1999) assigned the combined San Andres and Glorieta Formations a transmissivity range of 10,000–30,000 ft²/day. John Shomaker and Associates (1997) reported that in the Estancia Underground Water basin the transmissivity of the Glorieta Sandstone ranges from 4,010 to 51,778 ft²/day, with an average of 20,082 ft²/day.

Dissolved-solids concentrations in samples from 10 wells completed in the San Andres-Glorieta hydrostratigraphic unit ranged from 281 to 1,270 mg/L, and the median concentration was 348.5 mg/L. In two samples, concentrations were greater than the SMCL of 500 mg/L (table 6). Calcium and bicarbonate were the dominant ions in most of the samples, and the percentage of sulfate was greater than about 40 percent in two samples (fig. 17). Sulfate concentrations were greater in two samples (580 and 190 mg/L) than in any other samples from wells completed in the San Andres-Glorieta hydrostratigraphic unit. No samples exceeded the chloride SMCL of 250 mg/L, though one sample exceeded the sulfate SMCL of 250 mg/L. Nitrate concentrations ranged from 0.2 to 2.8 mg/L and no samples exceeded the MCL of 10 mg/L. Only one sample had a nitrate concentration greater than the assumed background concentration of 2 mg/L. Iron and manganese were generally less than 10 µg/L.

Table 6. Statistical summary of selected water-quality data for water from the San Andres-Glorieta hydrostratigraphic unit in the East Mountain study area.

[µS/cm, microsiemens per centimeter at 25 degrees Celsius; mg/L, milligrams per liter; Na, sodium; $CaCO_3$, calcium carbonate; SiO_2, silicon dioxide; N, nitrogen; P, phosphorus; µg/L, micrograms per liter; --, not applicable; MCL, U.S. Environmental Protection Agency maximum contaminant level; SMCL, U.S. Environmental Protection Agency secondary maximum contaminant level; ≤, less than or equal to]

Property or constituent	Number of samples	Number of samples less than detection limit	Number of samples greater than MCL or SMCL	Minimum	25th percentile	50th percentile	75th percentile	Maximum
pH (standard units)	8	--	--	7.3	7.33	7.45	7.57	7.8
Specific conductance (µS/cm)	9	--	--	478	485.5	577	656.5	766
Temperature (degrees Celsius)	8	--	--	11.7	13.05	13.75	14.425	15
Calcium (mg/L)	10	0	--	70	84.5	90.4	102.5	250
Magnesiuim (mg/L)	8	0	--	7.35	8.82	11.85	26	39
Potassium (mg/L)	9	0	--	0.7	0.715	0.89	1.18	2.1
Sodium plus potassium (mg/L as Na)	10	0	--	6.5	8.8	10.6	27.7	131.2
Sodium (mg/L)	9	0	--	6.11	7.85	9.74	31	130
Alkalinity (mg/L as $CaCO_3$)	11	0	--	110	220	239	247	286
Chloride (mg/L)	10	0	0	5.5	9.83	20.9	25.3	200
Fluoride (mg/L)	10	0	0	0.2	0.3	0.3	0.3	0.4
Silica (mg/L as SiO_2)	10	0	--	15.7	18	20	24.5	27
Sulfate (mg/L)	10	0	1	15	17	24	89.7	580
Dissolved solids (mg/L)	11	0	2	281	303	348.5	451	1,270
Nitrate (mg/L as N)	10	0	0	0.2	0.58	0.73	1.475	2.8
Ammonia (mg/L as N)	9	8	--	≤0.01	≤0.01	≤0.01	≤0.03	0.04
Orthophosphate (mg/L as P)	9	3	--	≤0.01	≤0.01	0.01	0.0165	0.02
Boron (µg/L)	9	0	--	10	12	20	110	410
Iron (µg/L)	9	5	0	≤3	≤4	6	7	11
Manganese (µg/L)	9	6	0	≤0.2	≤1	≤1	4	14

Triassic Moenkopi Formation and Chinle Group

The Moenkopi Formation of Triassic age is a sequence of maroon and brown micaceous sandstone and siltstone, that overlies the San Andres Formation. Thickness ranges from about 45 to 400 ft. The Moenkopi Formation is not a major aquifer in the study area and is combined in this report with the overlying Chinle Group into the Chinle-Moenkopi hydrostratigraphic unit.

The overlying Chinle Group, about 1,300 ft thick, is composed of reddish-brown, medium grained, cross-stratified sandstone and mudstone with pebble conglomerates near the base. The Chinle Group crops out at land surface and provides water to many wells west of NM 14 from about Cedar Crest to Sandia Park (fig. 2 and plate). The primary water-bearing sandstone is the basal rock unit of the Chinle Group, the Agua Zarca Formation. Initially identified by Smith (1957), Kelley and Northrop (1975), Titus (1980), Kues (1990), and White (1994) as the Santa Rosa Sandstone/Formation; Lucas and Heckert (1995) reclassified the Santa Rosa as the upper Triassic Agua Zarca Formation because of the lack of a medial mudstone.

A search of previous reports, including consultants' reports, found aquifer tests for about five wells completed in the Chinle Formation. Transmissivities ranged from 372 to

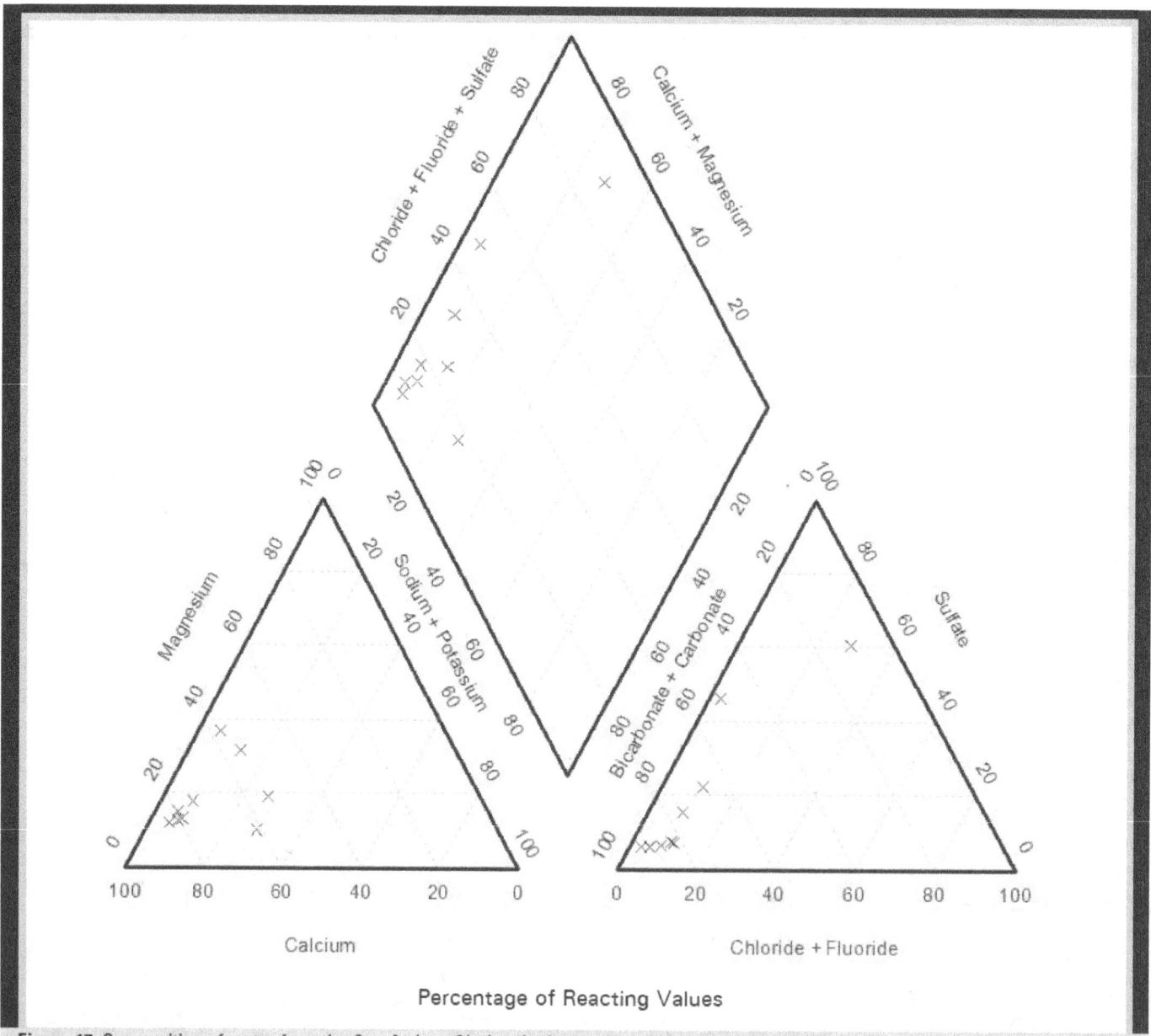

Percentage of Reacting Values

Figure 17. Composition of water from the San Andres-Glorieta hydrostratigraphic unit in the East Mountain study area.

2,280 ft²/day (Hydrotechnics, 1976; Molzen-Corbin, 1991; Rocky Mountain Geotech, Inc., 1989). The groundwater-flow model of Shafike and Flanigan (1999) assigned the combined Mesozoic formations a transmissivity range of 1–1,000 ft²/day.

Dissolved-solids concentrations in samples from 28 wells completed in the Chinle-Moenkopi hydrostratigraphic unit ranged from 268 to 1,950 mg/L; the median concentration was about 399.5 mg/L and concentrations in 8 samples were greater than the SMCL of 500 mg/L (table 7). Calcium and bicarbonate are the dominant ions in most samples (fig. 18). Several samples have high percentages of chloride or sulfate relative to most of samples. Samples with percentages of chloride greater than 30 generally have percentages of sulfate

less than 20 whereas samples with percentages of sulfate greater than 60 have percentages of chloride less than 20. Though water from wells completed in the Madera-Sandia and Abo-Yeso hydrostratigraphic units generally had high percentages of chloride and sulfate, samples from wells completed in the Chinle-Moenkopi hydrostratigraphic unit have either high chloride or high sulfate concentrations. This relation may be due to either the composition of recharge water or the mineralogy of the different geologic units. No samples from the Chinle-Moenkopi hydrostratigraphic unit had chloride concentrations greater than the SMCL of 250 mg/L; however, four samples had sulfate concentrations greater than the SMCL of 250 mg/L. The pH of one sample

Table 7. Statistical summary of selected water-quality data for water from the Chinle-Moenkopi hydrostratigraphic unit in the East Mountain study area.

[μS/cm, microsiemens per centimeter at 25 degrees Celsius; mg/L, milligrams per liter; Na, sodium; CaCO₃, calcium carbonate; SiO₂, silicon dioxide; N, nitrogen; P, phosphorus; μg/L, micrograms per liter; --, not applicable; MCL, U.S. Environmental Protection Agency maximum contaminant level; SMCL, U.S. Environmental Protection Agency secondary maximum contaminant level; ≤, less than or equal to]

Property or constituent	Number of samples	Number of samples less than detection limit	Number of samples greater than MCL or SMCL	Minimum	25th percentile	50th percentile	75th percentile	Maximum
pH (standard units)	31	--	1	6.5	7.2	7.4	7.6	9
Specific conductance (μS/cm)	32	--	--	448	570.25	715	983.75	3,200
Temperature (degrees Celsius)	29	--	--	10.5	13.5	14	15	20.5
Calcium (mg/L)	28	0	--	0.85	63.5	84.5	120	330
Magnesiuim (mg/L)	28	0	--	0.051	12.75	19	21.75	150
Potassium (mg/L)	26	0	--	0.07	0.775	1.1	1.5525	4.9
Sodium plus potassium (mg/L as Na)	28	0	--	8.5	22.2	28.5	50.3	168
Sodium (mg/L)	27	0	--	8	22	28	51	168
Alkalinity (mg/L as CaCO₃)	32	0	--	150	223.75	253	277.25	364
Chloride (mg/L)	33	0	0	5.6	17.5	43	87.4	203
Fluoride (mg/L)	30	0	0	0.1	0.2	0.3	0.3	2.2
Silica (mg/L as SiO₂)	29	0	--	10	18.5	23	25	28
Sulfate (mg/L)	30	0	4	16	25	31.5	47.25	1,100
Dissolved solids (mg/L)	28	0	8	268	345.25	399.5	537.75	1,950
Nitrate (mg/L as N)	33	1	1	≤0.1	0.8	2.3	4.885	21
Ammonia (mg/L as N)	29	15	--	≤0.01	≤0.01	≤0.015	0.03	0.71
Orthophosphate (mg/L as P)	29	8	--	≤0.01	≤0.01	0.01	0.025	0.07
Boron (μg/L)	26	0	--	10	69.25	100	175	684
Iron (μg/L)	25	14	0	≤3	≤3	≤4	9.5	60
Manganese (μg/L)	25	17	0	≤1	≤1	≤1	2.5	32.2

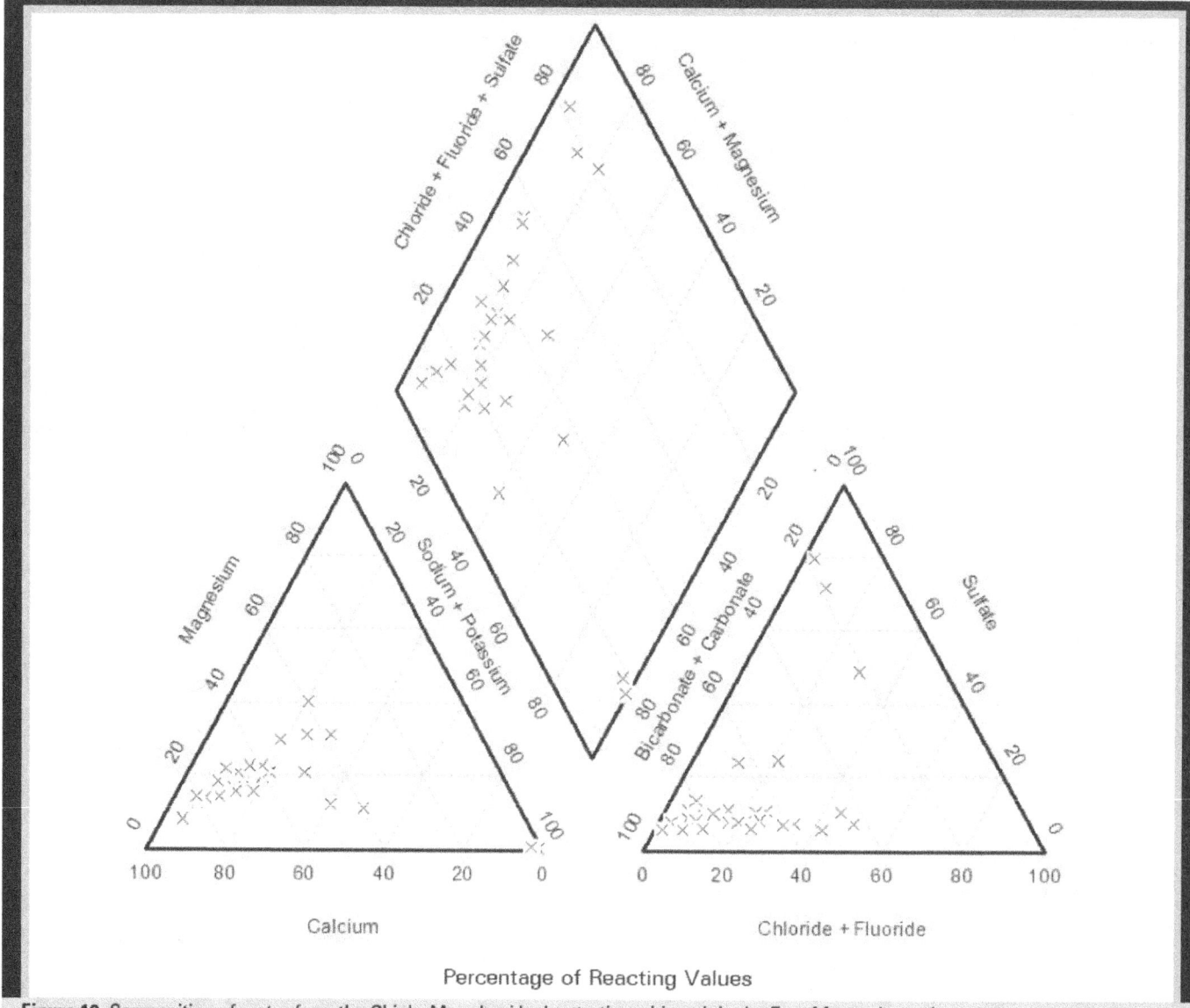

Figure 18. Composition of water from the Chinle-Moenkopi hydrostratigraphic unit in the East Mountain study area.

(9.0) exceeded the SMCL. One sample had a nitrate concentration greater than the MCL of 10 mg/L, and in 16 of 33 samples nitrate concentrations were greater than the assumed background concentration of 2 mg/L. Iron and manganese concentrations generally were less than 10 µg/L.

Jurassic Entrada Sandstone, Wanakah Formation, and Morrison Formation

The Entrada Sandstone and Wanakah Formation of lower Jurassic age are as much as 350 ft thick, and are composed of a sequence of sandstone, mudstone, dark limestone, and gypsum. The Morrison Formation of upper Jurassic age is about 850 ft thick and is composed of light colored sandstones with green to light brown mudstone in the study area.

Although previous authors have addressed these geologic units separately, in this report the Entrada Sandstone, Wanakah Formation, and Morrison Formation are grouped into the Jurassic hydrostratigraphic unit because recent mapping does not always differentiate the formations and because there are few wells completed in the Entrada Sandstone or the Wanakah Formation.

Jurassic rocks are exposed at land surface in several areas in the study area—the Tijeras Graben, Ortiz Mountains, and in the Hagen Basin (plate). These rocks are not commonly used as sources of water and apparently provide water only to a few wells in the north end of the Tijeras Graben, west of the Tijeras Fault near San Antonito, and near Placitas. The sandstone units have moderate porosity and permeability, though water quality is adversely affected by interbedded dark limestones and gypsum (Johnson, 2000).

A search of previous reports, including consultants' reports, found aquifer tests for three wells completed in the Jurassic hydrostratigraphic unit with reported transmissivities ranging from 16 to 910 ft²/day (Molzen-Corbin, 1991; Geohydrology Associates, Inc., 1994). The groundwater-flow model of Shafike and Flanigan (1999) assigned the combined Mesozoic formations a transmissivity range of 1-1,000 ft²/day.

Dissolved-solids concentrations in nine samples from wells completed in the Jurassic hydrostratigraphic unit ranged from 286 to 2,470 mg/L; the median concentration was 572 mg/L, and all but two of the samples had concentrations greater than 500 mg/L (table 8). Calcium was the dominant cation in water from wells completed in the Jurassic hydrostratigraphic unit; anion percentages varied widely

(fig. 19). Sulfate concentrations ranged from 10 to 1,500 mg/L and chloride concentrations ranged from 3.9 to 230 mg/L. Sulfate concentrations in three samples were greater than the SMCL of 250 mg/L. The large range in sulfate concentrations is due to the dissolution of the interbedded gypsum in the hydrostratigraphic unit though the source of the high chloride concentrations is not known. Nitrate concentrations varied from 0.02 to 3.9 mg/L, no samples had concentrations greater than the MCL of 10 mg/L, and only two samples had concentrations greater than the assumed background concentration of 2 mg/L. The highest nitrate concentrations were in samples with the highest chloride concentrations. Samples with the highest iron concentrations generally had the highest sulfate concentrations.

Table 8. Statistical summary of selected water-quality data for water from the Jurassic hydrostratigraphic unit in the East Mountain study area.

[µS/cm, microsiemens per centimeter at 25 degrees Celsius; mg/L, milligrams per liter; Na, sodium; $CaCO_3$, calcium carbonate; SiO_2, silicon dioxide; N, nitrogen; P, phosphorus; µg/L, micrograms per liter; --, not applicable; MCL, U.S. Environmental Protection Agency maximum contaminant level; SMCL, U.S. Environmental Protection Agency secondary maximum contaminant level; ≤, less than or equal to]

Property or constituent	Number of samples	Number of samples less than detection limit	Number of samples greater than MCL or SMCL	Minimum	25th percentile	50th percentile	75th percentile	Maximum
pH (standard units)	7	--	0	6.6	6.8	7.2	7.5	7.6
Specific conductance (µS/cm)	7	--	--	508	700	826	1,360	2,490
Temperature (degrees Celsius)	4	--	--	11.2	11.9	14.75	17.375	18
Calcium (mg/L)	9	0	--	84	92	120	305	610
Magnesiuim (mg/L)	9	0	--	4.4	14.85	25	42.5	56
Potassium (mg/L)	6	0	--	0.7	0.85	1.7	2.1	2.1
Sodium plus potassium (mg/L as Na)	9	0	--	12.4	20.9	26	44.6	77
Sodium (mg/L)	6	0	--	12	16.5	22.5	43	76
Alkalinity (mg/L as $CaCO_3$)	9	0	--	123	165	210	244	354
Chloride (mg/L)	9	0	0	3.9	6.3	20	119	230
Fluoride (mg/L)	9	0	0	0.1	0.2	0.3	0.35	0.6
Silica (mg/L as SiO_2)	9	0	--	18	19.5	22	23.5	40
Sulfate (mg/L)	9	0	3	10	19.5	130	735	1,500
Dissolved solids (mg/L)	9	0	7	286	465.5	572	1,270	2,470
Nitrate (mg/L as N)	9	0	0	0.02	0.1	0.66	2.55	3.9
Ammonia (mg/L as N)	6	4	--	≤ 0.01	≤ 0.01	0.01	0.0225	0.03
Orthophosphate (mg/L as P)	6	2	--	≤ 0.01	≤ 0.01	0.01	0.0325	0.04
Boron (µg/L)	6	0	--	20	35	65	150	210
Iron (µg/L)	6	1	0	≤ 3	3.75	12	22	43
Manganese (µg/L)	6	2	0	≤ 1	≤ 1	2	3	6

Cretaceous Dakota Sandstone, Mancos Shale, and Mesaverde Group

Despite a combined thickness of more than 3,000 ft in the Tijeras Graben, the Dakota Sandstone, Mancos Shale, and Mesaverde Group of Cretaceous age are primarily shale and wells completed in these units do not produce large quantities of water in the study area. The sandstone, siltstone, and limestone beds that produce water are generally thin. The Dakota Formation is primarily a fine to medium-grained sandstone. The Mancos Shale is primarily a dark-gray shale with limestone and sandstone beds. The Mesaverde Group is a complex unit of multicolored sandstone, shale, and

coal. The Cretaceous geologic units are treated as a single hydrostratigraphic unit in this report.

The Cretaceous hydrostratigraphic unit yields water to wells and springs in the Tijeras Graben, west of the Tijeras Fault near San Antonito and near Placitas. Titus (1980) and Johnson (2000) noted that wells completed in Cretaceous rocks tended to produce low volumes of poor-quality water. Previous reports, including consultants' reports, found aquifer tests for two wells completed in the Cretaceous hydrostratigraphic unit. Transmissivities ranged from 300 to 1,500 ft²/day (Molzen-Corbin, 1991). The groundwater-flow model of Shafike and Flanigan (1999) assigned the combined Mesozoic formations a transmissivity range of 1–1,000 ft²/day.

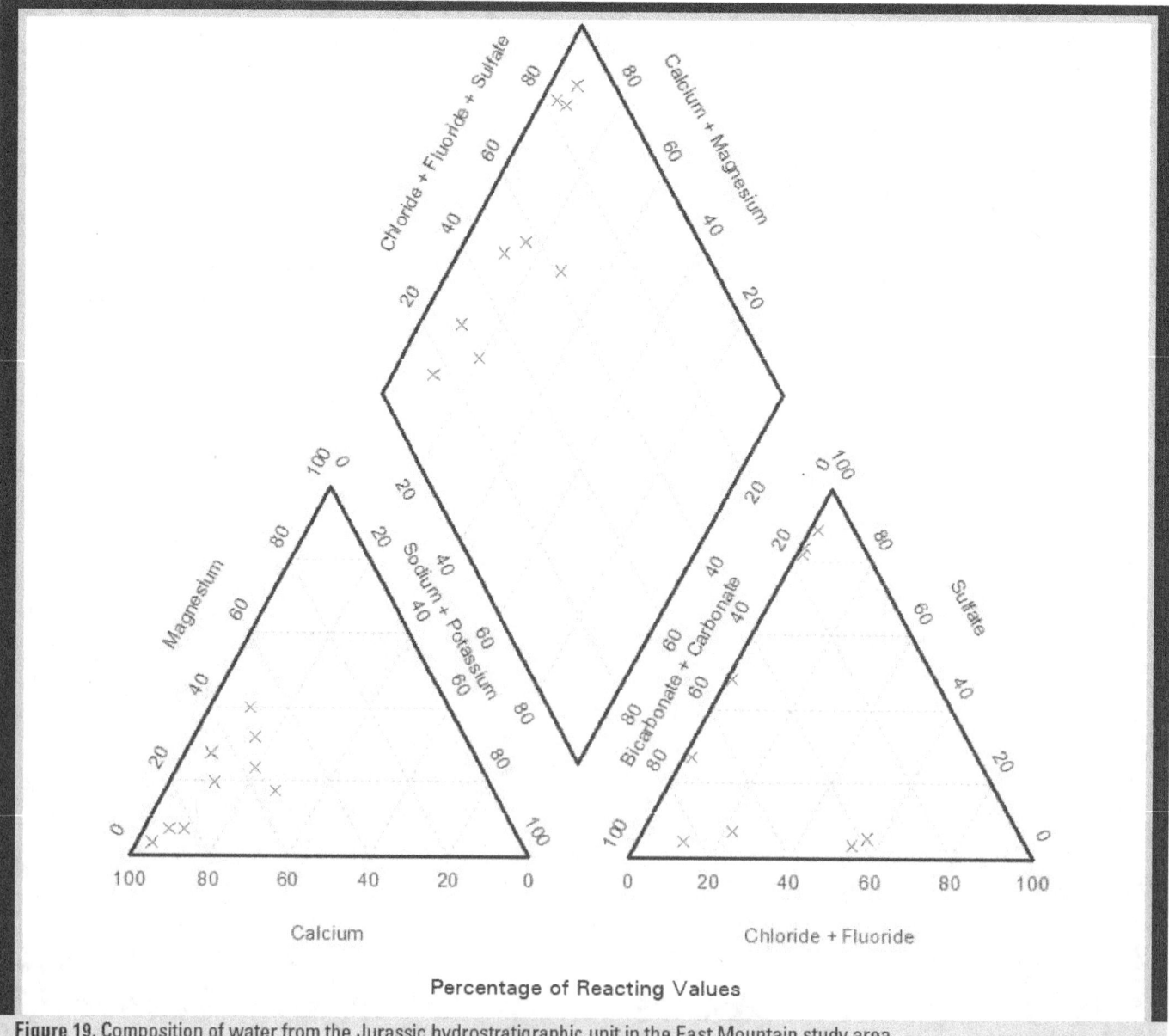

Figure 19. Composition of water from the Jurassic hydrostratigraphic unit in the East Mountain study area.

Dissolved-solids concentrations in samples from 30 wells completed in the Cretaceous hydrostratigraphic unit ranged from 407 to 3,540 mg/L, the median concentration was 1,022 mg/L and 28 samples had concentrations greater than the SMCL of 500 mg/L (table 9). Most wells completed in the Cretaceous hydrostratigraphic unit are along and east of NM 14 in the Cedar Crest area, and dissolved-solids concentrations in samples from this area generally were greater than 500 mg/L (fig. 20). No cations or anions were dominant in water from the Cretaceous hydrostratigraphic unit and the percentages of magnesium and chloride are mostly constant compared to the percentages of calcium, sodium, bicarbonate, and sulfate (fig. 21). The composition of water

from the Cretaceous hydrostratigraphic unit varies, which may be partly due to the range of rock types and the abundance of shale. In general, dissolved-solids and sulfate concentrations in water from the Cretaceous hydrostratigraphic unit are greater than dissolved-solids and sulfate concentrations in other hydrostratigraphic units in the study area. The chloride concentration in one sample was greater than the SMCL of 250 mg/L, and in 20 samples, sulfate concentrations were greater than the SMCL of 250 mg/L (in the area between NM 14 and Interstate 40) (fig. 13). In general, the pH of water from wells completed in the Cretaceous hydrostratigraphic unit was lower than the pH in samples from wells completed in other hydrostratigraphic units in the study area, and only one

Table 9. Statistical summary of selected water-quality data for water from the Cretaceous hydrostratigraphic unit in the East Mountain study area.

[μS/cm, microsiemens per centimeter at 25 degrees Celsius; mg/L, milligrams per liter; Na, sodium; CaCO$_3$, calcium carbonate; SiO$_2$, silicon dioxide; N, nitrogen; P, phosphorus; μg/L, micrograms per liter; --, not applicable; MCL, U.S. Environmental Protection Agency maximum contaminant level; SMCL, U.S. Environmental Protection Agency secondary maximum contaminant level; $\leq$, less than or equal to]

Property or constituent	Number of samples	Number of samples less than detection limit	Number of samples greater than MCL or SMCL	Minimum	25th percentile	50th percentile	75th percentile	Maximum
pH (standard units)	28	--	1	6.4	6.925	7.2	7.4	8.4
Specific conductance (μS/cm)	30	--	--	385	1077.5	1525	2452.5	4,010
Temperature (degrees Celsius)	27	--	--	9.5	13.9	15	16	19.1
Calcium (mg/L)	29	0	--	3	84	131	350	540
Magnesiuim (mg/L)	29	0	--	1.7	26.75	55	130.5	266
Potassium (mg/L)	27	0	--	0.85	2	4.2	7.4	50
Sodium plus potassium (mg/L as Na)	30	0	--	17.7	39.9	75.5	248.5	544.9
Sodium (mg/L)	27	0	--	17	45	173	290	540
Alkalinity (mg/L as CaCO$_3$)	32	0	--	210	316.5	402	514.75	809
Chloride (mg/L)	32	0	1	5.8	19	79.95	161.5	290
Fluoride (mg/L)	29	0	0	0.1	0.2	0.3	0.5	1.9
Silica (mg/L as SiO$_2$)	29	0	--	9.6	15	18.7	22.5	27
Sulfate (mg/L)	31	0	20	88	146	300	1,000	2,200
Dissolved solids (mg/L)	30	0	28	407	727.75	1,022.50	2,142.50	3,540
Nitrate (mg/L as N)	28	12	0	≤ 0.05	≤ 0.05	0.13	1.165	5.2
Ammonia (mg/L as N)	26	6	--	≤ 0.01	0.02	0.155	0.745	2
Orthophosphate (mg/L as P)	27	14	--	≤ 0.006	≤ 0.01	≤ 0.01	0.01	0.11
Boron (μg/L)	26	0	--	30	80	138.5	216.25	480
Iron (μg/L)	27	6	7	≤ 3	8	30	346	27,000
Manganese (μg/L)	27	3	6	≤ 1	6	18	30	260

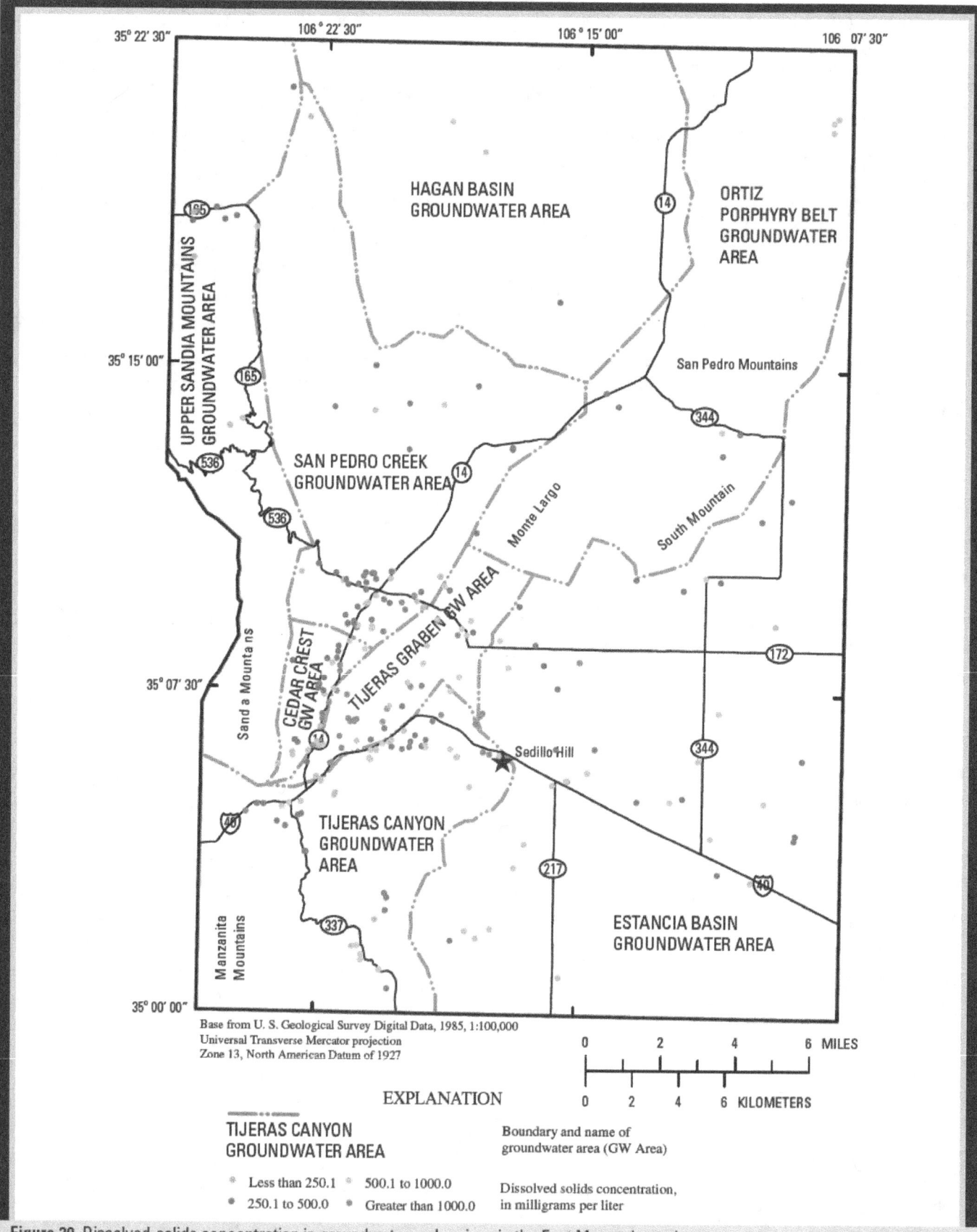

Figure 20. Dissolved-solids concentration in groundwater and springs in the East Mountain study area.

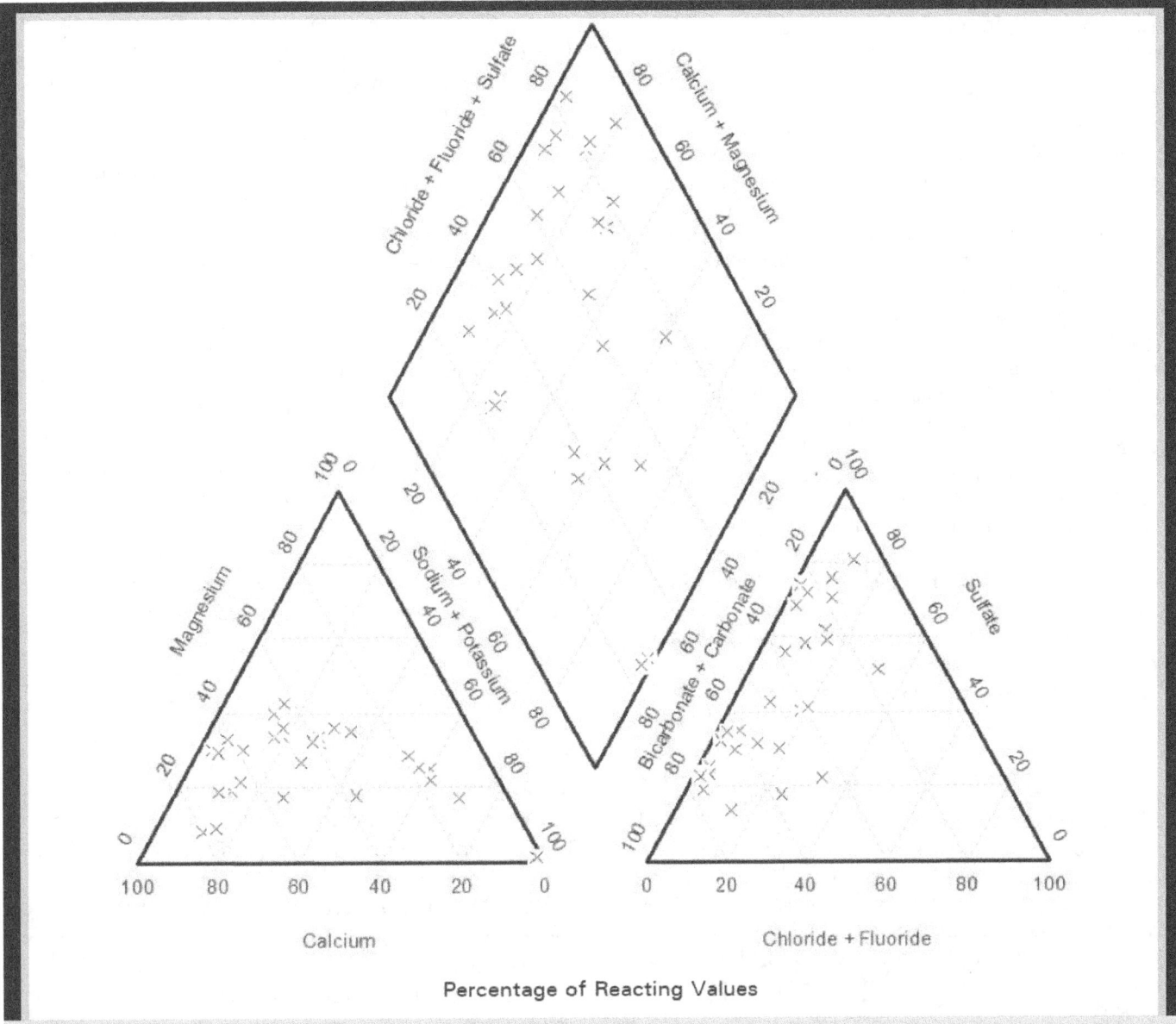

Percentage of Reacting Values

Figure 21. Composition of water from the Cretaceous hydrostratigraphic unit in the East Mountain study area.

sample with a pH of 6.4 was outside of the SMCL of 6.5 to 8.5 (table 9). Nitrate concentrations ranged from less than 0.05 to 5.2 mg/L; although no nitrate concentrations were greater than the MCL of 10 mg/L, concentrations in five samples were greater than the assumed background concentration of 2 mg/L. Dissolved iron and manganese concentrations were generally higher in water samples from the Cretaceous hydrostratigraphic unit than in samples from wells completed in other hydrostratigraphic units in the study area. Samples from seven wells exceeded the SMCL for iron (300 µg/L) and samples from six wells exceeded the SMCL for manganese (50 µg/L (table 9). Dissolved iron and manganese in water samples usually indicates the absence of dissolved oxygen;

conversely, nitrate concentrations are usually low in water without dissolved oxygen. Thus, in general, high nitrate concentrations are not expected in water from wells completed in the Cretaceous hydrostratigraphic unit because of the common lack of dissolved oxygen and the presence of dissolved iron and manganese.

Water from wells completed in Cretaceous rocks in the study area will generally contain higher dissolved solids, sulfate, iron, and manganese concentrations than water from wells completed in other hydrostratigraphic units in the East Mountain area. Nitrate concentrations, however, will generally be low in water from wells completed in the Cretaceous hydrostratigraphic unit.

Cenozoic Geologic Units

Rocks and sediment of the Cenozoic era in the study area include the Tertiary Diamond Tail, Galisteo, and Espinaso Formations and Santa Fe Group; and Quaternary alluvium and colluvium. All of these rocks and sediments are treated as a single Cenozoic hydrostratigraphic unit in this report.

The Diamond Tail Formation is the lowermost Cenozoic geologic unit in the northern part of the study area and is about 450 ft thick, but thickness varies. The Diamond Tail formation is composed of yellow, orange and gray sandstone and variegated mudstone. The overlying Galisteo Formation may be as much as 3,210 ft thick northwest of Galisteo and is composed primarily of red sandstone and mudstone (Lucas and others, 1997). Overlying the Galisteo is the 1,400-ft thick Espinaso Formation composed primarily of volcaniclastic conglomerate, sandstone, and volcanic debris-flow deposits, with a few volcanic interbeds (Pazzaglia and others, 1999a and Williams and Cole, 2007). All these geologic units crop out at land surface in the northern part of the study area.

Stratigraphically, the Tertiary Santa Fe Group overlies the Espinaso Formation; however, because of deformation and erosion in the northern Hagan Basin, the Santa Fe Group unconformably overlies many of the older geologic units exposed in the central and southern basin. Recent work by Connell (2001) and Connell and others (2001) on the stratigraphy of the Santa Fe Group have subdivided it and clarified the relation to other Tertiary deposits surrounding the Albuquerque Basin. In the Hagan Basin the Santa Fe Group has been divided into the Tanos, Blackshare, and Tuerto Formations (oldest to youngest, respectively).

Intrusive and extrusive igneous rocks of Tertiary age are in the northeastern part of the study area and emplacement of the igneous rocks resulted in South Mountain, the San Pedro Mountains, and other structural features of the Ortiz Porphyry Belt. These igneous rocks probably do not yield an appreciable quantity of water to wells or springs; these rocks probably act as barriers to flow.

Though little is known of the hydrologic properties of these Tertiary geologic units in the Hagan Basin, these units are not considered to be substantial aquifers because these rocks are generally thin, bounded by less permeable rocks, and are deep in much of the study area (Lewis and West, 1995; Grant, 1999; Johnson, 2000); however, a few wells are completed in these geologic units in the northern part of the study area.

Analyses are available for two samples collected from wells completed in the Galisteo Formation (appendix 3), though one sample was analyzed for few constituents and thus is not addressed in detail. The sample with the more complete analysis had a dissolved-solids concentration of 868 mg/L, the sulfate concentration was 374 mg/L, and the nitrate concentration was 1.5 mg/L. No dominant cations were detected, and sulfate was the dominant anion. The sulfate concentration was 660 mg/L in the second sample. Based on the high sulfate concentrations in these two samples, water in the Galisteo Formation may be of poor quality.

Locally, Quaternary alluvium provides water to wells and springs. The alluvium in the study area, is typically found in two settings: stream valleys and the Estancia Basin. Stream-valley alluvium is typically thin, such as in Tijeras Canyon, Arroyo San Antonito, and Frost Arroyo, but may be as much as 100 ft thick in some areas. Because water in the alluvium is well connected with streams, water levels in wells (and flows from springs) completed in the alluvium tend to fluctuate seasonally and with precipitation. Thus, these wells and springs are likely sensitive to drought.

The Quaternary alluvium in the Estancia Basin varies in thickness from 0 to about 450 ft; however, in most of the study area is probably less than 100 ft thick (Titus, 1980; Broadhead, 1997). Although many water wells have been drilled in the Estancia Basin alluvium, most are probably also screened in the underlying Madera (and occasionally Abo) Formations. Similarly, in those areas where the Quaternary alluvium is underlain by Precambrian granite, Tertiary volcanic rocks, or other consolidated geologic units, "Quaternary alluvium" wells may be completed in several units. Well completion in several units of wide ranging aquifer properties is probably reflected in the transmissivities recorded in previous reports for about six wells completed in Quaternary alluvium: these transmissivities ranged from 88 to 2,780 ft^2/day (Patterson, 1979; Geohydrology Associates, Inc., 1989; Molzen-Corbin, 1991; Clay Kilmer and Associates, Ltd., 1996b, 1997b; Balleau Groundwater Inc., 1997). The groundwater-flow model of Shafike and Flanigan (1999) assigned the Estancia Basin alluvium a transmissivity range of 2,000–8,000 ft^2/day. John W. Shomaker and Associates (1997) reported that in the Estancia Underground Water Basin the transmissivity of the Cenozoic valley fill ranges from 226 to 21,277 ft^2/day, with an average of 5,382 ft^2/day.

Dissolved-solids concentrations in samples from 10 wells completed in the Quaternary alluvium ranged from 250 to 1,860 mg/L, the median concentration was 395 mg/L, and in three of these samples, concentrations were greater than the SMCL of 500 mg/L (table 10). Calcium and bicarbonate are the dominant ions. In one sample the percentage of chloride plus fluoride was greater than 60 and in another the percentage of sulfate was about 50 (fig. 22). Chloride and sulfate concentrations in these two samples were much greater than in the remaining samples. In two samples, chloride concentrations were greater than the SMCL of 250 mg/L, and one sample had a sulfate concentration greater than the SMCL of 250 mg/L. Nitrate concentrations ranged from less than 0.02 to 9.2 mg/L, no concentrations were greater than the MCL of 10 mg/L. In five samples nitrate concentrations were greater than the assumed background concentration of 2 mg/L. Several of the samples with high nitrate concentrations also had high chloride concentrations compared to other samples from wells completed in the alluvium.

Table 10. Statistical summary of selected water-quality data for water from the Quaternary alluvium in the East Mountain study area.

[μS/cm, microsiemens per centimeter at 25 degrees Celsius; mg/L, milligrams per liter; Na, sodium; CaCO₃, calcium carbonate; SiO₂, silicon dioxide; N, nitrogen; P, phosphorus; μg/L, micrograms per liter; --, not applicable; MCL, U.S. Environmental Protection Agency maximum contaminant level; SMCL, U.S. Environmental Protection Agency secondary maximum contaminant level;≤, less than or equal to]

Property or constituent	Number of samples	Number of samples less than detection limit	Number of samples greater than MCL or SMCL	Minimum	25th percentile	50th percentile	75th percentile	Maximum
pH (standard units)	10	--	0	7.3	7.3	7.6	7.7	7.8
Specific conductance (μS/cm)	11	--	--	410	542	673	750	2650
Temperature (degrees Celsius)	6	--	--	11	11.75	14.5	18.125	21.5
Calcium (mg/L)	8	0	--	34	60.25	103	162.5	260
Magnesiuim (mg/L)	8	0	--	15	15.25	21	43	97
Potassium (mg/L)	5	0	--	0.6	0.95	1.9	3.2	4.3
Sodium plus potassium (mg/L as Na)	11	0	--	5.3	15	22	30.1	212.5
Sodium (mg/L)	5	0	--	5	13	29	125	210
Alkalinity (mg/L as CaCO₃)	11	0	--	171	211	250	303	358
Chloride (mg/L)	11	0	2	3	9	17	57	310
Fluoride (mg/L)	9	0	0	0.1	0.15	0.3	0.5	1
Silica (mg/L as SiO₂)	7	0	--	10	16	25	25	31
Sulfate (mg/L)	11	0	1	16	45	54	110	710
Dissolved solids (mg/L)	10	0	3	250	316.5	395	578.75	1,860
Nitrate (mg/L as N)	11	0	0	0.02	0.09	0.5	2.7	9.2
Ammonia (mg/L as N)	3	2	--	≤0.01	≤0.01	≤0.01	0.04	0.04
Orthophosphate (mg/L as P)	4	0	--	0.02	0.02	0.025	0.0375	0.04
Boron (μg/L)	3	0	--	50	50	110	110	110
Iron (μg/L)	4	1	1	16	17	45	467.5	600
Manganese (μg/L)	3	0	0	9	9	10	30	30

Groundwater Levels, Recharge, and Flow

Water-level contours were drawn on a regional scale assuming all hydrostratigraphic units are connected and function as one single regional aquifer (plate). The regional potentiometric map results in a coherent surface that shows general directions of groundwater flow, groundwater-flow divides, and can be used to estimate depth to water throughout the area. Some hydrologic connection between adjacent hydrostratigraphic units may exist although the connection varies depending on the hydrologic properties of the units. Several areas have large differences in water levels in small distances; however, these are generally adjacent to faults. On

a local scale, all hydrologic units may not function as a single aquifer because confining layers or low hydraulic-conductivity zones will impede movement of water on short time scales. The units in the area that have small hydraulic conductivity would restrict movement of water between units.

Not all water levels were used to construct the potentiometic map because of some large differences in water levels in short distances that could not be attributed to fault zones. Water levels in adjacent areas were then compared to determine which water levels were consistent with each other. Data were not sufficient to only use water levels measured during a short time period; therefore, water levels measured from many dates were used. Water levels vary with time in

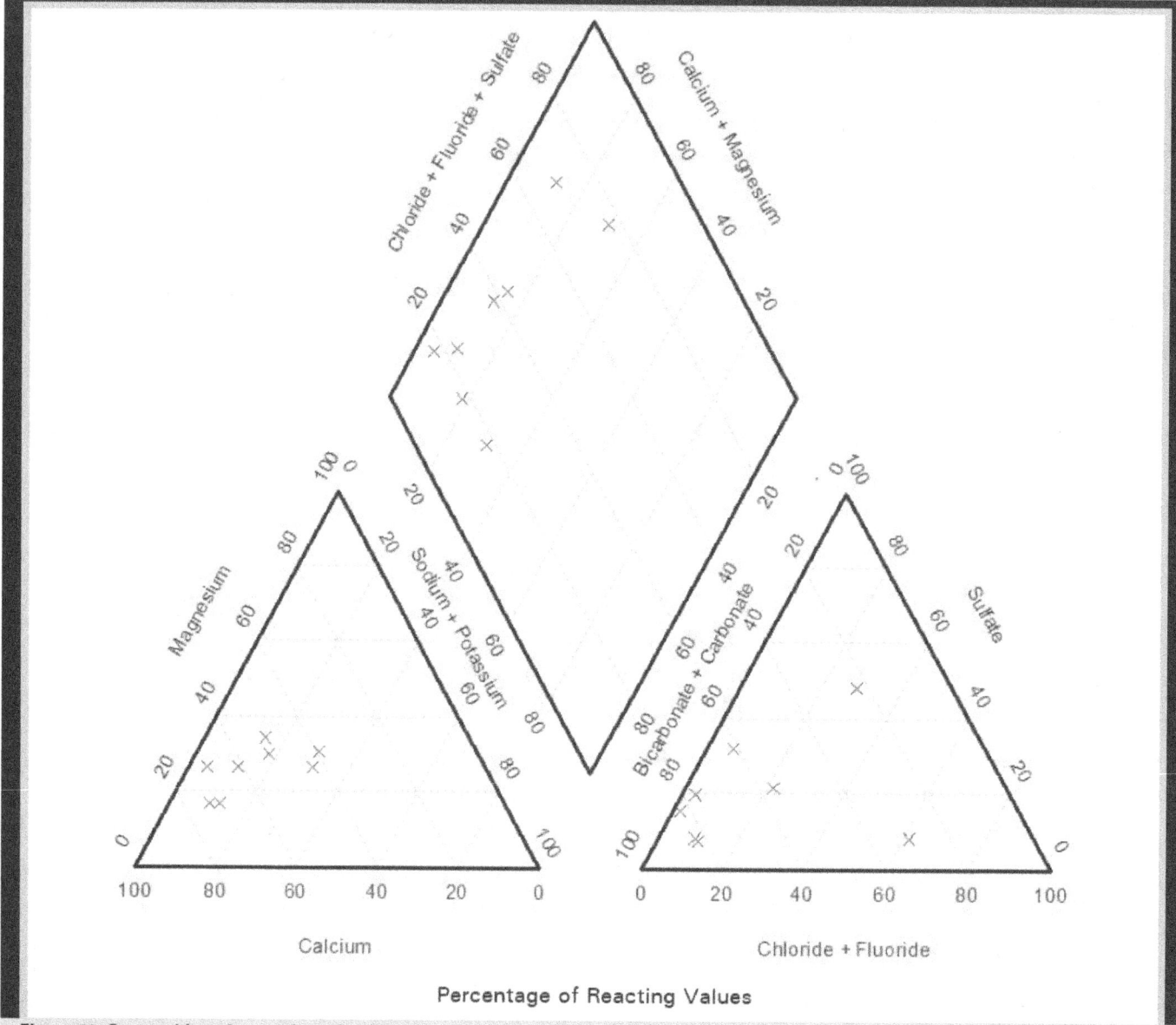

Figure 22. Composition of water from the Quaternary alluvium in the East Mountain study area.

the East Mountain area; however, small temporal water-level variations would not have a substantial effect on the regional potentiometric surface because the contour interval is 100 ft.

Among the previous groundwater-level maps of all or part of the East Mountain study area are Mourant (1980), Titus (1980), White (1994), Estancia Basin Planning Committee (1999), Shafike and Flanigan (1999), Bexfield and Anderholm (2000), D.B. Stephens and Associates (2003), and Bernalillo County (2006). In addition, many local scale water-level maps can be found in consultants' reports.

The highest water-level elevations as expected are associated with the Sandia, Manzanita, Ortiz and San Pedro

Mountains and South Mountains (plate). Groundwater moves eastward and northward from the Sandia and Manzanita Mountains. A groundwater-flow divide along the crest of the Ortiz Porphyry Belt corresponds to the area where flow moves eastward into the Estancia Basin and westward toward San Pedro synclinorium and the Hagen Basin. A groundwater-flow divide south of Frost Road first recognized by Titus (1980) runs roughly along the crest of the Manzanita Mountains or the surface-water divide between Tijeras Canyon and the Estancia Basin. This groundwater divide corresponds to the area where groundwater flows eastward to the Estancia Basin and westward to Tijeras Canyon (plate).

Groundwater flows out of the study area northward through the San Pedro synclinorium, into the Hagan Basin, and then into the Albuquerque Basin. In the southwest, groundwater flow is toward Tijeras Canyon and downgradient into the Albuquerque Basin. To the east, groundwater flow is into the Estancia (and Española) Basins, and then eastward out of the study area.

A potentiometric low corresponds to the location of the Barton Trough (discussed in the "Structural Features" section) mapped by Titus (1980). As he noted, the uplifted block on the east side of the trough blocks eastward flow and the Madera-Sandia hydrostratigraphic unit in the trough must have high values of hydraulic conductivity that allows groundwater from the surrounding uplands to drain into the trough and southeastward through a narrow gap into the Estancia Basin. As discussed in the earlier "Potential Sources of Alkalinity and Dissolved Carbon Section" high values of alkalinity may indicate carbon dioxide dissolution of carbonate rocks, resulting in increased permeability. Alkalinities in the Barton Trough area are high and thus, may confirm Titus's supposition of increased permeability. Titus (1980, p. 13) discussed several wells south and east of the Barton Trough that produced water charged with carbon dioxide and had high alkalinities. These wells were in a highly permeable zone in the Madera-Sandia hydrostratigraphic unit.

Water-level differences of about 600 ft were observed in a short distance in the area between South Mountain and the San Pedro Mountains (plate). The large difference is probably due to a large fault that offsets permeable rocks in the area. Whereas, the geologic map does not show a fault in this area, a splay fault associated with the Gutierrez Fault could extend northward in this area resulting in these large water-level differences.

Recharge

Recharge to the aquifers in the East Mountain area may originate as the result of direct infiltration of precipitation (diffuse recharge); infiltration of surface-water runoff in stream channels, arroyos, or road ditches (focused recharge); infiltration of wastewater discharged to septic tanks/drain fields; and groundwater inflow from adjacent aquifers. Direct and focused recharge are commonly estimated by using a variety of techniques. Most of these estimates assume a rate per unit area that implies that recharge rates are constant areally. During a groundwater study in Nevada, Maxey and Eakin (1949) developed a method, commonly used throughout the arid southwest, to estimate recharge on the basis of mean annual precipitation. They estimated no recharge happens in areas where mean annual precipitation is less than 8 inches and the rate of recharge increased to a maximum of 25 percent of mean annual precipitation in areas with more than 20 inches of mean annual precipitation. Since Maxey and Eakins work, several investigators have shown that direct infiltration of precipitation does not happen in large areas of the arid southwest even where mean annual precipitation is greater

than 8 inches (Anderholm, 1994; Phillips, 1994: and Scanlon, 1991). Focused recharge, however, does happen in many of the areas where there is no direct recharge.

Areal recharge (diffuse recharge plus focused recharge) is often the most uncertain component of water budgets and groundwater-flow models and is thus often calculated as the residual of other components. Without a priori knowledge of probable values, choosing between values of areal recharge calculated by different methods is difficult; thus, the larger context provided by water budgets and groundwater-flow model calibration is crucial in determining reasonable values.

Several investigators have estimated runoff and groundwater recharge in and near the East Mountain study area. Summers (1981) estimated recharge near the Ortiz Mountains as 1.06 inches per year. Molzen-Corbin and Associates and Lee Wilson and Associates (1991) cited recharge rates ranging from 0.1 to 1.0 inches per year, with a general rate of 0.5 inches per year. Among their assumptions were that as much as 8 percent of the precipitation falling on the Madera Formation outcrop in the Upper Sandia Mountains becomes groundwater recharge. In their study of the proposed San Pedro Creek Estates subdivision, Newcomer and Peery (1994, p. 10) used an estimate of 2.5 percent of precipitation on the Madera Formation outcrop in the lower Sandia Mountains as recharge to groundwater. By assuming an annual precipitation of 13.5 inches per year and an area of 4,660 acres (7.3 mi^2), Newcomer and Peery (1994, p. 10) arrived at a recharge volume of 132 arce-ft per year (0.34 inches per year). By using watershed modeling, Finch and others (1995) estimated that recharge at the San Pedro Mine ranged from 1.0 to 5.3 inches per year. In the course of determining minimum lot size in the East Mountain area of Bernalillo County, CH2M Hill (1992a) used a solute-transport model and specified recharge as 0.5 inches per year. Peterson (1999) used the Summers (1981) and CH2M Hill (1992a) estimates to determine recharge to the Sandia Basin as ranging from 2,000 to 4,100 acre-ft/year.

Meinzer (1911) in the first hydrologic study of the Estancia Basin, identified the primary sources of recharge and discharge and estimated discharge from the playas to be 81,000 acre-ft/year, but declined to quantify a recharge volume because of uncertainties regarding groundwater flow in and out of the basin. Smith (1957) noted that the primary source of recharge to the basin was runoff from the adjacent highlands but that direct infiltration of precipitation on the basin was substantially less. He calculated the average rate of recharge for the entire drainage area of the basin as 0.5 inches per year, or a total of about 50,000 acre-ft/year, on the basis of natural discharge from the playas (this estimate was made prior to large-scale groundwater development). This rate has been used by many subsequent authors as the best estimate of recharge to the Estancia Basin. DeBrine (1971) estimated that discharge to the playas was between 27,000 and 30,000 acre-ft/year. On the basis of recharge estimates in the Albuquerque Basin groundwater-flow model of Kernodle and others (1995), the Estancia Basin Planning Committee (1999) assigned recharge rates to the basin boundaries in the East Mountain area; these rates were 0.75 cubic feet per second mile (ft³/s-mi) from the Manzano Mountains and 0.15 ft³/s-mi for the area north of South Mountain. The groundwater-flow model of the Estancia Basin developed by the NMOSE (Shafike and Flanigan, 1999; Keyes, 2001) assigned three rates to recharge cells on the basis of runoff zones mapped by the Soil Conservation Service—2.993 inches per year, 0.397 inches per year, and 0.026 inches per year. Many cells in the Estancia Basin were assigned either no recharge or allowed evapotranspiration. Recharge in the model thus totaled 30,100 acre-ft/year— 22,000 acre-ft/year from direct infiltration (diffuse plus focused) and 8,100 acre-ft/year of mountain-front runoff.

The 2006 East Mountain Area plan (Bernalillo County, 2006) used a multistep approach to calculate recharge to East Mountain area. First, the Maxey-Eakin (1949) method was used to calculate a total annual recharge in the East Mountain area by using three recharge zones of 1.0, 2.4, and 5.3 in/yr resulting in a total recharge of 37,200 acre-ft/ year. (The Maxey-Eakin method assumes that the rate of groundwater recharge is proportional to the annual rainfall, and thus predicts recharge as a function of precipitation.) Next, the Shafike and Flanigan (1999) modeled recharge volume (using rates of 0.4 and 3 in/yr) for only the Estancia Basin part of the East Mountain area, 8,650 acre-ft/year, was compared to the Maxey and Eakin (1949) calculated recharge volume for the same area (12,320 acre-ft/year). Finally, the Shafike and Flanigan (1999) recharge rates were adjusted for precipitation changes with altitude and subdivided into five recharge rates ranging from 0.4 to 3.0 in/yr. These recharge rates were then applied to five watersheds to obtain recharge volumes: (1) West-facing slopes of the Sandias—1,027 acre-ft/ year; (2) West–facing slopes of the Manzano and Manzanita Mountains—2,861 acre-ft/year; (3) Estancia Basin in the East Mountain area—4,387 acre-ft/year; (4) Tijeras Canyon—3,037 acre-ft/year; and (5) San Pedro Creek—2,364 acre-ft/year. These analyses only included the parts of these watersheds within Bernalillo County, and are thus not directly comparable with watersheds described in this work.

As these and other investigations have noted, active springs along the lower slopes of the Sandia Mountains indicate that groundwater recharge happens on the upper slopes. In addition, flow in many of these springs increases in the spring especially during years of larger than normal snowpack. On the upper slopes, the recharge rate is probably greater than on the lower slopes because of the increase in precipitation with increasing elevation. Snowmelt is probably a primary source of recharge on the upper slopes of the Sandia Mountains and could be in other areas of the East Mountain area because transpiration is small during the snowmelt season compared to the summer.

Volumetric Precipitation Estimates

In order to estimate the volume of precipitation that falls on the study area and thus constrain the upper limit of

recharge to the aquifer system, nine watersheds in and near the study area were defined: (1) Galisteo Creek (2) San Pedro Mountain and South Mountain drainage to the Estancia Basin, (3) Arroyo Tonque except San Pedro Creek, (4) San Pedro Creek upstream from the confluence with Arroyo Cuchillo, (5) Tijeras Canyon upstream of Carnuel, (6) Las Huertas Creek, (7) Arroyo de San Francisco, (8) Arroyo de la Vega de los Tanos, and (9) an unnamed arroyo draining the area north of the study area near Santo Domingo Pueblo (fig. 23, table 11). Drainage areas for each watershed were defined by using geographic information system analysis of 10-meter, digital-elevation models and an average precipitation value on the basis of 1961–90 Parameter-elevation Regressions on Independent Slopes Model (PRISM) data (Daly and Taylor, 1998; Daly and others, 1994, 1997). Available through the Oregon Climate Service, PRISM is "a knowledge-based system that uses point data, a digital elevation model (DEM) and many other geographic datasets to generate gridded estimates of monthly and event-based climatic parameters" (Daly, 2002). PRISM data are available for the conterminous United States, and though originally developed for precipitation, temperature data are now available.

Table 11 shows the watersheds and drainage areas, ranges of mean annual precipitation and mean annual precipitation volume for each watershed. This precipitation volume is the maximum volume of water available for groundwater recharge in the watersheds—assuming that no water is lost to evapotranspiration or runoff. On the basis of previous estimates of recharge rates, groundwater recharge is probably a small percentage of the total precipitation; thus, table 11 shows percentages of the precipitation volume ranging from 10 to 0.5 percent.

The large range in estimates of recharge rates in and adjacent to the East Mountain area are due to variations in precipitation, soil-zone characteristics, and vegetation in the areas and the different methods used to calculate recharge. Recharge-rate estimates in and adjacent to the East Mountain area range from zero in some areas of the Estancia Basin (Shafike and Flanigan, 1999) to 5.3 in/yr (Finch and others, 1995) in the San Pedro Mountains. The larger recharge rates generally occur in the mountainous areas. Many of the estimates for the lower elevation areas in the study area range from 0.1 to 0.5 in/yr, which is generally less than 5 percent of mean annual precipitation (table 11).

Deuterium and Oxygen-18 Ratios in Groundwater

The ratios of deuterium and oxygen-18 and their relation to each other vary in response to a variety of processes; thus, deuterium and oxygen-18 can be used to evaluate the source of recharge and the flow of water in an aquifer (Fontes, 1980). Though a variety of factors affect the ratios and relation, the most relevant to the study area and effects of those factors are: (1) the ratios of deuterium and oxygen-18 tend to fall along a line with a slope of about 8; (2) winter precipitation is more depleted (lighter) in deuterium and oxygen-18 than summer

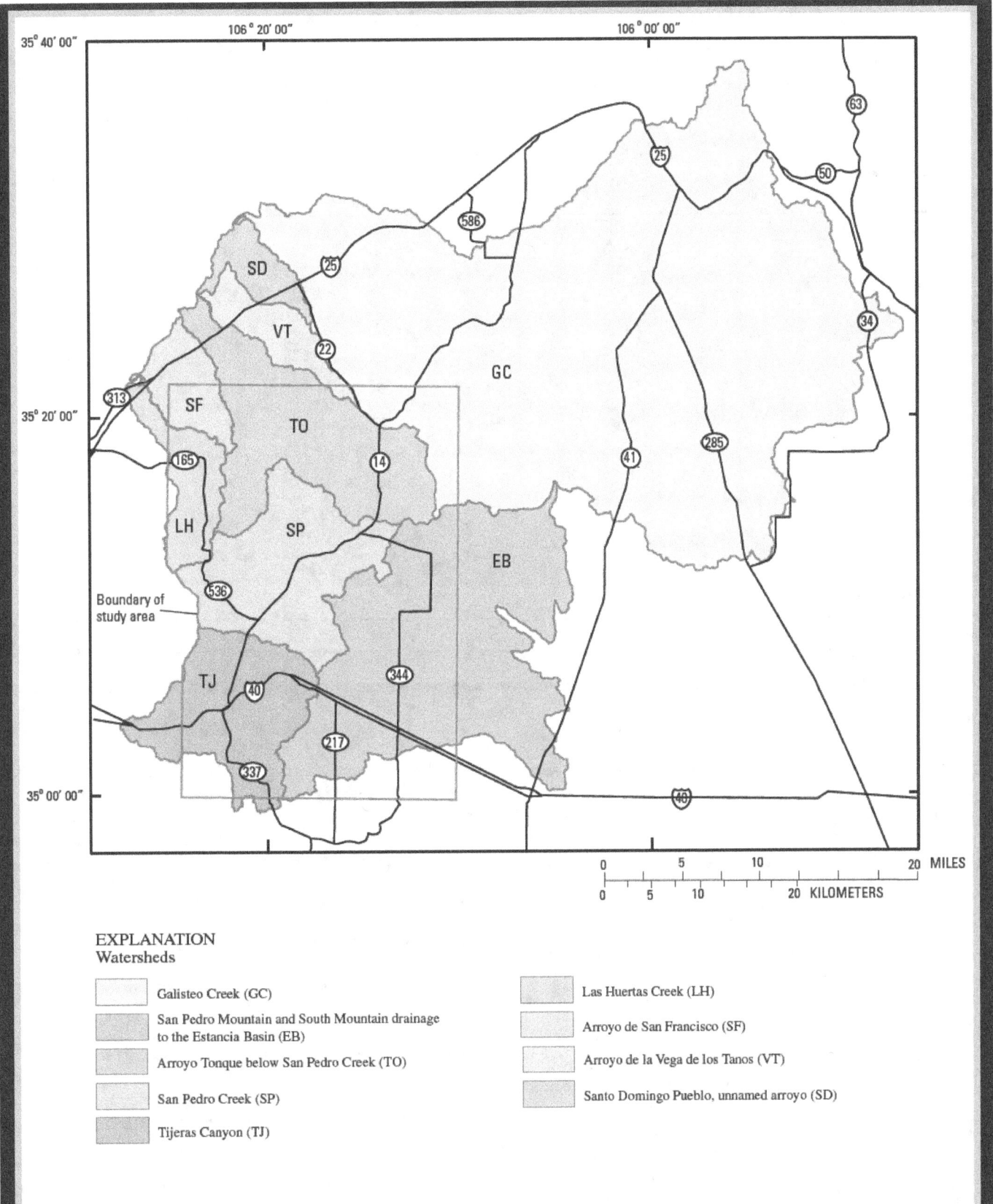

Table 11. Mean annual precipitation volumes (1961-90) for selected watersheds in or near the East Mountain study area.

[Locations of the watersheds are shown on figure 23. Annual precipitation amounts are from Daly and Taylor (1998) and Daly and others (1994, 1997). mi², square miles; in., inches; acre-ft/year, acre-feet per year]

Watershed (fig. 23)	Drainage area (mi²)	Annual precipitation range (in.)	Mean annual precipitation volume (acre-ft/yr)	Percent of mean annual precipitation				
				10 percent (acre-ft/yr)	5 percent (acre-ft/yr)	3 percent (acre-ft/yr)	1 percent (acre-ft/yr)	0.5 percent (acre-ft/yr)
Galisteo Creek; **GC**	670	8-24	490,000	49,000	24,500	14,700	4,900	2,450
San Pedro Mountain and South Mountain drainage to the Estancia Basin; **EB**	210	14-20	160,000	16,000	8,000	4,800	1,600	800
ArroyoTonque below San Pedro Creek; **TO**	100	8-20	71,000	7,100	3,550	2,130	710	355
San Pedro Creek, **SP**	90	10-24	77,000	7,700	3,850	2,310	770	385
Tijeras Canyon; **TJ**	77	14-24	68,000	6,800	3,400	2,040	680	340
Las Huertas Creek; **LH**	31	8-24	26,000	2,600	1,300	780	260	130
Arroyo de San Fransisco; **SF**	26	8-14	14,000	1,400	700	420	140	70
Arroyo de la Vega de los Tanos; **VT**	25	8-14	14,000	1,400	700	420	140	70
Santo Domingo Pueblo, unnamed arroyo; **SD**	19	8-12	9,400	940	470	282	94	47
Totals:	1,248	8-24	929,400	92,940	46,470	27,882	9,294	4,647

precipitation; (3) precipitation at higher elevations tends to be more depleted in both isotopic ratios than at lower elevations; (4) evaporation of water prior to recharge tends to enrich the content of both isotopes (however, oxygen-18 is enriched at a greater rate) causing analyses to plot below the meteoric water line on a trend with lesser slope; and (5) water recharged during the Pleistocene tends to be more depleted in deuterium (Coplen, 1993). The isotopic ratios and relation of deuterium and oxygen-18 can be affected by several other factors such as geothermal activity, interaction of water with rock units along the flow path, and mixing of water from different sources. Transpiration, unlike evaporation, does not affect the composition of deuterium and oxygen-18.

Deuterium and oxygen-18 ratios were determined for 21 groundwater samples from wells and springs in and adjacent to the study area (fig. 24). Most water samples from the study area plot near the local meteoric water line for the Santa Fe area developed by Anderholm (1994), indicating little evaporation of precipitation during recharge (fig. 25). The deuterium compostion of samples from wells in the Estancia Basin generally range from -77 to -69 parts per thousand (per mil); whereas, the samples from the area north and west of NM 14 generally range from -85 to -81 per mil (fig. 24). The difference in isotopic composition of groundwater in these two areas probably indicates different source areas of recharge for groundwater. The few isotopic analyses available for the study area indicate that the isotopic composition of groundwater could be a useful tool for determining source areas of recharge and tracing groundwater in the area although the available data were insufficient to determine sources or flow paths during this study.

Groundwater Areas

The complex geology of the East Mountain area leads to a division into groundwater areas of similar hydrogeologic characteristics, an approach that has been used by previous authors. In his discussion of groundwater resources of the East Mountain area, Titus (1980, p. 29) delimited groundwater areas thusly: "Each area comprises a terrane in which a particular formation or sequence of formations crops out." Similarly, Kues (1990, p.13), who studied only eastern Bernalillo County, divided the study area into three regions on the basis of "generalized types of outcropping units." Johnson (2000, p.11) defined three hydrologic systems in the Placitas area on the basis of physiographic regions, then further divided each into hydrogeologic zones on the basis of "unique

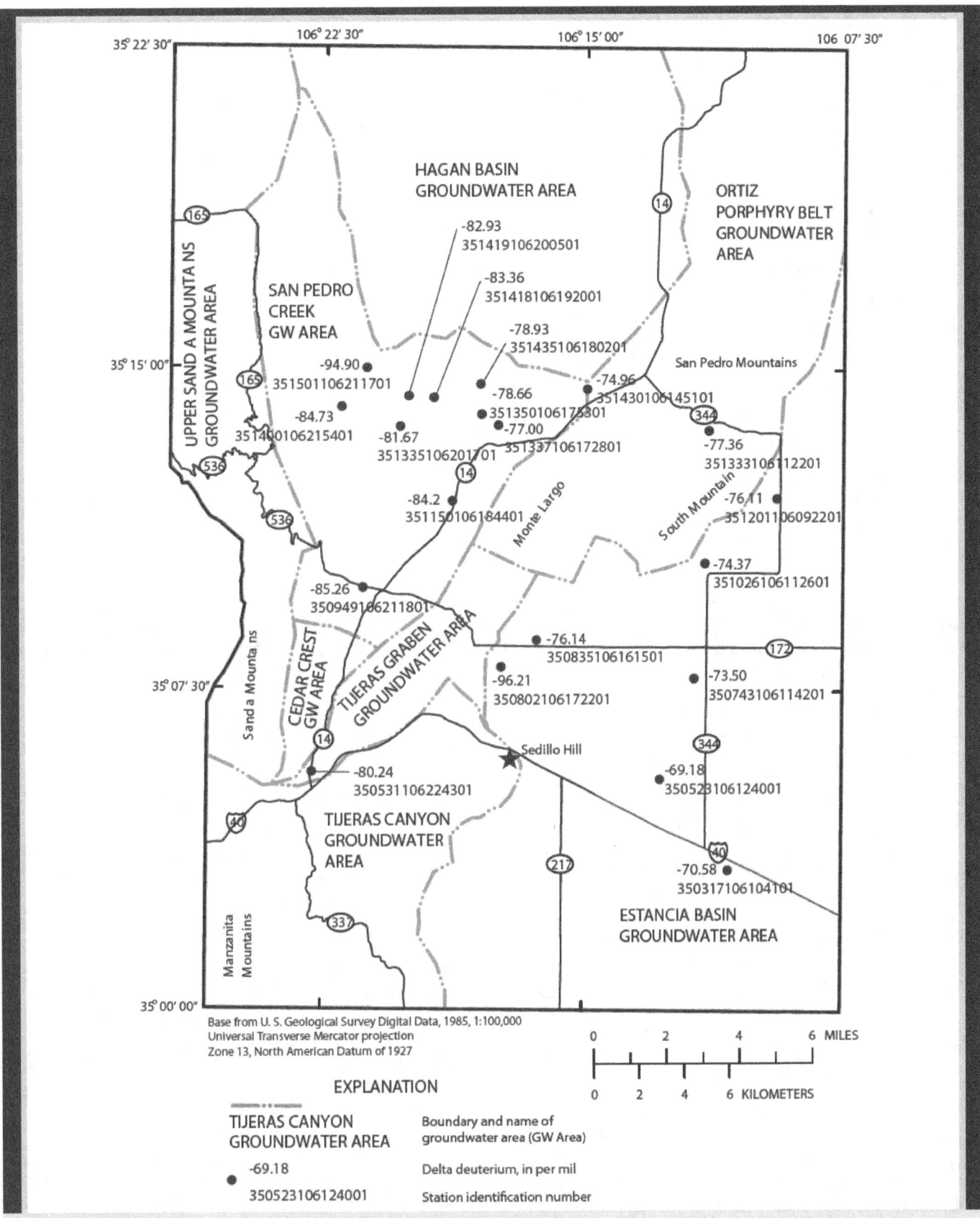

Figure 24. Delta deuterium compostion of groundwater and springs in the East Mountain study area.

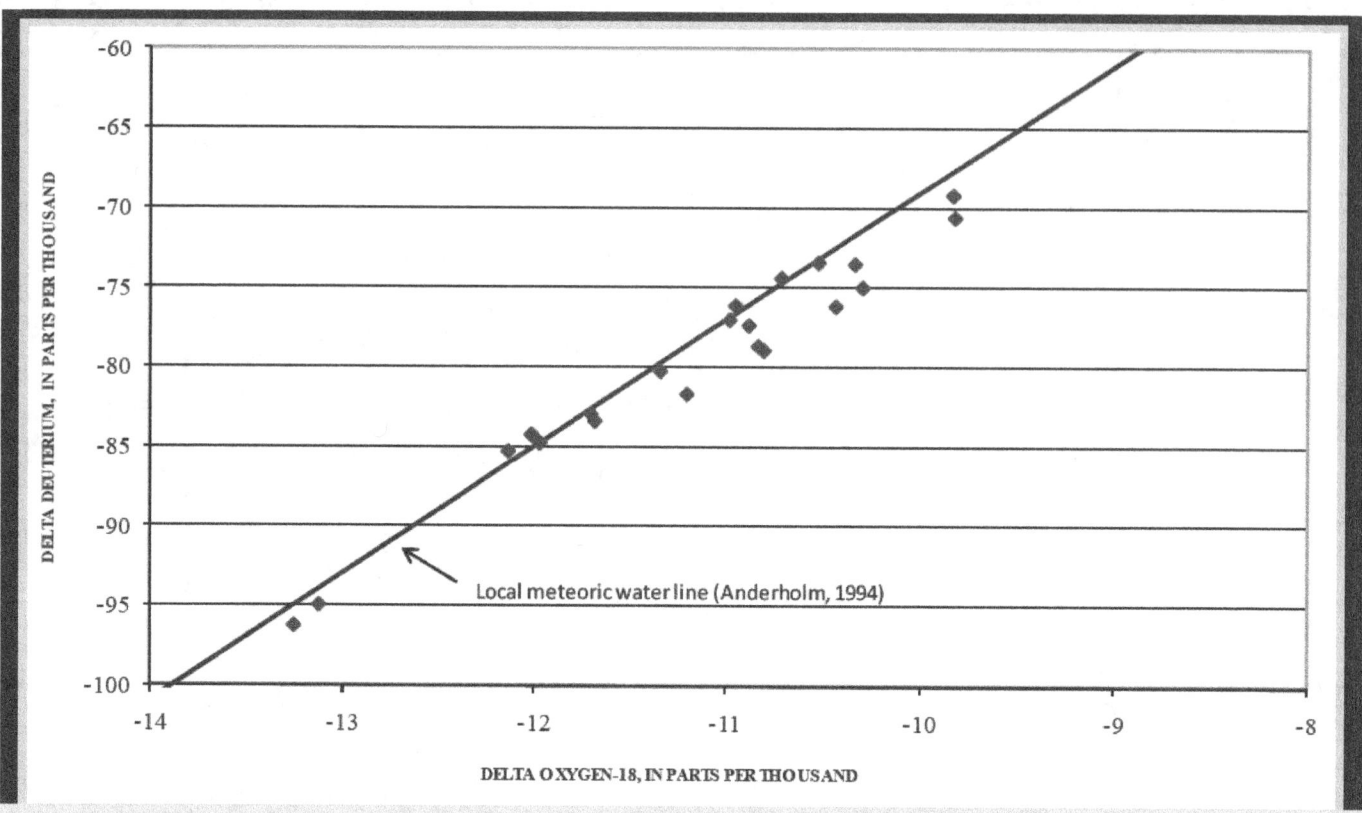

Figure 25. Relation between deuterium and oxygen-18 composition in water from selected wells and springs in the East Mountain study area.

combinations of hydrostratigraphic units, recharge sources and mechanisms, groundwater residence time, and water quality."

This report also uses the concept of groundwater areas/ regions/zones (fig. 26 and table 12) and because much of the study area was addressed by Titus (1980), these areas resemble his groundwater areas. Though the division into groundwater areas based on surficial geology is still a highly useful way to characterize water resources in the East Mountain area, more than 25 years of additional data collection and interpretation since Titus's work have allowed the current authors to expand and refine Titus's classification scheme in a manner similar to Johnson (2000). These areas, defined on the basis of geologic, hydrologic, and geochemical information, are presented in this report with some modification and redefinition from the original Titus paper. In addition, because the boundaries of the two study areas are different, the lower Tijeras Canyon area of Titus is not discussed here.

Table 12 summarizes important information about each groundwater area. The dominant dissolved ions in groundwater in the groundwater area listed in table 2 are based on the Piper diagrams discussed in the "Geologic units and water-bearing characteristics" section. A general estimate of depth to water below land surface for each groundwater area is also given in table 12. The typical depth to water listed in table 12 is based on the altitude of land surface at wells and water level information given in appendix 2. The water types and the

depths to water are general estimates for the groundwater area, water types and depths to water much different than those listed in table 12 could be encountered in the groundwater area.

Hydrographs are plotted for selected wells in each groundwater area that met the following criteria: (1) four or more water-level measurements and (2) the most recent water-level measurements were made in 2002–03. Mean monthly precipitation at the Estancia weather station, smoothed by a 3-point moving median, was plotted for comparison. Water-level data for these hydrographs were from the USGS Groundwater Site Inventory (GWSI) database. Because land in the Hagan Basin and Ortiz Porphyry Belt areas is largely undeveloped or only recently developed, no wells were found in these areas meeting the criteria. Visual comparison of water levels and precipitation on the hydrographs is useful; but should be approached with caution because "studies have shown that visual inspection of data may not be very reliable" (Fisch and Porto, 1994). Water levels in many wells declined after 2000, possibly in response to less than average precipitation (drought); however, whether water-level declines are affected by humans or by climate is difficult to determine. Water-level data collected after the drought will be useful in determining how water levels are related to precipitation. Periods of missing record plot as straight lines

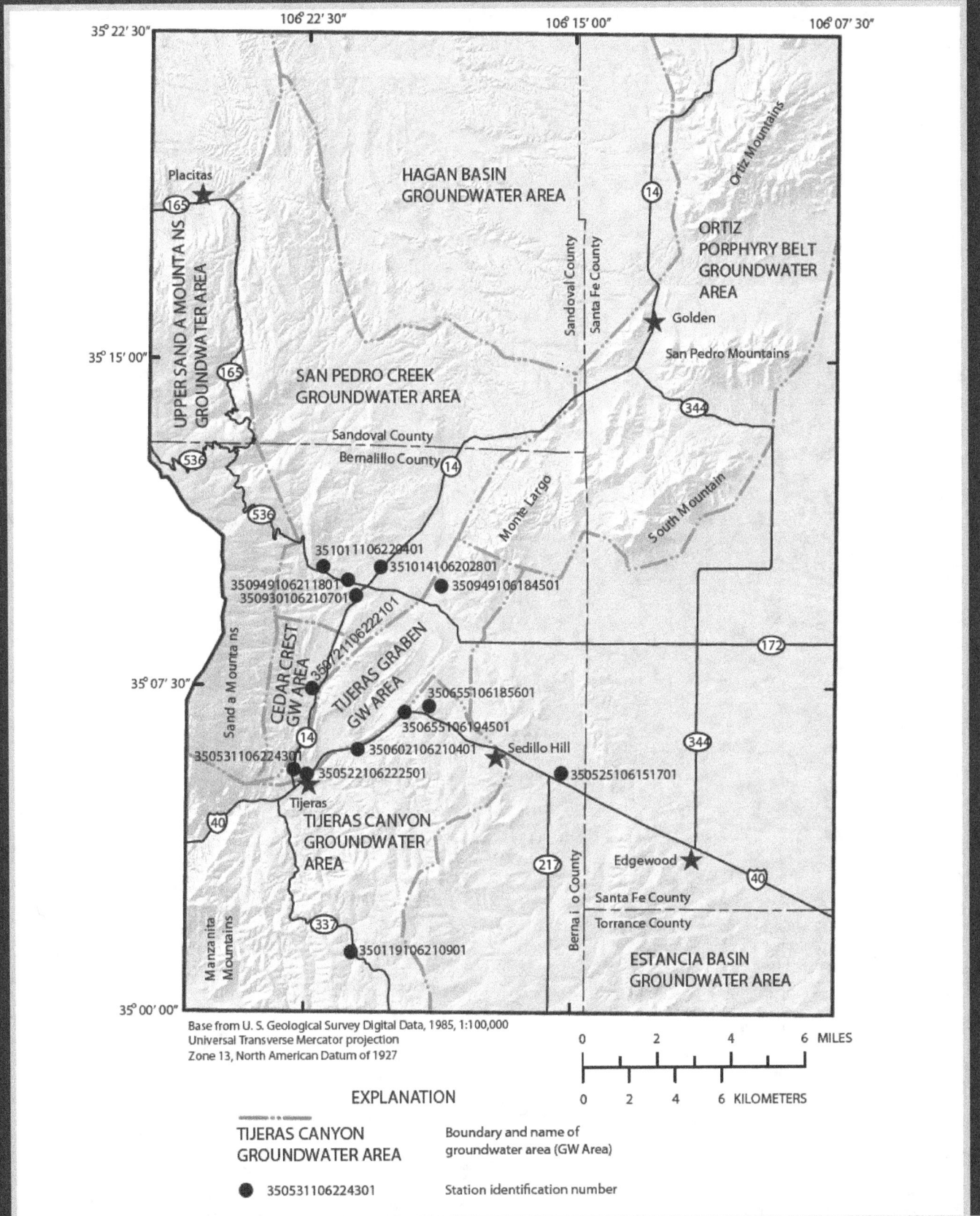

Table 12. Summary of East Mountain groundwater areas and generalized defining characteristics.

[>, greater than; <, less than; --, no data or inadequate data; ft, feet]

Groundwater Area	Primary hydrostatigraphic units	Primary structural feature	Dominant dissolved ions in groundwater	Primary source of recharge	Primary groundwater discharge	Typical depth to water
Tijeras Canyon	Madera-Sandia and Abo-Yeso	Tijeras Fault, Sandia and Manzanita Mountains	Calcium-bicarbonate	[a]Precipitation and infiltration of runoff from Sandia, Manzanita, and Manzano Mountains	Withdrawals, springs, and groundwater flow to Albuquerque Basin	<100 ft
Cedar Crest	Madera-Sandia, Abo-Yeso, San Andres-Glorieta, and Chinle-Moenkopi	Sandia Mountains	Sodium-bicarbonate	Precipitation, infiltration of runoff from Sandia Mountains, and groundwater flow from Upper Sandia Mountains groundwater area	Withdrawals, springs, and groundwater flow to Tijeras Canyon	<100 ft
Tijeras Graben	Abo-Yeso, San Andres-Glorieta, Chinle-Moenkopi, Jurassic, and Cretaceous	Tijeras Graben	Calcium-sulfate	Precipitation and infiltration of runoff from Monte Largo	Withdrawals and springs	<100 ft
Estancia Basin	Madera-Sandia and Cenozoic	Estancia Basin	Calcium-bicarbonate, high alkalinity	Precipitation and infiltration of runoff from the Manzano and San Pedro Mountains, South Mountain, and Monte Largo	Withdrawals and groundwater flow to Estancia Basin	>100 ft
San Pedro Creek	Madera-Sandia, Abo-Yeso, San Andres-Glorieta, and Chinle-Moenkopi	San Pedro synclinorium and Sandia Mountains	Calcium-bicarbonate	Precipitation and infiltration of runoff from Sandia Mountains and Monte Largo	Withdrawals, springs, and groundwater flow to Hagan Basin	100- 400 ft
Ortiz Porphyry Belt	Madera-Sandia, Abo-Yeso, Jurassic, and Cretaceous	San Pedro, Ortiz, and South Mountains and Monte Largo Horst	Calcium-bicarbonate	Precipitation	Withdrawals, springs, and groundwater flow to Estancia and Hagen Basins	<200 ft
Hagan Basin	Chinle-Moenkopi, Jurassic, Cretaceous, and Cenozoic	Hagan Basin	Sodium-bicarbonate	Precipitation and groundwater flow from San Pedro Creek and Ortiz Porphyry Belt groundwater areas	Withdrawals and groundwater flow to Albuquerque Basin	<25- 400 ft
Upper Sandia Mountains	Madera-Sandia and Abo-Yeso	Sandia Mountains	Calcium-bicarbonate	Precipitation	Springs and groundwater flow to San Pedro Creek and Cedar Crest groundwater areas	--

[a]Precipitation indicates infiltration of precipitation or runoff caused by precipitation and not groundwater inflow from adjacent areas.

on hydrographs, but a glance at a more complete period of record for the same well indicates the unmeasured probable fluctuation.

Tijeras Canyon Groundwater Area

The Tijeras Canyon groundwater area (fig. 26 and table 12) includes Tijeras Canyon, parts of the Manzanita and Manzano Mountains, and the southernmost Sandia Mountains. This groundwater area is bounded by the Gutierrez Fault (Tijeras Graben and Estancia Basin groundwater areas); the groundwater divide represented on the surface by the chain of 7,700-ft peaks trending northwest, then northeast between NM 14 and NM 217 south of Interstate 40 (Estancia Basin groundwater area); and by the approximate contact between Pennsylvanian and underlying Precambrian geologic units (Upper Sandia Mountains groundwater area). The Tijeras Canyon groundwater area extends south and west beyond the study area.

The primary hydrostratigraphic units are Madera-Sandia and Abo-Yeso; however, locally the Cenozoic and Precambrian hydrostratigraphic units produce water to wells and springs. Aquifer properties and hydrochemistry of each of these units is discussed in the "Geologic units and water-bearing characteristics" section. Drakos and others (1999) concluded from aquifer tests done for remediation of a contaminated site near Zuzax that the upper Madera and lower Abo Formations are in hydrologic communication and that fracturing related to faults is the main source of permeability.

Ten wells in the Tijeras Canyon area have four or more water-level measurements and two wells have at least yearly measurements from 1988 to 2003—350602106210401 and 350655106185601 (figs. 26 and 27). Well 350602106210401 is completed in the Abo-Yeso hydrostratigraphic unit, though the Cenozoic and Madera-Sandia units may contribute some water, and well 350655106185601 is completed in the Madera-Sandia hydrostratigraphic unit. Water levels in well 350602106210401 (fig. 27) have varied about 17 ft from 1988–2004 and water levels in well 350655106185601 (fig. 27) have varied about 25 ft from 1990–2002. Water levels in both wells were generally the lowest measured in 2002 possibly in response to lower than average precipitation from about 2000 to 2004.

In general, chloride and dissolved-solids concentrations were high near Interstate 40 and NM 14, but low elsewhere (figs. 10 and 20). Whether this trend is the result of road de-icing, development along road corridors, the Abo-Yeso hydrostratigraphic unit along Interstate 40, or movement of water across the Tijeras Fault zone from the Tijeras Graben groundwater area is unknown.

The source of groundwater in the Tijeras Canyon groundwater area is primarily infiltration of runoff from higher elevations in the Sandia, Manzano, and Manzanita Mountains, direct infiltration of precipitation, and infiltration of domestic wastewater from septic systems. Groundwater flow from adjacent groundwater areas may be small: the eastern boundary is a groundwater divide, and the Precambrian

hydrostratigraphic unit is a meager source of groundwater. Drakos and others (1999) also concluded little flow crosses faults related to the Tijeras Fault zone in the Zuzax area. Groundwater typically moves westward or toward the surface-water drainages in this area (plate). Discharge is from wells, springs, evapotranspiration along streams, and groundwater flow into the Albuquerque Basin.

Although the 77-mi^2 Tijeras Canyon watershed includes parts of the Tijeras Canyon, Cedar Crest, Tijeras Graben, Estancia Basin, and Upper Sandia Mountains groundwater areas (fig. 23), the watershed can be used to approximate recharge to the Tijeras Canyon groundwater area. Mean annual precipitation on the watershed is about 68,000 acre-ft/year (table 11). The Bernalillo County (2006) report cites an estimate of 3,037 acre-ft/year of recharge for the Tijeras Canyon area. Previous general estimates of recharge in the East Mountain area discussed in the "Recharge" section generally range from 0.1 to 3.0 in/yr: applied to the Tijeras Canyon watershed these rates yield 410 to 12,000 acre-ft/year of recharge (or 1 and 18 percent of average annual precipitation, respectively). Another estimate of recharge can be made with the McAda and Barroll (2002) groundwater-flow model of the Middle Rio Grande Basin. Though groundwater and surface water from Tijeras Canyon discharges into the Albuquerque Basin, surface-water flow seldom reaches the Rio Grande. The model applied 1,400 acre-ft/year for recharge from Tijeras Canyon and Tijeras Arroyo with about 700 acre-ft/year of that subsurface groundwater discharge from Tijeras Canyon to the Middle Rio Grande Basin. This 700 acre-ft/year from the Tijeras Canyon drainage is equivalent to 1 percent (or 680 acre-ft/year) of the precipitation that falls on the Tijeras Canyon watershed (fig. 23, table 11). Based on the McAda and Barroll (2002) recharge estimate, groundwater recharge on the Tijeras Canyon groundwater area likely is less than several percent of average annual precipitation.

Cedar Crest Groundwater Area

The Cedar Crest groundwater area (fig. 26 and table 12) includes the lowermost eastern slopes of the Sandia Mountains. The Cedar Crest groundwater area is bounded by the Tijeras Fault to the southeast (Tijeras Graben groundwater area), the upslope contact between the Madera Formation and younger rocks to the west (Upper Sandia Mountains groundwater area), and the east-west trending groundwater divide several miles south of NM 536 to the north (San Pedro Creek groundwater area).

The primary water-bearing geologic units are Triassic and older. The primary hydrostratigraphic units are the Madera-Sandia, Abo-Yeso, San Andres-Glorieta, and Chinle-Moenkopi, though locally the Cenozoic hydrostratigraphic unit produces water. The aquifer properties and hydrochemistry of each of these units is discussed in the "Geologic Units and Water-Bearing Characteristics" section.

In the Cedar Crest area, 22 wells have four or more water-level measurements. The last water-level measurement

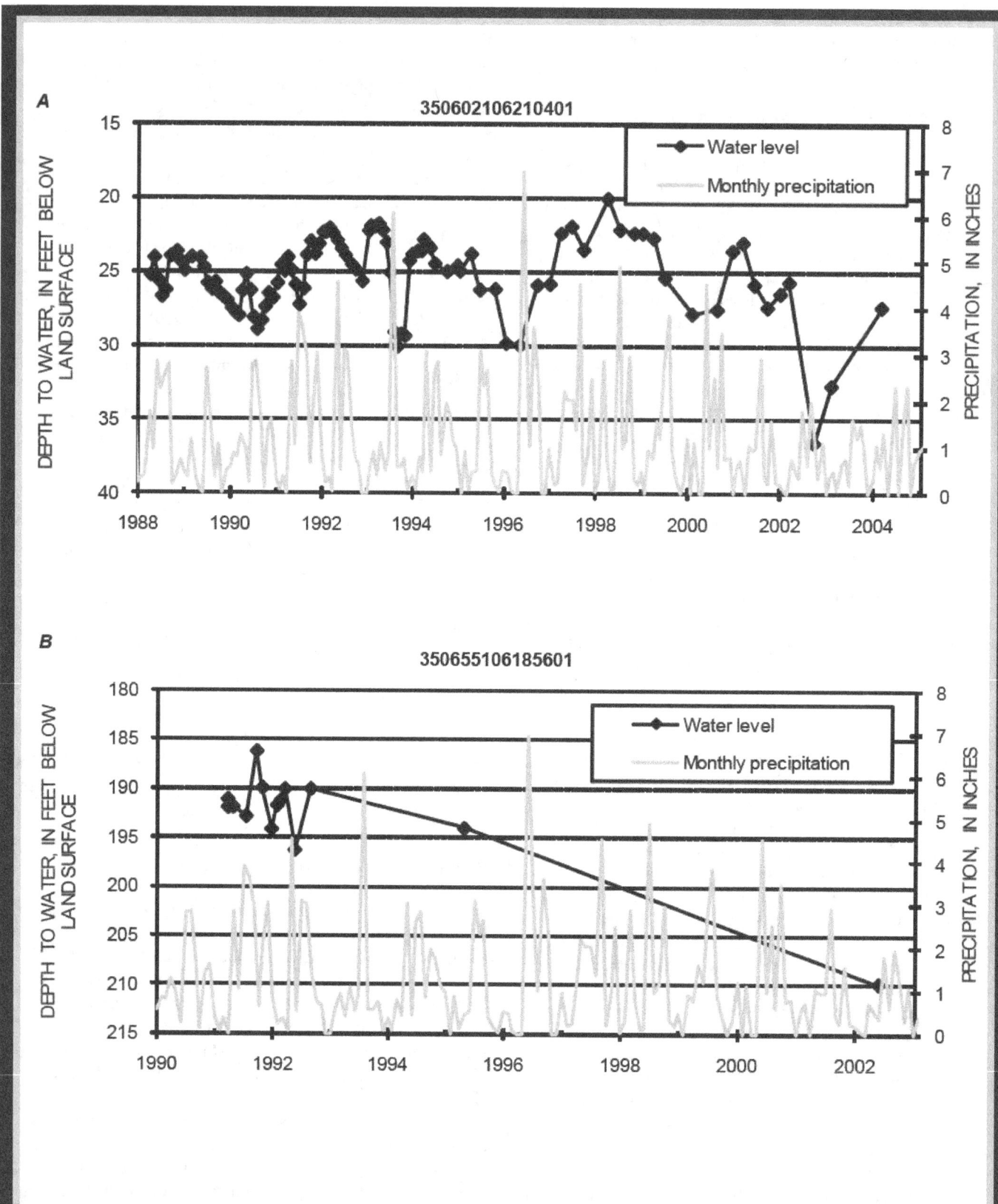

Figure 27. Water levels for selected wells in the Tijeras Canyon groundwater area (350602106210401 and 350655106185601). Monthly precipitation measured at the Estancia weather station is shown for comparison (data from Western Regional Climate Center, 2006).

in well 350721106222101 (Chinle-Moenkopi) was in 2002 (fig. 28); however, this graph was included to represent water-level variations in the area. Water levels in well 350721106222101 have fluctuated nearly 160 ft from 1990–2002. Water level variations in this well are probably due to variations in withdrawals from other wells in the area.

In general, except for wells along NM 14, concentrations of chloride, sulfate, dissolved solids, and nitrate were low in this groundwater area (figs. 10, 11, 13, and 20). Because geologic units in this area generally strike parallel to NM 14, whether high concentrations of some constituents are related to development along Highway 14, road de-icing, or the generally poorer water quality of Permian and younger units is difficult to determine.

The source of groundwater in the Cedar Crest groundwater area is primarily infiltration of runoff from higher elevations in the Sandia Mountains, direct infiltration of precipitation, infiltration of domestic wastewater from septic systems, and groundwater flow from the Upper Sandia Mountains groundwater area. This latter source is probably the major source of groundwater in the Cedar Crest groundwater area. Groundwater flow from the adjacent San Pedro Creek and Tijeras Graben groundwater areas is probably meager because the northern boundary is a groundwater divide and there may be little flow across faults related to the Tijeras

Fault zone (Drakos and others, 1999). Groundwater typically moves eastward in the Cedar Crest groundwater area. Titus (1980, p. 23) indicated that tributaries to Tijeras Canyon act as drains to the groundwater system in this area. Discharge is from wells, springs, evapotranspiration along streams, and possible groundwater flow into the Tijeras Graben groundwater area. Development in this area is extensive and predates that in many other areas, thus consumptive use may be substantial.

Estimated recharge volumes to the Cedar Crest groundwater area was not attempted because this area straddles the drainage divide between the Tijeras Canyon and San Pedro Creek watersheds though the Cedar Crest groundwater area only encompasses a small part of each. Based on previous estimates of recharge in the area, the percentage of precipitation resulting in recharge to the aquifer is probably less than 3 percent.

Tijeras Graben Groundwater Area

The Tijeras Graben groundwater area (fig. 26 and table 12) mostly corresponds to the southern, Tijeras Graben part of the structural Frost Fault Block discussed in the "Structural features" section. The Tijeras Graben groundwater area is bounded by the Tijeras Fault to the west (Cedar

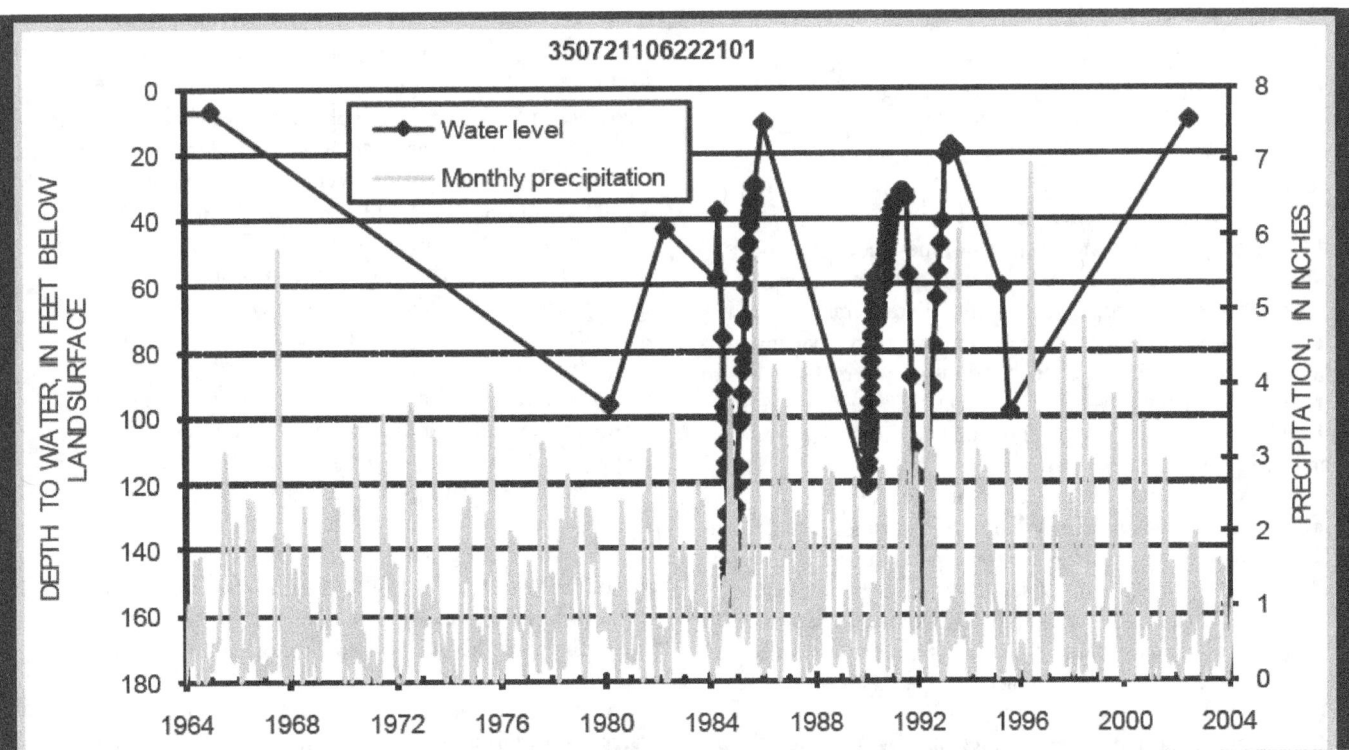

Figure 28. Water levels for a selected well in the Cedar Crest groundwater area (350721106222101). Monthly precipitation measured at the Estancia weather station is shown for comparison (data from Western Regional Climate Center, 2006).

Crest groundwater area), and the Gutierrez Fault to the east (Estancia Basin and Tijeras Canyon groundwater areas). This groundwater area differs from the structural Tijeras Graben in that the groundwater area has been extended to the Precambrian outcrop of Monte Largo Horst to the northeast.

Most of the groundwater area in the southwest has Mesozoic geologic units cropping out at the surface, whereas the northeastern third primarily has Permian and Pennsylvanian rocks at the surface. In general, wells are completed in the Chinle-Moenkopi, Jurassic, and Cretaceous hydrostratigraphic units to the southwest and the Abo-Yeso and San Andres-Glorieta hydrostratigraphic units to the northeast. Locally the Madera-Sandia and Cenozoic hydrostratigraphic units produce water. The aquifer properties and hydrochemistry of each of these units is discussed in the "Geologic Units and Water-Bearing Characteristics" section.

Three wells in the Tijeras Graben groundwater area have four or more water-level measurements: 350531106224301 (Cretaceous), and 350655106194501 and 350949106184501 (San Andres-Glorieta); hydrographs are shown in figures 29A, 29B, and 29C. Water levels in wells 350531106224301 and 350949106184501 have fluctuated about 30 and 40 ft respectively. Water levels in well 350655106194501 have varied about 25 ft. The most recent water-level measurements are some of the lowest on record. The water levels in well 350531106224301show annual drawdown and recovery cycles in the early 1990s. The low water-level measurements in 2001–04 seem to correspond to the general downward trend in precipitation since 2000.

Although nitrate concentrations (fig. 11) in the Tijeras Graben groundwater area were primarily low, sulfate and dissolved-solids concentrations were among the highest in the study area (figs. 13 and 20). Chloride concentrations were generally high in the southwestern part of the area but not in the northeastern part (fig. 10). The difference in water quality between these two areas is probably a reflection of the generally higher concentrations of these constituents in water from the Chinle-Moenkopi, Jurassic, and Cretaceous hydrostratigraphic units. Water in the Tijeras Graben area may be hydrologically isolated from groundwater in adjacent areas because the high sulfate concentrations in water from wells in the Tijeras Graben area are not evident in water from wells in the adjacent Tijeras Canyon and Estancia Basin groundwater areas (fig. 13)

The source of groundwater in the Tijeras Graben groundwater area is primarily infiltration of runoff from Monte Largo Horst, direct infiltration of precipitation, and infiltration of domestic wastewater from septic systems. Probably little or no groundwater flows from adjacent groundwater areas because the Tijeras and Gutierrez Faults and the Precambrian geologic units of Monte Largo act as impermeable boundaries. That the faults are mostly impermeable in the transverse direction is supported by the findings of Drakos and others (1999) as discussed in the "Tijeras Canyon Groundwater Area" section. Groundwater seems to move toward the major arroyos in the area (plate). Discharge is from wells, springs, and evapotranspiration along streams.

Estancia Basin Groundwater Area

The Estancia Basin Groundwater Area (fig. 26 and table 12) includes the Estancia Basin, the easternmost extensions of the Manzanita and Manzano Mountains, and the southernmost Espanola Basin north of the indeterminate boundary of the Estancia Basin and the Espanola Basin. The western boundaries of the area are the approximate contact between pre-Quaternary/Quaternary geologic units (Ortiz Porphyry Belt groundwater area), the Gutierrez Fault (Tijeras Graben groundwater area), and the groundwater divide represented on the surface by the chain of 7,700-ft peaks trending northwest then northeast between NM 14 and NM 217 south of Interstate 40, respectively (Tijeras Canyon groundwater area). The Estancia Basin groundwater area extends south and east beyond the study area.

The main geologic units that crop out in the Estancia Basin groundwater area are the Madera Formation and Quaternary alluvium. The primary hydrostratigraphic units in this area are the Madera-Sandia and Cenozoic units, though the Abo-Yeso is a primary water-bearing unit along the boundary with the Ortiz Porphyry Belt groundwater area. Wells are commonly completed across the boundary between the Cenozoic and underlying hydrostratigraphic unit, either Madera-Sandia or Abo-Yeso. The aquifer properties and hydrochemistry of these units are discussed in the "Geologic Units and Water-Bearing Characteristics" section.

One well in the Estancia Basin area has four or more water-level measurements, with the latest made in 2002 or 2003; location and hydrographs are shown in figures 26 and 30. Well 350525106151701 (fig. 30) is completed in the Madera-Sandia hydrostratigraphic unit. Water levels in this well generally have fluctuated about 15 ft during the period of record. The lowest water level in well 350525106151701 was the first measurement in 1980. No obvious relation exists between water levels in well 350525106151701 and precipitation at the Estancia weather station.

In general, chloride, sulfate, dissolved solids, and nitrate concentrations were not high except in an area along Interstate 40 approximately west of NM 217 (figs. 10, 20, 13, and 11). The concentrations along Interstate 40 may be the result of subsurface eastward flow from the Tijeras Graben area, development, road deicing, or a combination. Several wells in this same area had high values of pH for unknown reasons (fig. 14).

The source of groundwater in the Estancia Basin groundwater area is the infiltration of runoff from higher elevations in the Manzano and San Pedro Mountains, South Mountain, and other areas outside of the study area; direct infiltration of precipitation; and infiltration of domestic wastewater from septic systems (and infiltration of irrigation water east of the study area). Groundwater flow from adjacent groundwater areas is probably small: the southwest boundary with the Tijeras Canyon groundwater area is a groundwater divide, the western boundary is the mostly impermeable

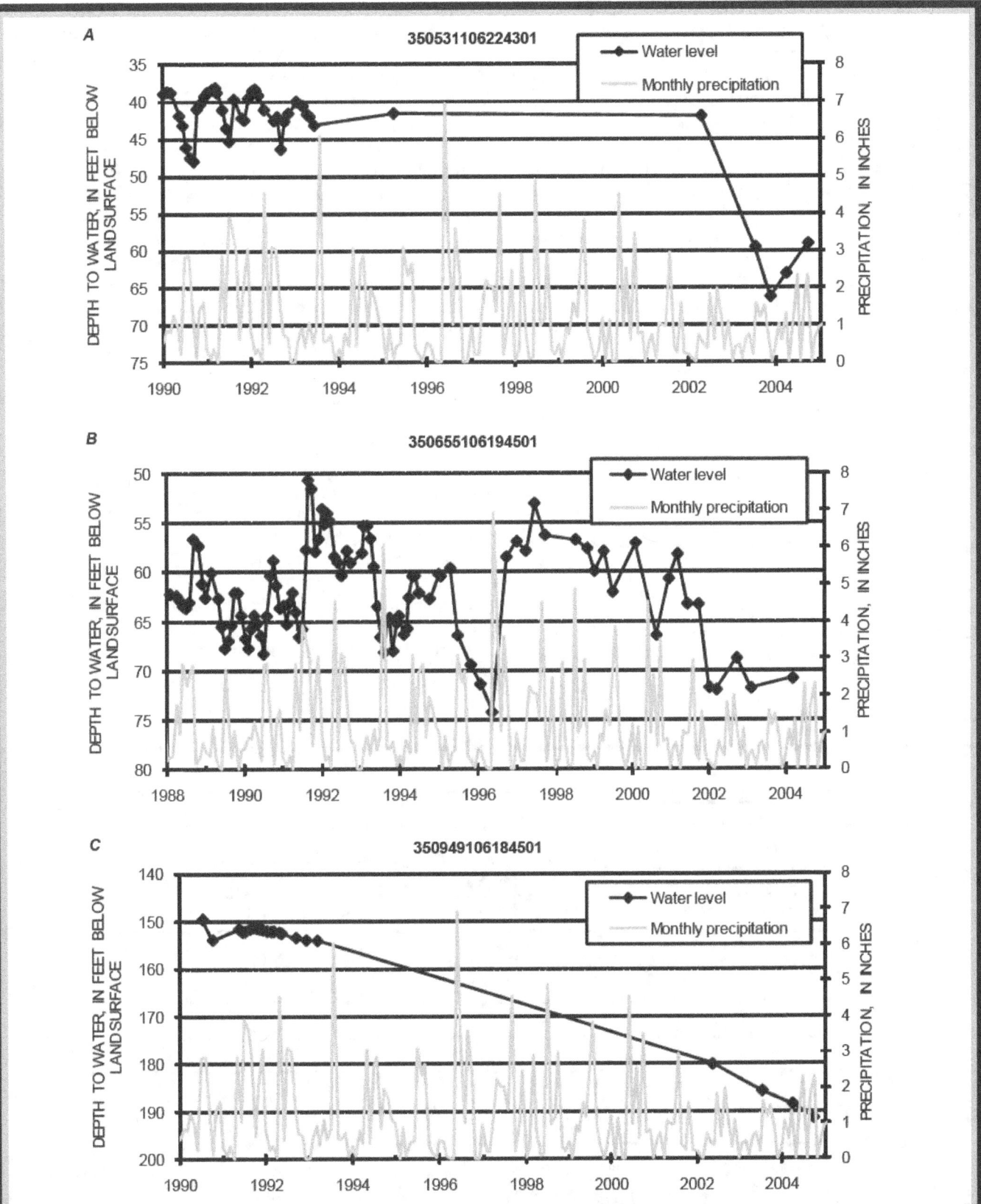

Figure 29. Water levels for selected wells in the Tijeras Graben groundwater area (350531106224301, 350655106194501, and 350949106184501). Monthly precipitation measured at the Estancia weather station is shown for comparison (data from Western Regional Climate Center, 2006).

Tijeras Fault zone (Drakos and others, 1999), and the northwestern boundary is with the mostly impermeable geologic units of the Ortiz Porphyry Belt groundwater area. Because deuterium and oxygen-18 ratios are typically greater than those ratios from other groundwater areas except the Ortiz Porphyry Belt and San Pedro Creek areas, the source of recharge likely is infiltration of precipitation on these lower elevation areas, not underflow from the Sandia Mountains. The rates and volume of recharge to the Estancia Basin are discussed in the "Recharge" section. Groundwater typically flows eastward out of the Estancia Basin groundwater area. Discharge is from wells, springs, evapotranspiration along streams (and the playas east of the study area), and possible underflow north into the Espanola Basin or south into the Tularosa Basin.

San Pedro Creek Groundwater Area

The San Pedro Creek groundwater area (fig. 26) is bounded to the west by the west Las Huertas fault and the San Francisco Fault (Upper Sandia Mountains groundwater area), to the south by the groundwater divide south of NM 536 (Cedar Crest groundwater area), to the east by the Tijeras Fault (Tijeras Graben and Ortiz Porphyry Belt groundwater areas), and to the north by the approximate contact between Permian and Triassic geologic units (Hagan Basin groundwater area). The primary hydrostratigraphic units in this area are Madera-Sandia, Abo-Yeso, San Andres-Glorieta, and Chinle-Moenkopi; locally the Cenozoic hydrostratigraphic unit

produces water to wells and springs. The aquifer properties and hydrochemistry of each of these units is discussed in the "Geologic Units and Water-Bearing Characteristics" section.

Surface-water drainage from the San Pedro Creek groundwater area is by San Pedro Creek (an area of about 90 mi² upstream from the confluence with Arroyo Cuchillo).

Four wells have measurements from 1990 through 2003: 350930106210701 (Chinle-Moenkopi) (fig. 31A), 350949106211801 (San Andres-Glorieta) (fig. 31B), 351011106220401 (Abo-Yeso) (fig. 31C) and 351014106202801(Chinle-Moenkopi) (fig. 31D). Water levels in these wells have fluctuated about 8 ft in well 351011106220401 to about 40 ft in well 350930106210701 during the period of record. Annual drawdown and recovery cycles are apparent in wells 350930106210701, 351011106220401, and 351014106202801 in years with sufficient water-level measurements, though the magnitude varies from year to year. The decrease in water-levels from the late 1990s to 2002–2004 may correspond to the general downward trend in precipitation since 2000.

In general, concentrations of chloride, sulfate, dissolved solids, and nitrate and values of pH were among the lowest in the study area (figs. 10, 11, 13, 20, and 14). These low concentrations probably reflect the composition of recharge in the area prior to development.

The source of groundwater in the San Pedro Creek groundwater area is primarily infiltration of runoff from higher elevations in the Sandia Mountains and Monte Largo, direct infiltration of precipitation, infiltration of domestic

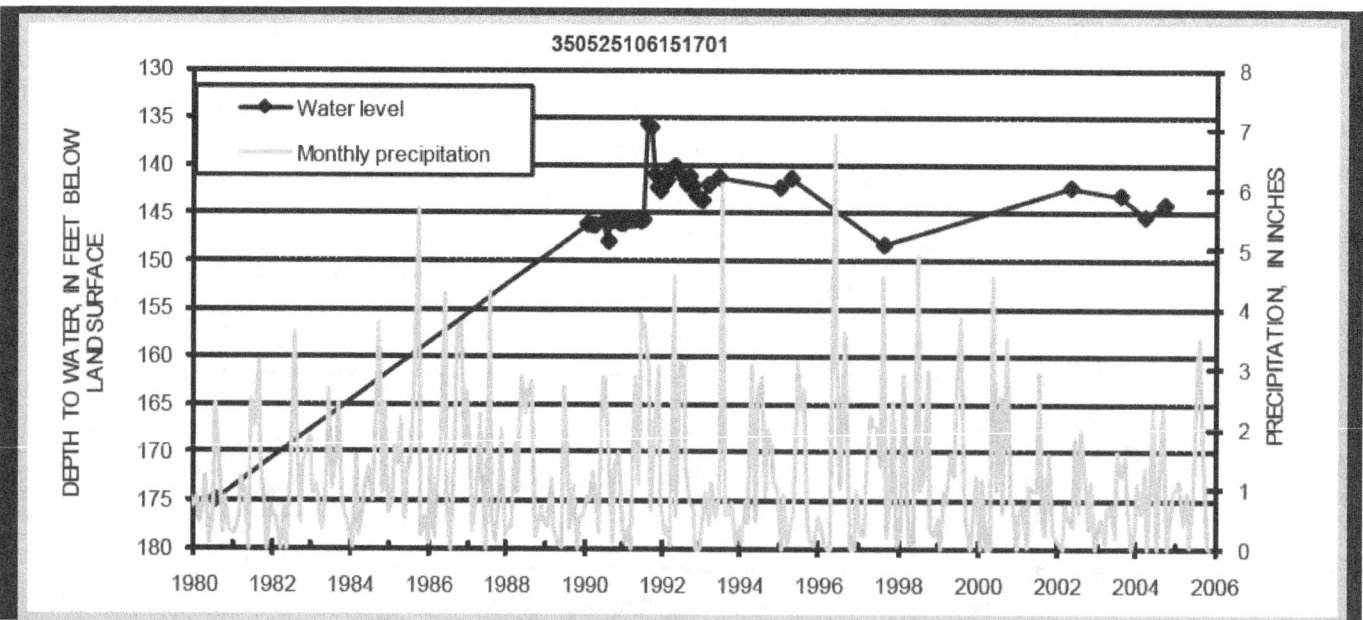

Figure 30. Water levels for a selected well in the Estancia Basin groundwater area (350525106151701). Monthly precipitation measured at the Estancia weather station is shown for comparison (data from Western Regional Climate Center, 2006).

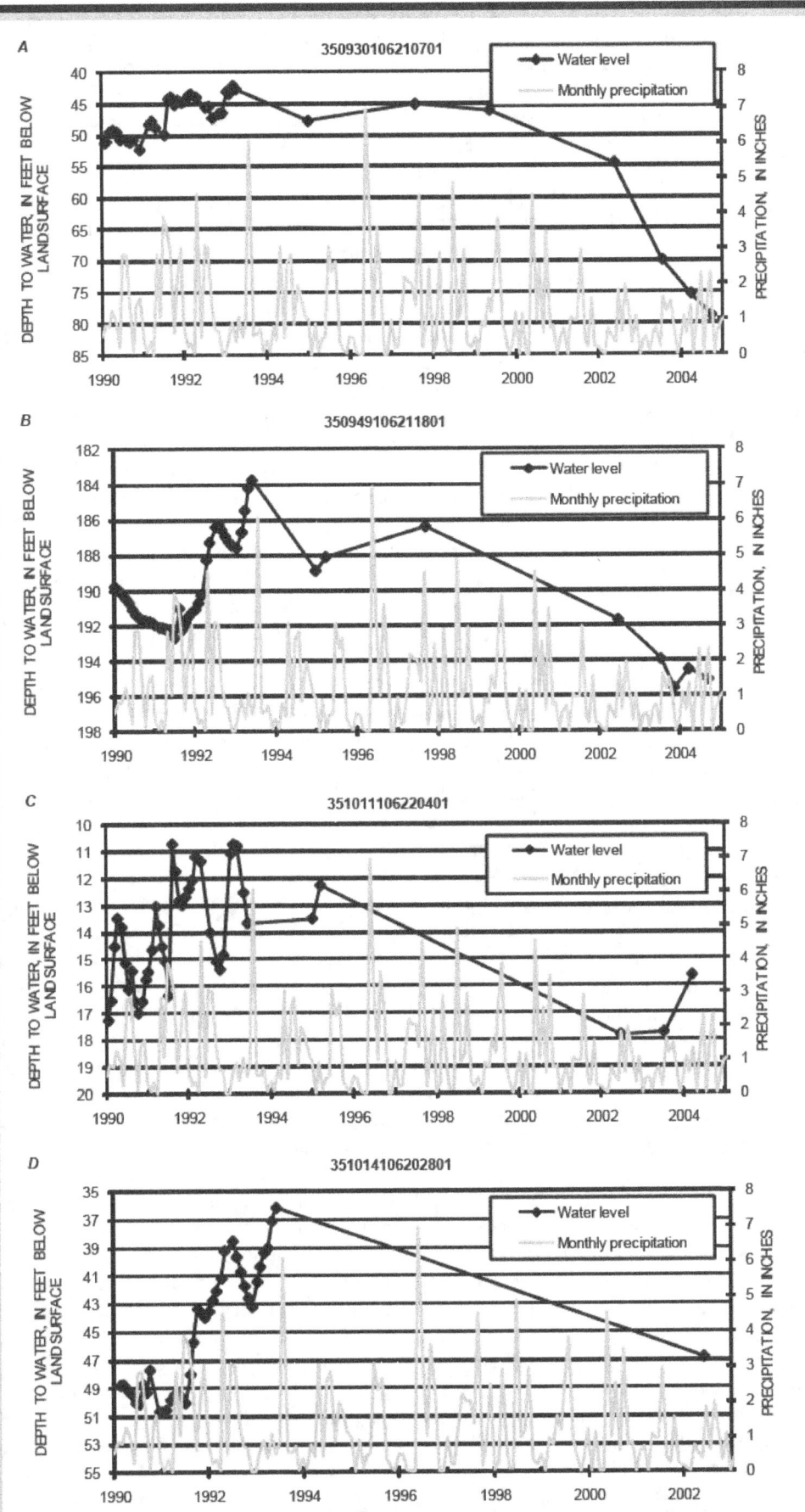

Figure 31. Water levels for selected wells in the San Pedro Creek groundwater area (350930106210701, 350949106211801, 351011106220401, and 351014106202801). Monthly precipitation measured at the Estancia weather station is shown for comparison (data from Western Regional Climate Center, 2006).

wastewater from septic systems, and groundwater flow from the Upper Sandia Mountains groundwater area. Groundwater flow from the adjacent Cedar Crest, Tijeras Graben, and Ortiz Porphyry Belt groundwater areas is probably small because the southern boundary is a groundwater divide and the Tijeras Fault zone may be fairly impermeable across the fault (Drakos and others, 1999). Groundwater flows north and eastward in the San Pedro Creek area. Discharge is from wells, springs, evapotranspiration along streams, and groundwater flow into the Hagan Basin groundwater area.

Although the 90-mi^2 San Pedro Creek watershed includes parts of the Upper Sandia Mountains, Cedar Crest, Tijeras Graben, and Ortiz Porphyry Belt groundwater areas, San Pedro Creek watershed can be used to approximate recharge to the San Pedro Creek groundwater area. Mean annual precipitation on the watershed is about 77,000 acre-ft/year (fig. 23 and table 11). The Bernalillo County (2006) report cites an estimate of 2,364 acre-ft/year of recharge for the Bernalillo County part of the San Pedro Creek watershed. Previous general estimates of recharge in the East Mountain area discussed in the "Recharge" section generally range from 0.1 to 3.0 in/yr: applied to the San Pedro Creek watershed these rates yield 480 to 14,000 acre-ft/year of recharge (or about 0.5 and 18 percent of average annual precipitation, respectively).

Source of Water to San Pedro Creek

San Pedro Creek is one of several streams in the East Mountain area with perennial reaches, though the creek seldom flows along the entire length. A question regarding the creek is whether development can affect the flows from the springs or flow in the perennial reaches of the creek. Groundwater withdrawals from aquifers that discharge to the creek or to the springs adjacent to the creek could result in decreases in flow in the creek if water levels decrease near the creek/springs.

San Pedro Spring is the first major spring on San Pedro Creek (plate and fig. 32) downstream from the junction with Frost Arroyo and Arroyo Armijo, and provides flow for the perennial reach downstream from the spring. Three sources of water to the spring are possible—discharge from alluvium in the San Pedro Creek drainage, subsurface discharge from the Yeso and Abo Formations, or subsurface discharge from the San Andres and Glorieta Formations. The areally extensive Quaternary alluvium in the San Pedro Creek drainage could serve as a minor aquifer, allowing water to move downgradient until forced to the surface at San Pedro Spring by underlying consolidated rock. Alternatively, groundwater also may discharge after moving downgradient through the Yeso and Abo Formations from recharge areas at higher elevations in the Sandia Mountains. The San Andres and Glorieta Formations are exposed in the streambed at the spring and the spring appears to discharge from these formations. Though the southward-plunging San Pedro synclinorium nears the northward extent here, water levels in nearby test wells indicate that sufficient potentiometric head is present in the

San Andres-Glorieta Formations for groundwater discharge to San Pedro Spring. Ascertaining whether discharge is from the Abo-Yeso or San Andres-Glorieta Formations is difficult because the contacts are overlain by younger alluvium in the stream channel. A combination of these three sources also is possible.

An unnamed spring is shown on the USGS Sandia Park 7.5-minute quadrangle near the Bernalillo-Sandoval County line (fig. 32). During several visits to the area the spring was not found, nor was the spring mentioned by Titus (1980). Consequently the spring is not included in this discussion.

Rock Spring is in the channel of a tributary several yards upstream from San Pedro Creek (fig. 32). There is little alluvium in the channel of San Pedro Creek near Rock Spring and limestone of the Madera Formation crops out in San Pedro Creek channel bottom for about 1,000 ft upstream from near where flow from Rock Spring enters San Pedro Creek.

Figure 33 is a nearly west-east diagrammatic cross section through San Pedro Creek near Rock Spring showing geologic units and the approximate potentiometric surface. At the spring, the contact between the Abo and Madera Formations is overlain by several feet of alluvium. Water levels in nearby wells completed in the Abo and Madera Formations are higher than Rock Spring, and thus both formations are potential sources of water to the spring. The contact between the Abo and Madera Formations is covered by alluvium at the spring, though the driller's log for well 351348106173001 shows a probable contact between the Abo and Madera Formations at a depth of 415 ft; thus, the Abo-Madera contact coincides with measured dips for the Abo and Madera Formations in the area (plate). Because of differences in hydraulic conductivity between different units, springs are commonly found at geologic contacts, and it seems likely that Rock Spring is such a spring. With currently (2005) available information however, whether the source of water to the spring is the Madera, Abo, or both units cannot be answered. If the Madera and Abo are hydraulically connected, both units likely contribute some flow to the spring. In addition, because the potentiometric surface slopes toward Rock Spring from the east and west sides of San Pedro Creek (fig. 32), groundwater development in either direction will likely affect flows at Rock Spring by the interception of water that would discharge at the spring under natural conditions.

The most probable source of water to Cottonwood Spring (fig. 32) is groundwater flow in the alluvium that is forced to the surface by a buried constriction of consolidated rock or downdip/downgradient flow in the Abo-Yeso hydrostratigraphic unit west of the creek that discharges at the buried contact with alluvium in and near the channel. Because the updip extent of the Abo Formation is within 2,500 ft of the spring, some or all this water may originate in the Madera Formation and cross into the Abo Formation before discharging to the spring. If measured dips are used to project the Madera Formation eastward, the formation passes well below the streambed and thus is unlikely to be a direct water source to the spring. Water levels in wells east of San Pedro Creek are lower than the spring.

From July 14, 2003, through January 23, 2005, streamflow and (or) specific conductance were measured on six occasions at various locations between San Pedro Spring and Cottonwood Spring (fig. 34). On December 20, 2004, flow about 800 ft downstream from San Pedro Spring was about 0.23 cubic feet per second (ft³/s). Flow increased to about 0.4 ft³/s about 4,000 ft downstream of San Pedro Spring. In general, flow and specific conductance reach the maximum in the stream reach near the convergence of two arroyos, one from each side of the main channel, with the main channel (figs. 32 and 34) and then decrease downstream. Streamflow increases in the 4,000-ft stream reach downstream from San Pedro Spring indicate groundwater discharge to the creek in this area. Flows generally decrease along San Pedro Creek from about 4,000 ft downstream from San Pedro Spring until near Rock Spring. In general, streamflow increases downstream from Rock Spring to Cottonwood Spring, which also indicates groundwater discharge to the creek. Specific conductance decreases and then increases from about 4,000 to 9,000 ft below San Pedro Spring. This increase and then decrease could indicate groundwater discharge to the creek although streamflow does not increase in this reach indicating the creek probably is gaining and losing water in this reach. Specific conductance decreases in the reach about 9,000 to 12,000 ft downstream from San Pedro Spring also indicating groundwater discharge to the creek. The decrease in flow in the creek in this reach indicates groundwater with relatively low specific conductance is discharging to the creek; however, overall the creek is losing water to the groundwater system in this reach. Specific conductance ranged from 570 to 728 microsiemens per centimeter at 25°Celsius (µS/cm) and measured streamflow ranged from 0 to 0.407 ft³/s (fig. 34). The temporal variation in specific-conductance at a site along San Pedro Creek upstream from Rock Spring may indicate evaporation of water through the alluvial reach upstream from Rock Spring.

If no additional groundwater entered San Pedro Creek downstream from Rock Spring, evaporation would decrease flow and increase specific conductance as the water moved downstream. Instead, downstream from Rock Spring, flows decrease almost in tandem with specific conductance that indicates flow is indeed being lost in this reach but that additional, low-conductance water is gained at a rate less than the loss, similar to what was observed upstream from Rock Spring. As is noted in the "Geologic Units and Water-Bearing Characteristics" section and tables 4 and 5, the median and range of dissolved-solids concentrations in the Madera/Sandia and Abo/Yeso units are similar; thus, with available information, whether the Madera, Abo, or both formations are the source of water to San Pedro Creek downstream from Rock Spring can not be determined.

Based on the streamflow measurements, specific-conductance measurements, and the geology and hydrology of the area between San Pedro Spring and Cottonwood Spring, there are probably several hydrostratigraphic units that discharge to San Pedro Creek and the springs along San Pedro Creek. There appears to be differences in the water quality in these hydrostratigraphic units based on the specific-conductance measurements along the creek. There is also probably infiltration of water from the creek to the underlying hydrostratigraphic units along the creek based on the streamflow measurements. Additional streamflow and specific conductance measurements would be useful in improving the understanding of the groundwater/surface-water interactions along San Pedro Creek as well as the effect development could have on the perennial reaches of the creek.

Ortiz Porphyry Belt Groundwater Area

The Ortiz Porphyry Belt groundwater area (fig. 26) includes the Monte Largo Horst, South Mountain, and the San Pedro and Ortiz Mountains in the northeast part of the study area. Boundaries are the approximate contact between pre-Quaternary and Quaternary geologic units (Estancia Basin groundwater area), the Tijeras and La Bajada Faults (San Pedro Creek and Hagan Basin groundwater areas), and the contact between Precambrian rocks and the Madera Formation (Tijeras Graben groundwater area). The eastern boundary with the Estancia Basin groundwater area is mapped as the contact between pre-Quaternary rocks and sediment to the west and Quaternary deposits to the east. The eastern boundary becomes arbitrary in the areas between South Mountain and the San Pedro Mountains and between the San Pedro and Ortiz Mountains. The Ortiz Porphyry Belt groundwater area extends north and east beyond the study area.

Geologic units that outcrop in this area include the Precambrian rocks of Monte Largo Horst, Tertiary igneous rocks, and Pennsylvanian to Tertiary sedimentary rocks. The primary hydrostratigraphic units in the South Mountain and San Pedro Mountain areas are the Madera-Sandia and Abo-Yeso units. In the Ortiz Mountains, the Jurassic and Cretaceous hydrostratigraphic units are probably the main source of water, though fractured Tertiary igneous rocks and alluvium of the Cenozoic hydrostratigraphic unit may produce water in localized settings. The aquifer properties and hydrochemistry of each of these units is discussed in the "Geologic Units and Water-Bearing Characteristics" section.

Much of the area in the Ortiz Porphyry Belt is too steep for development and most current (2005) wells are concentrated on the northern slopes of South Mountain. Of the three wells in the Ortiz Porphyry Belt area with four or more water-level measurements, none have been measured more recently than 1993; hence, no hydrographs are shown for this area. For the same reason, few water-quality analyses are available for the area. Chloride, sulfate, dissolved solids, and nitrate concentrations in groundwater were generally low and pH is generally slightly alkaline (figs. 10, 11, 13, 14, and 20). One well near NM 344 on the north end of the San Pedro Mountains has high concentrations of sulfate and dissolved solids, and a high value of pH. This well may be

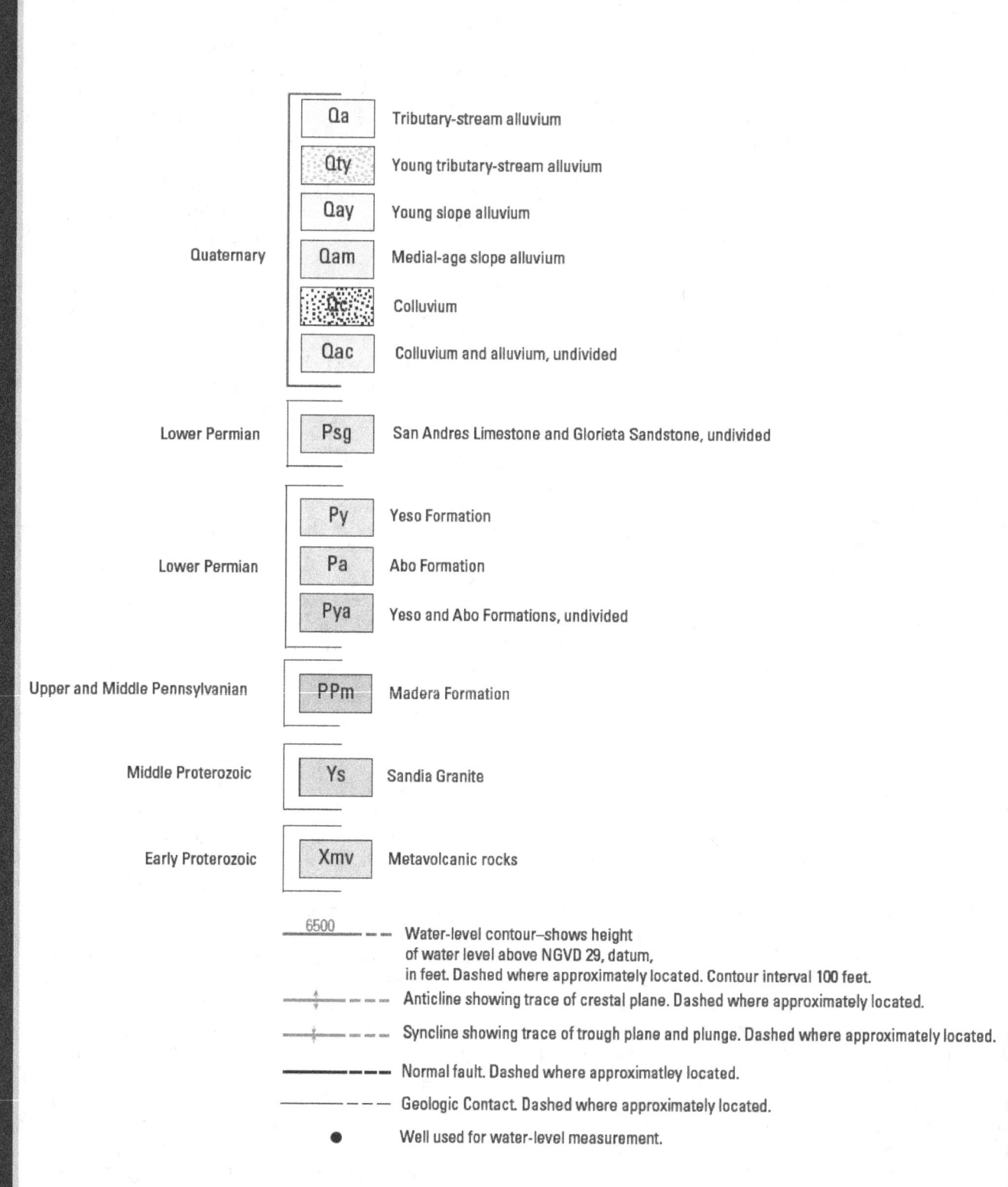

Figure 32. Geohydrologic map of the San Pedro Creek area.

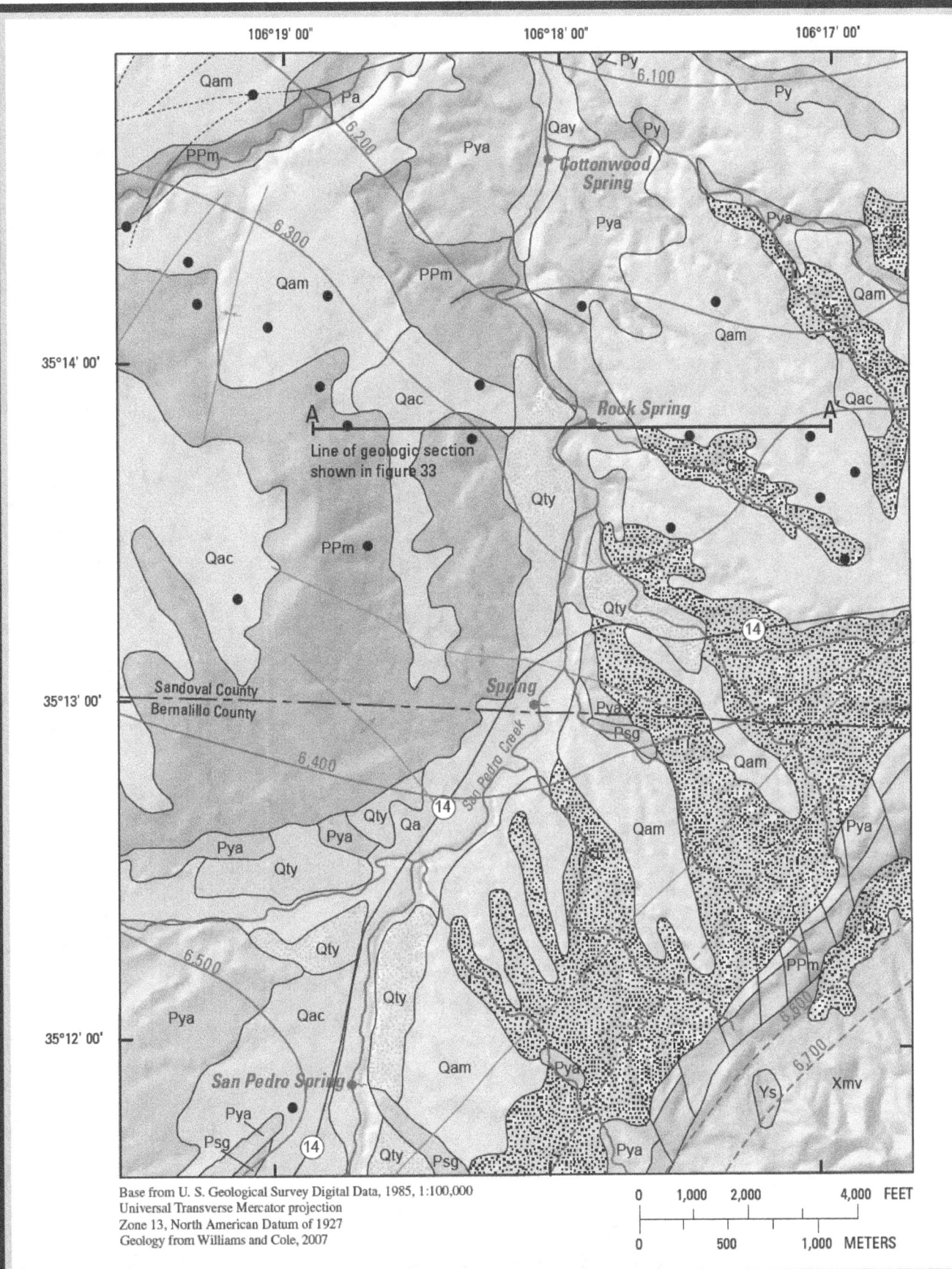

106°19' 00"   106°18' 00"   106°17' 00"

35°14' 00'

35°13' 00'

35°12' 00'

Qam
Pa
Py
6,100
Py
6,200
Pya
Qay
Py
Cottonwood Spring
PPm
Pya
6,300
Qam
PPm
Pya
Qam
Qam
Qac
Rock Spring
Qac
A   A
Line of geologic section shown in figure 33
Qty
Qac
PPm
Qty
14
Sandoval County
Bernalillo County
Spring
Pya
6,400
Psg
Qam
14
San Pedro Creek
Qty   Qa
Pya
Pya
Qty
Qam
Pya
Qty
6,500
Qty
Pya
Qac
Qty
PPm
6,600
San Pedro Spring
Qam
6,700
Pya
Ys
Xmv
Psg
14
Qty
Psg
Pya

Base from U. S. Geological Survey Digital Data, 1985, 1:100,000
Universal Transverse Mercator projection
Zone 13, North American Datum of 1927
Geology from Williams and Cole, 2007

0   1,000   2,000   4,000   FEET

0   500   1,000   METERS

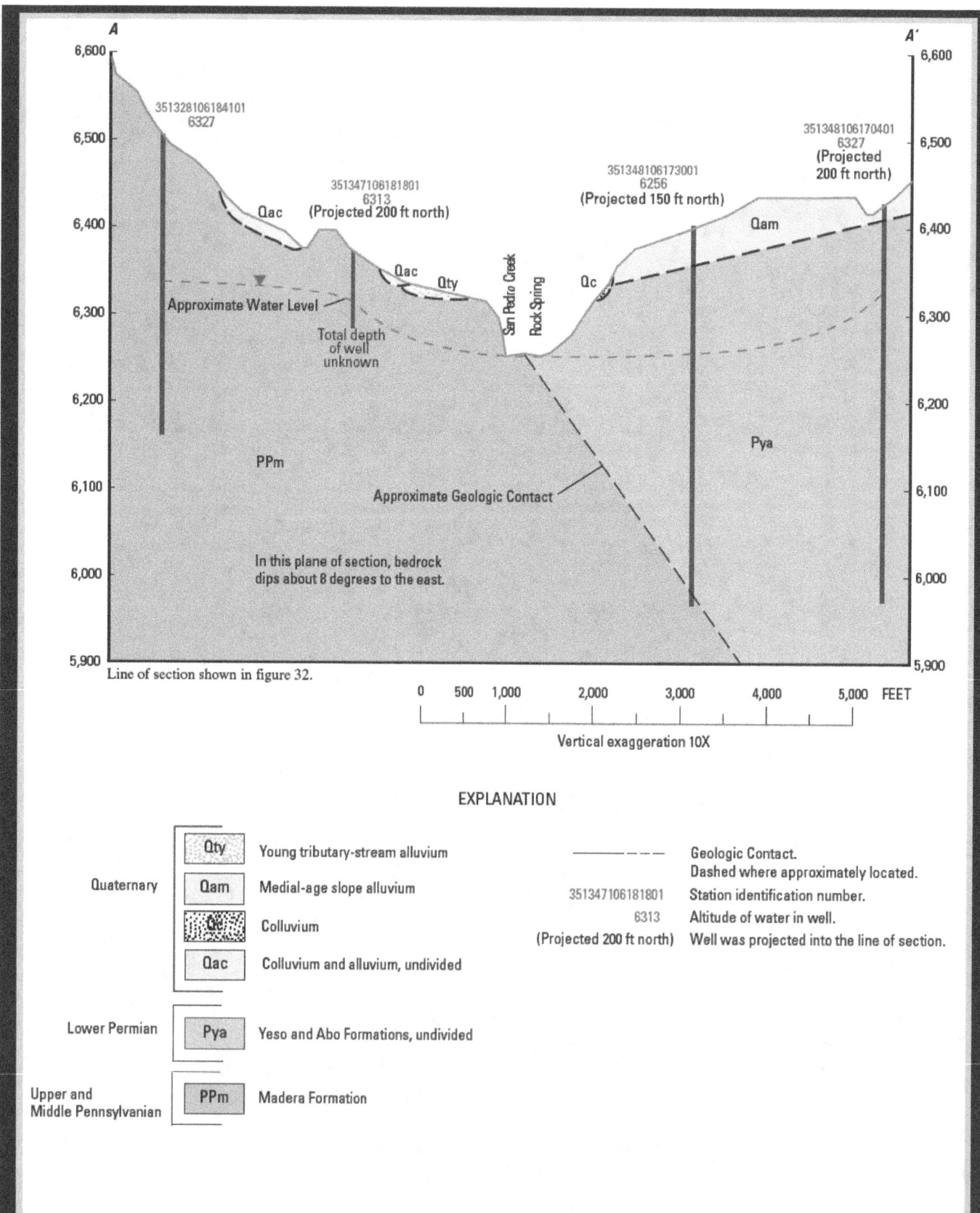

Figure 33. Geohydrologic section of the San Pedro Creek area.

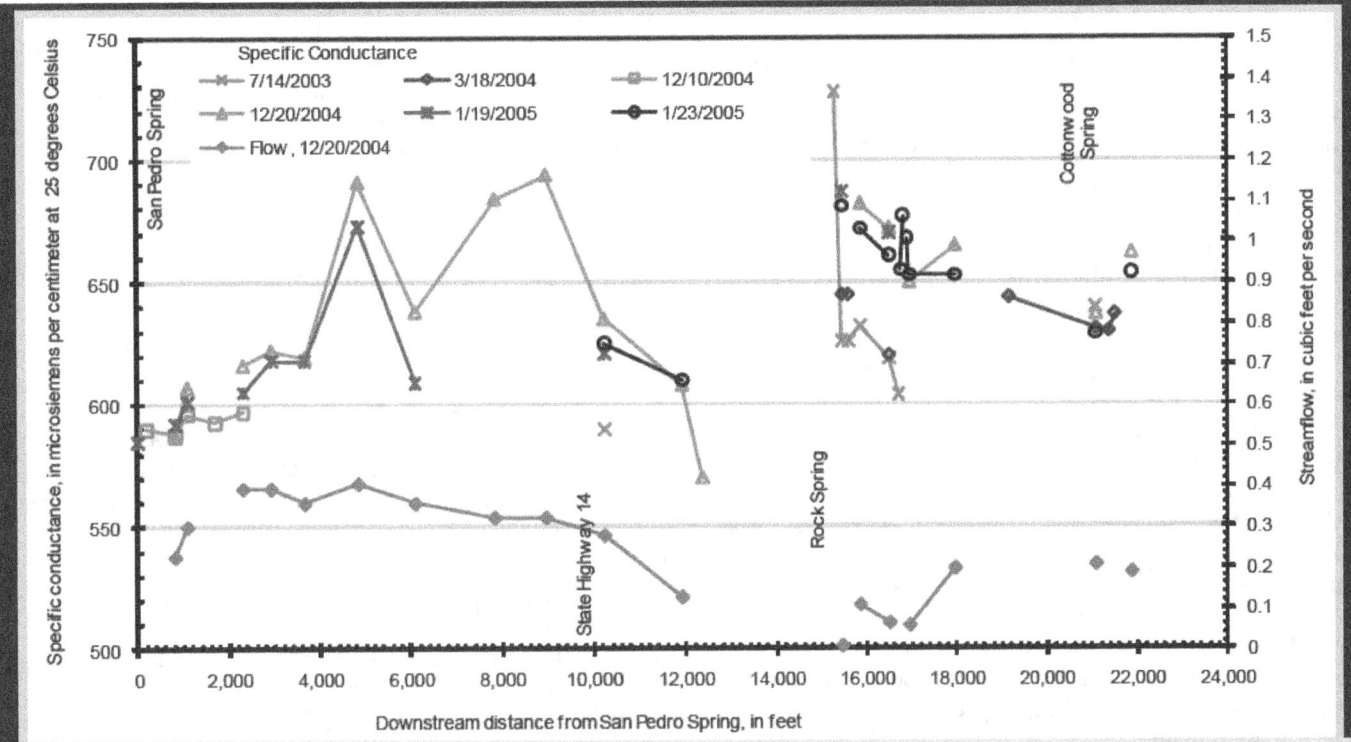

Figure 34. Selected measurements of specific conductance and discharge along San Pedro Creek between San Pedro Spring and Cottonwood Spring.

anomalous because of the proximity to igneous intrusions and the Gutierrez Fault.

Much of the Ortiz Porphyry Belt groundwater area is higher than the surrounding area so groundwater recharge by direct infiltration of precipitation might be an important source of recharge. Infiltration of domestic wastewater from the few septic systems in the area would also be a source of recharge. Groundwater typically flows east and west off the higher areas. Discharge is from wells, springs, evapotranspiration along streams, and groundwater flow into the Estancia Basin and Hagan Basin groundwater areas.

Hagan Basin Groundwater Area

Most land in the Hagan Basin groundwater area (fig. 26 and table 12) is owned by large ranches, the Federal Government, and Pueblos that have used the land primarily for rangeland. As a result, little is known about the hydrogeology of the area except for meager information from a few wells, several consultant reports, and surficial geologic mapping. The groundwater area defined here largely corresponds to the basin as discussed in the "Structural Features" section. The area is bounded on the east by the Tijeras and La Bajada Faults and on the west by limestone of the Madera Formation in the Sandia Mountains and the San Francisco Fault. The

southern boundary of the area, with the San Pedro Creek and Upper Sandia Mountains groundwater area, is the approximate contact between Permian and Triassic rocks. The Hagan Basin extends north beyond the study area.

The few wells in the Hagan Basin are primarily completed in the Chinle-Moenkopi, Jurassic, Cretaceous, and Cenozoic hydrostratigraphic units, though wells are completed in other hydrostratigraphic units on the basin margins. The Cenozoic hydrostratigraphic unit becomes the primary water bearing unit as Hagan Basin transitions into the Albuquerque Basin to the north. The aquifer properties and hydrochemistry of each of these units is discussed in the "Geologic Units and Water-Bearing Characteristics" section.

No wells in the area have more than one water-level measurement; thus, no hydrographs are shown. Similarly, few wells have been sampled for water quality. Of those sampled wells, chloride and nitrate concentrations were low, whereas sulfate and dissolved-solids concentrations were high (figs. 10, 11, 13, and 20). These high concentrations are probably found in water produced from the three Mesozoic-age hydrostratigraphic units or the Tertiary Galisteo Formation in the Cenozoic hydrostratigraphic unit.

Surface-water drainage from the Hagan Basin is primarily by Arroyo Tonque and San Pedro Creek (190 mi^2) to the south and Galisteo Creek (670 mi^2) to the north. Arroyo de San Francisco, Arroyo de la Vega de los Tanos, and an unnamed arroyo draining the area near the Santo Domingo school collectively drain an additional 70 mi² (fig. 23 and table 11).

The source of groundwater in the Hagan Basin is infiltration of precipitation, infiltration of runoff from adjacent highlands, and possible groundwater flow from the San Pedro Creek and Ortiz Porphyry Belt areas. Groundwater flows from the margins of the Hagen Basin toward the basin axis and into the Albuquerque Basin. Aside from wells, a few springs, and probable evapotranspiration along streams, discharge probably is limited to groundwater flow to the Albuquerque Basin. Jurassic strata on the north and east of the Hagan Basin adjacent to the La Bajada Fault are folded into a tight, faulted anticline (Maynard, 2000) that likely acts at least as a partial barrier to groundwater flow. Johnson (2000) described the San Francisco Fault in the area north of Tecolote as "a broad zone of deformation…roughly 100 to 1,000 feet" across. She noted that the fault zone had substantially less permeability than the surrounding geologic units, though more permeable sections of the fault exist in the area. North of this area the fault can be traced along the boundary between the Quaternary deposits of the Albuquerque Basin and the Mesozoic and Tertiary rocks of the Hagan Basin before the fault becomes poorly expressed beneath the alluvium.

A geochemical study of the Albuquerque Basin (Plummer and others, 2004) confirmed that groundwater from the Hagan Basin discharges north into the Albuquerque Basin. The Albuquerque Basin groundwater-flow model (McAda and Barroll, 2002) included four sources of recharge to the Albuquerque Basin from this area: (1) 300 acre-ft/year of mountain-front recharge along the approximate 6-mi reach of the San Francisco Fault that includes Arroyo Tonque and the area north to about Santo Domingo, (2) 1,000 acre-ft/year of groundwater flow northward from the Hagan Basin, (3) 1,750 acre-ft/year tributary recharge from Galisteo Creek, and (4) about 835 acre-ft/year of groundwater discharge in the area surrounding Galisteo Creek. Thus, the Albuquerque Basin groundwater-flow model shows a contribution of 3,885 acre-ft/year from the Hagan Basin area—about 0.6 percent of the precipitation that falls on the five watersheds that drain the Hagan Basin (fig. 23 and table 11).

Upper Sandia Mountains Groundwater Area

The Upper Sandia Mountains groundwater area (fig. 26 and table 12) is defined as the upper slopes of the Sandia Mountains underlain by Pennsylvanian and older geologic units. The Upper Sandia Mountains groundwater area is bounded to the northeast by the West Las Huertas Fault and other faults extending north from the West Las Huertas Fault (San Pedro Creek and Hagan Basin groundwater areas), to the southeast by the contact between the Madera Formation and younger rocks (Cedar Crest groundwater area), to the far southeast by the Tijeras Fault (Tijeras Graben groundwater area), and to the south by the approximate contact between Pennsylvanian and underlying Precambrian geologic units

(Tijeras Canyon groundwater area). The Upper Sandia Mountains groundwater area extends north and west beyond the study area. The hydrogeology of the northernmost part of the area near Placitas has been described in detail by Johnson (2000).

The primary hydrostratigraphic units in the Upper Sandia Mountains groundwater area are the Madera-Sandia and the Abo-Yeso units; locally the Cenozoic hydrostratigraphic unit produces water to wells and springs. The aquifer properties and hydrochemistry of each of these units is discussed above in the "Geologic Units and Water-Bearing Characteristics" section.

Because nearly all the area is in the Cibola National Forest, few wells have been installed and none have sufficient water-level measurements to plot hydrographs. In general, concentrations of chloride, sulfate, dissolved solids, and nitrate are low in wells sampled near Placitas (figs. 10, 11, 13, and 20).

The source of groundwater in the Upper Sandia Mountains groundwater area is primarily direct infiltration of precipitation on the eastern slopes of the Sandia Mountains and infiltration of domestic wastewater from a few septic systems. Probably no groundwater flows from adjacent groundwater areas because the Upper Sandia Mountains groundwater area includes the highest elevations within the study area. Groundwater probably flows eastward in the southern part of the area and northward in the northern part of the area. Discharge is from a few wells, numerous springs, evapotranspiration along streams, and groundwater flow into the Cedar Crest and San Pedro Creek groundwater areas.

Effects of Development on Water Resources

Concern exists in the East Mountain community and government entities about the effects of development on water resources in the area. Such effects could manifest in terms of groundwater supply or by changes in water quality. Groundwater withdrawals or pumpage can result in decreases in water levels, changes in groundwater-flow directions, and decreases in discharge to springs or streams. Water-quality changes can result from infiltration of effluent from onsite wastewater-disposal systems (septic tanks/drain fields); infiltration of runoff from roofs, driveways, and roads; and infiltration of water from irrigated fields or garden plots.

Water-Quantity Effects

Under predevelopment and constant climatic conditions, over the long term, aquifer systems are generally assumed to be under steady state conditions where recharge to an aquifer system equals discharge from the aquifer. Changes in recharge or discharge rates will result in changes in the amount of water stored in the aquifer (changes in water levels). During development, wells are installed and groundwater is withdrawn or pumped. The source of water for pumpage is either increased recharge, decreased discharge, removal of water from storage, or some combination of the three. Recharge in the study area can be increased from more than predevelopment amounts only by infiltration of wastewater, infiltration of runoff from roads or home sites (driveways, roofs, and so on), groundwater flow from other aquifer systems or adjacent areas, or conversion of stream reaches from gaining by discharge of groundwater to losing surface water to the ground system. Predevelopment groundwater discharge can be reduced by intercepting water that formerly discharged at springs and gaining stream reaches or by reductions in groundwater flow to other aquifer systems or adjacent areas. A decrease of water in storage results in water-level declines; thus, water levels decrease (water is removed from storage) if the rate of groundwater recharge is less than groundwater discharge from the aquifer. If no water withdrawn from wells were used consumptively (water is removed from the area by evaporation or evapotranspiration) and all well pumpage was returned to the aquifer, there would be no long-term net change in the aquifer system. Because some of the withdrawals are lost to consumptive use, the equilibrium is upset, and the resulting deficit causes increased recharge, decreased discharge, removal of water from storage, or some combination of the three. Water-level declines are generally the first effects that are observed because of the slow movement of groundwater from recharge areas to discharge areas. Effects of groundwater withdrawals on recharge or discharge in most aquifers can take many years.

The actual water used by a household varies depending on many things, including the number of individuals in the home, the type of appliances used in the home (washing machines, dishwashers, evaporative coolers, and so on), and the amount of landscape or gardening use (Wilson and others, 2003). Groundwater use and consumptive use (depletion) of water in the East Mountain area in 2000 can be estimated by using the 2000 population of 33,000 and the NMOSE estimate of 80 gallons daily per capita water use (U.S. Census Bureau, 2005; Wilson, and others, 2003, p. 19). By assuming 80 gallons daily per capita water use, the total domestic water use is about 2.6 million gallons per day or about 2,950 acre-ft/year. Water use is about 0.27 acre-ft/year for a household of three.

Most domestic water is discharged to the septic tank/drainfield as wastewater though during the summer some water is used consumptively by evapotranspiration for landscaping and irrigation or by evaporation for cooling by evaporative coolers. Wastewater discharged to a septic tank and then to a drain field or dry well is either lost to evapotranspiration or infiltrates below the root zone and recharges area aquifers. The percentage of water use that is used consumptively varies depending on many factors including outdoor water use and the use of evaporative coolers. Wilson and Lucero (1997, p. 13) estimated that about half of domestic water is lost to the atmosphere by evaporation or transpiration (consumptive use). The remaining half would be available to recharge area aquifers. By using

these assumptions, annual consumptive use from domestic use in the East Mountain area is about 1,475 acre-ft/year and the amount of water available for recharge to the aquifers as the result of infiltration of water from septic tanks also is about 1,475 acre-ft/year. Consumptive use for a household of three is about 0.135 acre-ft/year assuming consumptive use is one-half of water use.

Recharge rates in developed areas could be increased relative to predevelopment conditions if runoff from roofs, driveways, and roads accumulates and this water infiltrates below the root zone. The amount of recharge, if this circumstance actually happens, would be small, however, because of the small runoff areas. Further investigation of this possible source of recharge would be necessary to document if recharge originates from this process in the East Mountain area.

The East Mountain area contains little irrigated agriculture with the exception of residential garden plots. Most water used for irrigation in this setting is withdrawn from the groundwater system, and therefore, the net effect would be removal of water from the aquifers as part of the water applied would be used consumptively.

Water-Quality Effects

Much of the population in the study area is served by private or individual wells; in these areas the water that is returned to the area aquifers from septic-tank infiltration occurs near where water is withdrawn from the well. Areas served by community water systems may have their water pumped a substantial distance from the supply well, though wastewater is still discharged to a septic system. Thus, in areas served by community water systems, the location of recharge from domestic-wastewater disposal is removed from the community supply well.

The composition of water used in the home that is discharged to a septic tank and then to a drain field or dry well can change relative to supply water. The concentrations of many constituents in the effluent would be similar the concentration in the supply water because for many activities little is added to the water during use in the home and what is added settles out as solids in the septic tank. Sodium, chloride, and nitrate concentrations increase in wastewater discharging to a drain field compared to the same constituent concentrations in the supply water (Cantor and Knox, 1985; Umari and others, 1993). Umari and others (1993) found considerable variation in the amount of this increase—sodium increased by 29 to 158 mg/L, chloride increased by 9 to 80 mg/L, and total nitrogen increased by 15 to 62 mg/L as nitrogen. The increase in sodium and chloride in areas where water softeners are used could be much greater because of the salt (sodium chloride) used in water softeners. Groundwater withdrawn from the aquifer for domestic use will infiltrate from drain fields with an altered water quality. In areas served by distant community supply wells, the chemical signature of the supply water also may differ; thus, infiltrating water may have a markedly different water quality than the native groundwater in the area of the residence.

Sodium and chloride concentrations in water would tend to increase as water moves through the soil zone or aquifer; whereas, nitrate concentrations can decrease under some conditions. Constituent concentrations in water interacting with the rocks would generally increase as the result of chemical reactions and may be further increased by evaporation or transpiration. Nitrate concentrations can decrease as the result of biological reactions or uptake by plants. Under some conditions, dissolved nitrate is converted to nitrogen gas (denitrification), thus reducing the nitrate concentration. In areas where such denitrification happens, groundwater receiving wastewater recharge could have low nitrate concentrations and higher concentrations of sodium and chloride.

Precipitation also contains sodium, chloride, and nitrate; evaporation or transpiration of precipitation in the soil zone can concentrate these constituents resulting in elevated concentrations in soil water relative to precipitation. Recharge of this soil water also may result in high sodium, chloride, and nitrate concentrations in groundwater. In general, such soil zone concentration of constituents from precipitation and subsequent recharge would not be localized, but instead have a more regional distribution and, therefore, affect the composition of groundwater in large areas.

Walvoord and others (2003) have shown that in areas with little or no recharge, chloride and nitrate in precipitation accumulates in the soil zone and concentrations in the soil zone can be large (greater than 1,000 mg/L). These constituents can be stored in the soil zone for long periods if recharge rates are small. Recharge rates in the East Mountains area probably vary depending on precipitation, soil-zone characteristics, and vegetation. Some areas probably have little or no diffuse recharge based on studies in the area and areas similar to the East Mountains area (Scanlon, 1991; Phillips, 1994; and Anderholm, 1994). In areas where no diffuse recharge happened during predevelopment, installation of septic tanks or focused runoff could cause leaching of chloride and nitrate from the soil zone and movement of water with large concentrations of these constituents to the groundwater system.

Road salt used for deicing in the winter also contains sodium and chloride. Recharge of the resulting runoff increases sodium and chloride concentrations in groundwater. Areas where snow is piled after removal or where road salt is stored also may be local sources of sodium and chloride.

Nitrate concentrations at the scale of the study area are typically higher in samples with higher chloride concentrations (fig. 35). The larger concentrations could be due to variations in the composition of recharge or effects of development. Large areas with similar or elevated concentrations would be expected in areas where natural factors are important. Nitrate concentrations throughout much of the study area are less than the assumed background concentration of 2 mg/L (fig. 11). Localized areas with high concentrations of chloride

and nitrate (figs. 10 and 11) could indicate the effects of development. Water from wells with nitrate concentrations greater than 2 mg/L is generally found in areas along the major roads (I-40 and NM 14, fig. 11). These areas were probably developed prior to other areas and the density of homes in these areas is generally greater than in other areas, which may indicate development is resulting in the larger nitrate concentrations in these areas; however, determining the precise source of these high concentrations is difficult.

Temporal Water-Level and Water-Quality Variations

Identification of human-related effects on the water resources of an area is often difficult because of confounding factors such as climate and natural variability in groundwater, and scientists working in the East Mountain area have struggled with this issue. The USGS has done periodic monitoring of water levels and water quality in selected wells in the East Mountain area to evaluate short-(monthly) and long-term variations. Short-term changes in water level and water quality would indicate effects caused by local-scale recharge or withdrawals and long-term changes would be more indicative of regional changes in climate and land use. Kues and Garcia (1995), Rankin (1996), Rankin (2000), and Blanchard (2004) present water-quality and water-level data collected from wells in the study area. Based on monthly monitoring from January 1990 through June 1993 and periodic monitoring thereafter, they found seasonal variations in water levels and, occasionally, in water quality. Figure 26 is a map showing the location of selected wells for which some of this earlier data are plotted. Temporal plots of water levels, chloride concentrations, and nitrate concentrations from selected wells are shown to demonstrate typical short- and long-term variations that have been observed in the area (figs. 27, 28, 29, 30, 31, 36, and 37). Water from 4 of the 6 wells shown in figures 36 and 37 had nitrate concentrations greater than 2 mg/L indicating groundwater in the area of these wells could be affected by development.

Short-term variations in water levels are more apparent than variations in chloride and nitrate concentrations. In several wells (350531106224301, 350930106210701, and 351011106220401, figs. 29 and 31), water levels decrease (that is, the depth to water below land surface increases) to a low in the summer (June and July) and increase in the late winter. These variations are probably because of larger withdrawal in the summer as residents water outdoors and use evaporative coolers in the summer. Seasonal variations seem more apparent in wells with water levels less than 50 ft below land surface. Large changes in water levels were observed in many of the wells (350602106210401, 350655106185601, 350531106224301, 350655106194501, 350525106151701, 350930106210701, 351011106220401, and 351014106202801) in August–September 1991 (figs. 27, 29, 30, and 31), which is discussed in more detail later

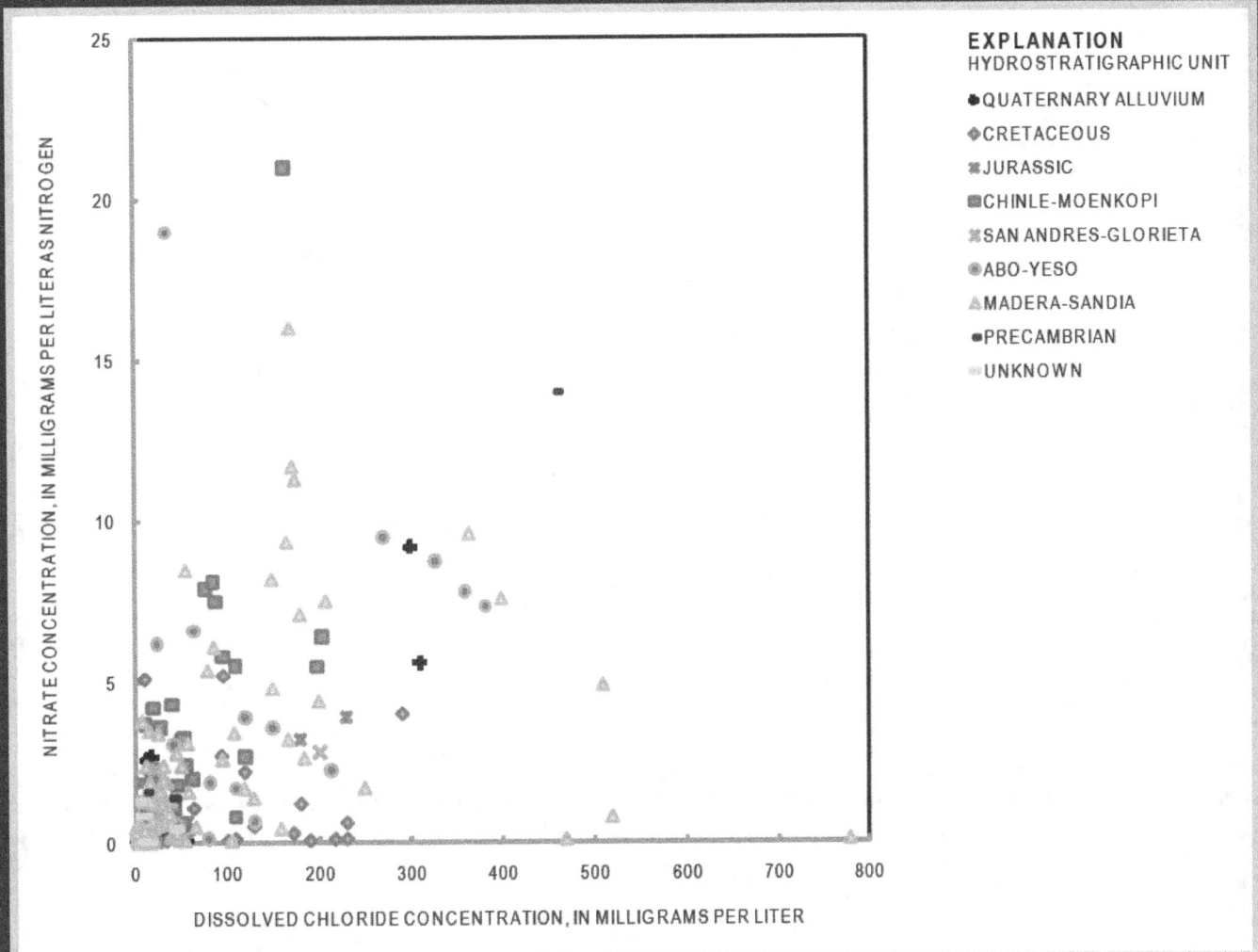

Figure 35. Relation between nitrate concentration and dissolved chloride concentration in water from selected wells in the East Mountain study area.

in this section. Seasonal variations in chloride and nitrate concentrations in water from the selected wells are not as common as were seen in water levels although there is short-term variation in chloride and nitrate concentrations (figs. 36 and 37). A large change in water quality was observed in several wells similar to what was seen in water levels. Such abrupt changes are probably the result of infrequent conditions as defined by the available data. These step changes had substantial and long-lasting effects on water levels and especially water quality

Water levels in many wells that were monitored monthly increased rapidly in August–September 1991 (Kues and Garcia, 1995). The water-level increase in many wells was about 5 ft. Blanchard and Kues (1999, p. 32–39) noted that the water-level increases in late summer 1991 were due to infiltration of precipitation as the result of an anomalously large amount of precipitation in July 1991 (7.4 inches). They

pointed out that increases in water levels in the wells indicated "an effective hydraulic connection between the land surface and the groundwater system" and that the groundwater was susceptible to land-surface contamination (Blanchard and Kues, 1999, p. 39). Chloride and nitrate concentrations also changed in several wells as the result of the precipitation in July 1991 (figs. 36 and 37). Chloride concentrations increased shortly after July 1991 in samples from wells 350522106222501 (Abo-Yeso) and 351014106202801 (Chinle-Moenkopi) and decreased in samples from wells 350655106185601 (Madera-Sandia), 350525106151701 (Madera-Sandia) and 350119106210901 (Madera-Sandia). Nitrate concentrations decreased shortly after July 1991 in samples from well 350655106185601 (Madera-Sandia). This extreme climatic event had a profound and long-lasting effect on water levels and water quality in the area based on the existing data. For example, the chloride concentration in water

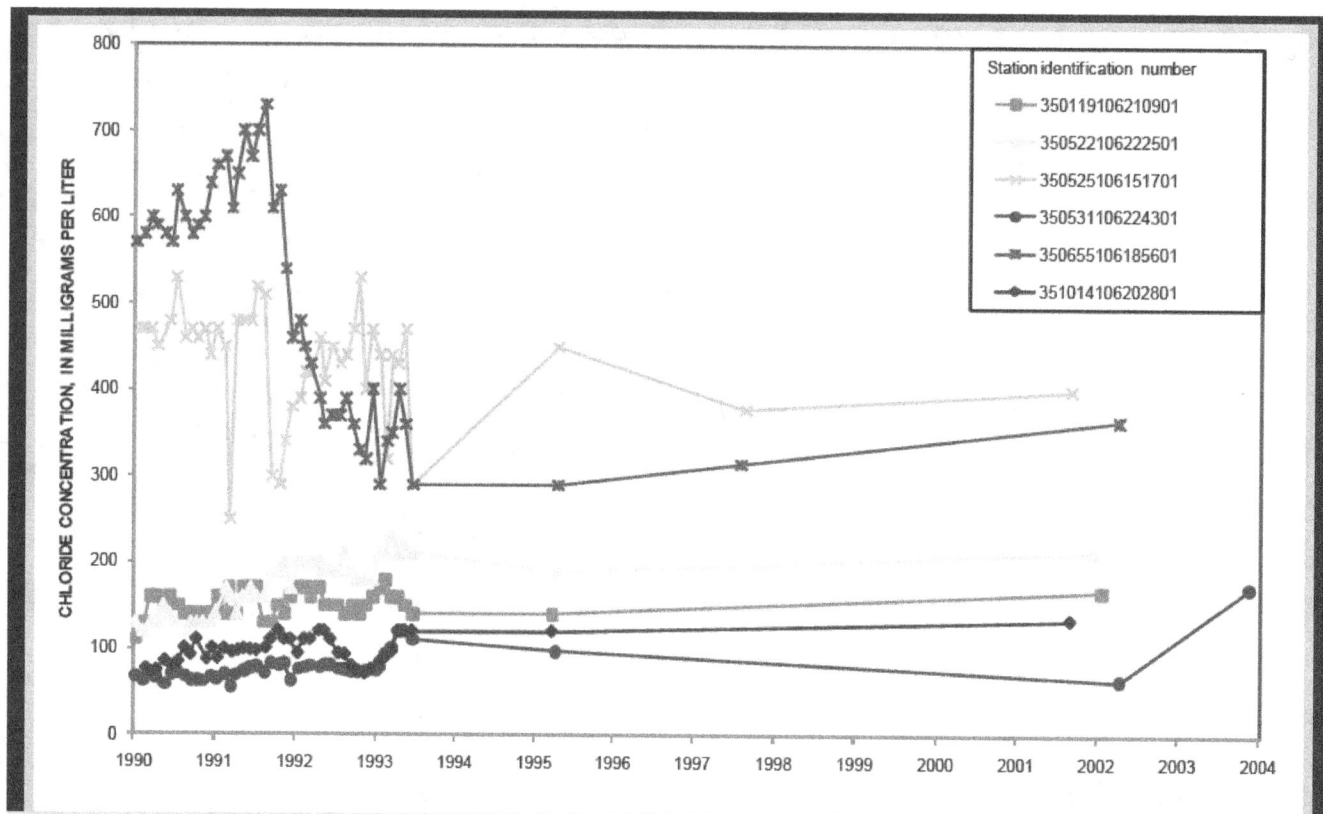

Figure 36. Seasonal variation in dissolved chloride concentration in water from selected wells in the East Mountain study area.

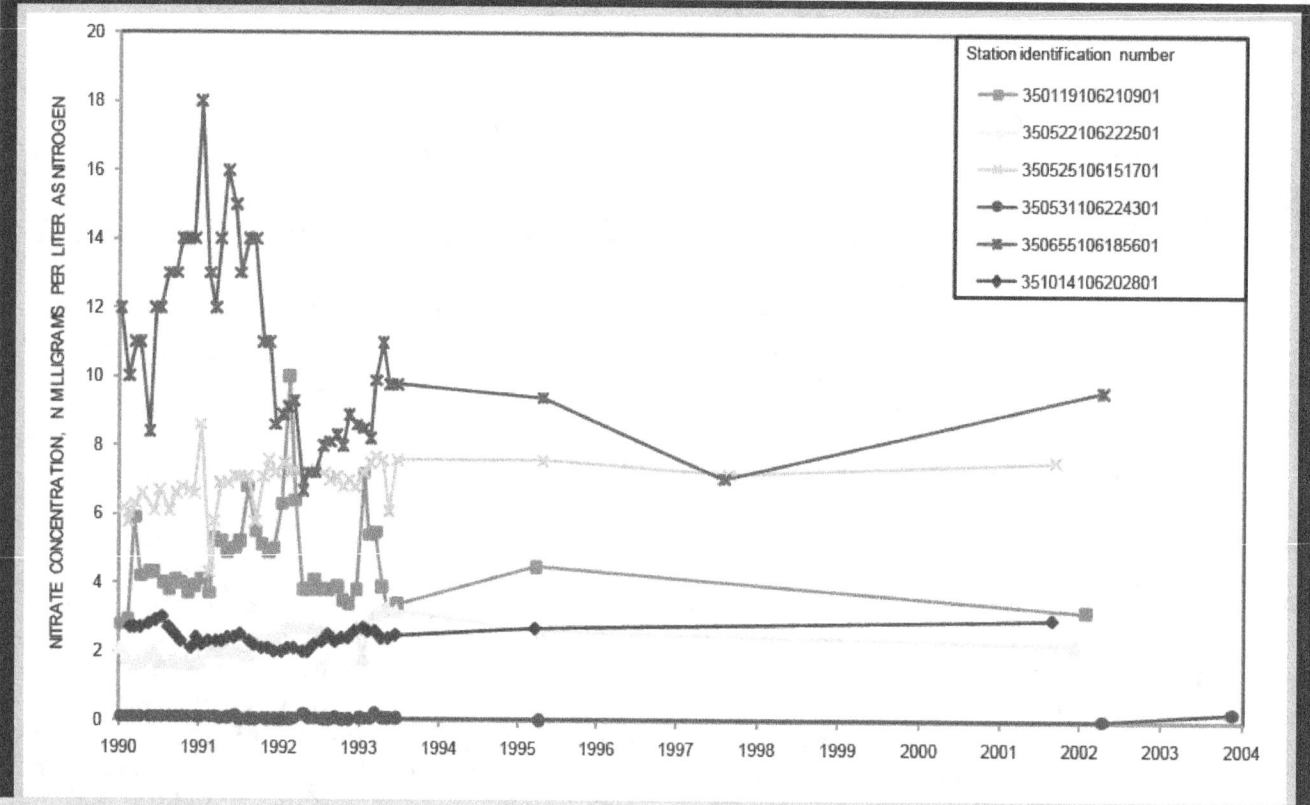

Figure 37. Seasonal variation in nitrate concentration in water from selected wells in the East Mountain study area.

from well 350655106185601 (Madera-Sandia) decreased from 720 to 300 mg/L and nitrate concentrations decreased from 15 to 8 mg/L (figs. 36 and 37).

Long-term water-level variations in most wells indicated relatively stable water levels until about 2000 after which water levels decreased in most wells (figs. 27, 28, 29, 30, and 31). The water-level decreases in the wells after 2000 were probably the result of groundwater withdrawals and decreases in recharge during the drought that existed from about 1995 to 2005. The large decreases in water levels in many wells in the area during the drought indicated that changes in precipitation had a substantial effect on the water resources of the area. Large increases in groundwater withdrawals could have a similar effect.

Blanchard and Kues (1999) compared chloride and nitrate concentrations in samples from wells in and adjacent to the study area that were sampled in 1962 or 1984 and again in 1990. They found chloride concentrations increased in 7 of 8 wells, most by more than 10 mg/L and nitrate concentrations increased in 6 of 11 wells, generally by more than 1 mg/L, decreased in 3 wells, and did not change in 2 wells. Blanchard (2004, p. 24) found similar nitrate concentrations in samples collected from wells in the East Mountain area in 2001–02 and the late 1990s. Based on data presented by Rankin (2000), long-term (1990–99) systematic increases in chloride and nitrate concentration also are not apparent in water from most wells in the area that have been frequently monitored. Data presented by Rankin show that chloride and nitrate concentrations in groundwater vary over time, possibly indicating variations in the composition of recharge and groundwater moving through the area. Long-term (1990 to 2002) increases in chloride and nitrate are also not evident in water from wells shown on figures 36 and 37. Water from many of these wells had nitrate concentrations greater than the assumed background of 2 mg/L, possibly indicating effects from development; however, a consistent increase in nitrate or chloride concentrations is not apparent in the long term data.

Chlorofluorocarbons (CFCs) are synthetic organic compounds first manufactured in the 1930s whose changing concentrations in the atmosphere have been measured or reconstructed since 1940. CFC concentrations in precipitation and in soil water in contact with the atmosphere reflect the current atmospheric concentration. Once this water passes the water table and enters groundwater, the water is isolated from the atmosphere and the CFC concentration in this water is a function of the date the water was isolated from the atmosphere. Consequently, CFC concentration in water can be used to determine when the water recharged and the approximate length of time the water has been in the aquifer. In practice, several factors can complicate the analysis or otherwise affect results. A comprehensive discussion of CFC dating can be found in Plummer and Busenberg (1999).

Blanchard (2004) measured CFCs (CFC-11, CFC-12, and CFC-113) in samples from five wells in the study area. The concentrations of CFC-11 or CFC-12 in three wells were much greater than could be imparted from the atmosphere

(Paul Blanchard, U.S. Geological Survey, written comm., November 2005). Because other organic compounds can affect CFC analyses and many household products and septic-tank additives can contain CFCs (Neil Plummer, US Geological Survey, oral commun., 1999), such "contamination" of the sample may indicate septic-tank effluent; thus, elevated CFC concentrations measured in water from wells in the study area may indicate that infiltrating water from domestic-wastewater disposal is mixing with groundwater near the sampled wells. Blanchard (2004, p. 17) used the CFC samples to determine that the length of time the water had been in the aquifer. Because well screens in the area are generally below the water table, however, water withdrawn for analysis is from deeper parts of the aquifer. If water is recharged near the well, water at or near the water table has probably been in the aquifer much less time than the water used for analysis that is pumped from deeper in the aquifer. Water levels in the wells sampled for CFCs by Blanchard ranged from about 45 to 130 ft above the bottom of the wells where well depth is known. The time needed for water to move from the water table to deeper parts of the aquifer varies depending on aquifer properties and pumpage. The CFC dating of water in the wells sampled by Blanchard (2004, p. 17) indicated that the minimum time for water to move from the water table to the well screens was 14 to 19 years, though the location of the recharge may be at or near the site or upgradient.

The lack of widespread, long-term increases in chloride and nitrate concentrations in groundwater in the study area does not rule out that domestic-wastewater disposal is not resulting in recharge to the aquifer or affecting groundwater quality. Because groundwater quality at the water table would be most affected by the composition of recharge from onsite wastewater-disposal systems, such effects may not have reached deeper parts of the aquifer where many wells are completed. To what degree water mixes in the aquifer and the time needed for water to move from the water table or point of recharge downward to well screens or pump intakes is not known. The short-term variation in water levels indicated recharge happens in the area and the variation in chloride and nitrate concentrations indicated the varying chemical composition of recharge. Additional groundwater sampling and continuous water-level monitoring would aid in a better understanding of recharge, timing, composition, and the effects of development on water levels and groundwater quality in the area.

Summary

The groundwater resources of about 400 mi² of the East Mountain area of Bernalillo, Sandoval, Santa Fe, and Torrance Counties in central New Mexico were evaluated by using groundwater levels and water-quality analyses, and updated geologic mapping. Substantial development in the study area (population increased by 11,000, or 50 percent, from 1990 through 2000 has raised concerns about the effects of growth on water resources. The last comprehensive examination of the water resources of the study area was done in 1980; this study examines a slightly different area and incorporates data collected in the intervening 25 years.

Because most aquifers in the East Mountain area appear to respond to precipitation, climatic conditions are important. Of the 132 months from January 1995 through December 2005, 67 had Palmer drought severity index values of less than -0.5, indicating drier than normal climate. Of those months, 61 experienced mild to extreme drought while 45 months experienced slightly to very wet climate. Because the drought persisted at least until September 2005, whether water level declines are affected by humans or by climate is difficult to determine.

The East Mountain area is geologically and hydrologically complex—in addition to the geologic units, such features as the Sandia Mountains, Tijeras and Gutierrez Faults, Tijeras Graben, and the Estancia Basin affect the movement, availability, and water quality of the groundwater system.

The stratigraphic units of the study area can be separated into eight hydrostratigraphic units, each having distinct hydraulic and chemical properties. Overall, the primary hydrostratigraphic units are the Madera-Sandia and Abo-Yeso; however, other units are the primary source of supply in some areas.

Despite the eight previously defined hydrostratigraphic units, water-level contours were drawn on the generalized regional potentiometric map assuming all hydrostratigraphic units are connected and function as a single aquifer system. Groundwater originates as infiltration of precipitation in upland areas (Sandia, Manzano, and Manzanita Mountains, and the Ortiz Porphyry Belt) and moves downgradient into the Tijeras Graben, Tijeras Canyon, San Pedro synclinorium, and the Hagan, Estancia, and Española Basins. Isotopic analyses indicate that different source areas of recharge can be identified with more comprehensive sampling.

The study area can be divided into eight groundwater areas defined on the basis of geologic, hydrologic, and geochemical information. These areas and their main characteristics are as follows:

1. Tijeras Canyon groundwater area: The primary hydrostratigraphic units are Madera-Sandia and Abo-Yeso; depth to water is generally less than 100 ft; chloride and dissolved-solids concentrations are high near Interstate 40 and NM 14, and low elsewhere.

2. Cedar Crest groundwater area: The primary hydrostratigraphic units are Madera-Sandia, Abo-Yeso, San Andres-Glorieta, and Chinle-Moenkopi; depth to water is generally less than 100 ft; except for wells along NM 14, concentrations of chloride, sulfate, dissolved solids and nitrate are low.

3. Tijeras Graben groundwater area: The primary hydrostratigraphic units are Abo-Yeso, San Andres-Glorieta, Chinle-Moenkopi, Jurassic, and Cretaceous; depth to water is generally less than 100 ft; nitrate concentrations in the Tijeras Graben are primarily low, sulfate and dissolved-solids concentrations are among the highest in the study area, chloride concentrations are generally high in the southwestern part of the area but not in the northeastern part.

4. Estancia Basin groundwater area: The primary hydrostratigraphic units are Madera-Sandia and Cenozoic; depth to water is generally greater than 100 ft; chloride, sulfate, dissolved-solids, and nitrate concentrations are not high except in an area along Interstate 40 west of NM 217.

5. San Pedro Creek groundwater area: The primary hydrostratigraphic units are Madera-Sandia, Abo-Yeso, San Andres-Glorieta and Chinle-Moenkopi; depth to water is generally between 100 and 400 ft; concentrations of water-quality constituents were among the lowest in the study area.

6. Ortiz Porphyry Belt groundwater area: The primary hydrostratigraphic units are Madera-Sandia, Abo-Yeso, Jurassic, and Cretaceous; depth to water is generally less than 200 ft; chloride, sulfate, dissolved-solids, and nitrate concentrations in groundwater were generally low.

7. Hagan Basin groundwater area: The primary hydrostratigraphic units are Chinle-Moenkopi, Jurassic, Cretaceous, and Cenozoic; depth to water is generally less than 25 ft to 400 ft; chloride and nitrate concentrations were low, whereas sulfate and dissolved-solids concentrations were high in some wells.

8. Upper Sandia Mountains groundwater area: The primary hydrostratigraphic unit is Madera-Sandia; depth to water is poorly defined; water-quality concentrations were low in wells sampled near Placitas.

San Pedro Creek is one of several streams in the area with perennial reaches; thus, the source of water to springs that discharge to the creek and whether development can affect these flows is of concern. The source of water to San Pedro Spring could be discharging from Quaternary alluvium or the Abo-Yeso or San Andres-Glorieta hydrostratigraphic units or from all three. Water at Rock Spring could be discharging from the Madera-Sandia or Abo-Yeso hydrostratigraphic units, or possibly both. The most probable source of water to Cottonwood Spring is subsurface downstream flow in the alluvium forced to the surface by a buried constriction of consolidated rock or downdip/downgradient flow in the Abo-Yeso hydrostratigraphic unit west of the creek that discharges at the buried contact with alluvium in and near the channel.

Streamflow and specific conductance of the water in San Pedro Creek vary downstream from San Pedro Spring in response to groundwater inflow and leakage from the stream. On December 20, 2004, flow about 800 ft downstream from San Pedro Spring was about 0.23 cubic feet per second. Flow increased to about 0.4 cubic feet per second about 4,000 ft downstream from San Pedro Spring. In general, flow and specific conductance reach the maximum in the stream reach near the convergence of two arroyos, one from each side of the main channel, with the main channel and then decrease downstream. Streamflow increases in the 4,000-ft stream reach downstream of San Pedro Spring indicate groundwater discharge to the creek in this area. Flows generally decrease along San Pedro Creek from about 4,000 ft downstream of San Pedro Spring until near Rock Spring.

Based on the streamflow measurements, specific conductance measurements, and the geology and hydrology of the area between San Pedro Spring and Cottonwood Spring, there are probably several hydrostratigraphic units that discharge to San Pedro Creek and the springs along San Pedro Creek. There appears to be differences in the water quality in these hydrostratigraphic units based on the specific conductance measurements along the creek. There is also probably infiltration of water from the creek to the underlying hydrostratigraphic units along the creek based on the streamflow measurements.

Development and groundwater withdrawals in the area could affect the groundwater flow system and water quality because groundwater withdrawals upset the natural equilibrium of the flow system and because infiltration and recharge of onsite wastewater has elevated concentrations of sodium, chloride, and nitrate relative to supply water. Annual water use in the East Mountains area was estimated to be 2,950 acre-ft in 2000, and consumptive use was estimated to be 1,475 acre ft. Consumptive use of groundwater could affect the groundwater-flow system because this water is removed from the area as the result of evaporation and transpiration. Short-term water-level variations indicate water levels decrease during the summer months and increase in the winter months probably in response to varying seasonal pumping rates. Nitrate concentrations less than the assumed background of 2 mg/L are found in many parts of the East Mountain area. Nitrate concentrations greater than 2 mg/L are generally found along the major roads that had initial development and where home density is generally largest.

Long-term trends in water quality are difficult to determine in the area. The apparent lack of large, widespread, long term increases in chloride and nitrate concentrations in water from wells in the area may be due to the length of time it takes for water from onsite wastewater systems to move to deeper parts of the aquifer where many wells are completed. Because groundwater quality at the water table would be affected by the composition of recharge from onsite wastewater-disposal systems initially, such effects may not have reached deeper parts of the aquifer where many wells are completed. The degree to which water mixes in the aquifer and the time it takes for water to move from the water table or point of recharge downward to well screens or pump intakes is unknown. More groundwater sampling and continuous water-level monitoring would help lead to a better understanding of recharge and the effects of development on water levels and groundwater quality.

Selected References

Abbott, J.C., 1995, Constraints on the deformational history of the Tijeras-Canoncito fault system, north-central New Mexico: Socorro, New Mexico, New Mexico Institute of Mining and Technology, M.S. thesis, 161 p.

Abbott, J.C., Cather, S.M., and Goodwin, L.B., 1995, Paleogene synorogenic sedimentation in the Galisteo basin related to the Tijeras-Canoncito fault system, in Bauer, P.W., Kues, B.S., Dunbar, N.W., Karlstrom, K.E., and Harrison, B., eds., Geology of the Santa Fe region: New Mexico Geological Society Guidebook 46, p. 271-278.

Abbott, J.C., and Goodwin, L.B., 1995, A spectacular exposure of the Tijeras fault system, with evidence for Quaternary motion, in Bauer, P.W., Kues, B.S., Dunbar, N.W., Karlstrom, K.E., and Harrison, B., eds., Geology of the Santa Fe region: New Mexico Geological Society Guidebook 46, p. 117-125.

Abbott, J.C., Goodwin, L.B., Kelley, S.A., Maynard, S.R., and McIntosh, W.C., 2004, The anatomy of a long-lived fault system—structural and thermochronologic evidence for Laramide to Quaternary activity on the Tijeras fault, New Mexico, in Cather, S.M., McIntosh, W.C., and Kelley, S.A., eds., Tectonics, geochronology, and volcanism in the Southern Rocky Mountains and Rio Grande rift: New Mexico Bureau of Geology and Mineral Resources Bulletin 160, p. 113-138. Available online at: http://geoinfo.nmt.edu/publications/bulletins/160/downloads/06abbot.pdf

Allen, B.D., 1993, Late Quaternary lacustrine record of paleoclimate from Estancia basin, central New Mexico, USA: Albuquerque, University of New Mexico, Ph.D. dissertation, 94 p.

Allen, B.D., 2000, Geology of the Edgewood 7.5-min. quadrangle, Santa Fe and Torrance Counties, New Mexico: New Mexico Bureau of Geology and Mineral Resources, Open-File Geologic Map OF-GM 35, scale 1:24,000. Available online at: http://www.geoinfo.nmt.edu/publications/maps/geologic/ofgm/details.cfml?Volume=35

Allen, B.D., and Anderson, R.Y., 2000, A continuous, high-resolution record of late Pleistocene climate variability from the Estancia basin, New Mexico: Geological Society of America Bulletin, v. 112, no. 9, p. 1,444-1,458.

Allen, B.D., and Shafike, N.G., 2003, Groundwater loss from playa lakes in the Estancia Basin, central New Mexico [abs.], *in* New Mexico symposium on hydrologic modeling: Socorro, New Mexico, August 12, 2003, New Mexico Water Resources Research Institute, p. E-17.

Amato, Ron, Cook, Casey, Cotter, Jeff, Diehl, Danielle, Grassel, Kathleen, Hunter, Andrea, Mandeville, Debra, Nims, Josh, O'Neil, Joy, Romero, Orlando, Vardaro-Charles, Patricia, Walters, Toby, 2001, The East Mountain area septic system user's guide to the Bernalillo County wastewater ordinance: Water Resources Program, Albuquerque, University of New Mexico, Publication No. WRP-3, 29 p., 4 appendices. Available online at: *http://www.unm.edu/~wrp/wrp-3.pdf*

American Ground Water Consultants, 1997, 100-year water availability report for the Entranosa Water and Wastewater Cooperative using water supplied by the Horton family interests: Albuquerque, New Mexico, American Ground Water Consultants, August 11, 1997.

American Ground Water Consultants, 1998, 100-year water availability report for the Horton family well field at 2615.7 and 4215.7 acre feet per year: Albuquerque, New Mexico, American Ground Water Consultants, 18 p.

Anderholm, S.K., 1994, Groundwater recharge near Santa Fe, north-central New Mexico: U.S. Geological Survey Water-Resources Investigations Report 94-4078, 68 p.

Anderson, R.Y., and Allen, B.D., 1999, Third-day, trip 2 road log, Geomorphic and hydrologic response in Estancia basin to late Pleistocene and Holocene climate change, *in* Pazzaglia, F.J., Lucas, S.G., and Austin, G.S., eds. Albuquerque geology: New Mexico Geological Society Guidebook 50, p. 75-82.

Associated Development, Inc., undated, Water availability report for Wellborn/Maguire subdivision: Moriarty, New Mexico, Associated Development, Inc., 152 p.

Atkinson, W.W., Jr., 1961, Geology of the San Pedro Mountains, Santa Fe County, New Mexico: New Mexico Bureau of Geology and Mineral Resources Bulletin 77, 49 p.

Bachhuber, F.W., 1982, Quaternary history of the Estancia Valley, central New Mexico, *in* Grambling, J.A., and Wells, S.G., eds., Albuquerque country II: New Mexico Geological Society Guidebook 33, p. 343-346.

Bachman, G.O., 1975, Geologic map of the Madrid Quadrangle, Santa Fe and Sandoval Counties, New Mexico: U.S. Geological Survey Geologic Quadrangle Map GQ-1268, scale 1:62,500, 1 sheet.

Baker, J.A., undated, Water availability report for Futures II subdivision: Moriarty, New Mexico, Associated Development, Inc., variously paged, 3 tables, 3 figs., 6 appendices, 1 plate in pocket.

Balleau Groundwater, Inc., 1997, Exploratory drilling and testing north-central Estancia basin, New Mexico: Balleau Groundwater, Inc., 27 p.

Balleau Groundwater, Inc., 2000, Geohydrology and water availability for The Overlook at San Pedro Creek, Sandoval County, New Mexico: Albuquerque, New Mexico, Balleau Groundwater, Inc., consultant's report prepared for San Pedro Creek Land Company, 22 p., 2 pls. in pocket.

Barrow, Ronald, and Keller, G.R., 1994, An integrated geophysical study of the Estancia Basin, central New Mexico, *in* Keller, G.R., and Cather, S.M., eds., Basins of the Rio Grande Rift-structure, stratigraphy, and tectonic setting: Geological Society of America Special Paper 291, p. 171-186.

Basham, W.L., 1951, Structure and metamorphism of Pre-Cambrian rocks of the south Manzano Mountains: Evanston, Ill., Northwestern University, M.S. thesis.

Behnke, R. J., Platts, W. J., and Bachhuber, F. W., 1989, The occurrence and paleolimnologic significance of cutthroat trout (*Oncorhynchus clarki*) in pluvial lakes of the Estancia Valley, central New Mexico: Geological Society of America Bulletin, v. 101, No. 12, p. 1,543-1,551.

Behnke, R. J., Platts, W. J., and Bachhuber, F. W., 1990, The occurrence and paleolimnologic significance of cutthroat trout (*Oncorhynchus clarki*) in pluvial lakes of the Estancia Valley, central New Mexico: Discussion and reply: Geological Society of America Bulletin, v. 102, p. 1,731-1,732.

Bernalillo County, 2006, East Mountain area plan, 2006: Albuquerque, N. Mex., Bernalillo County, 150 p. Available at: *http://www.bernco.gov/live/departments. asp?dept=7346&submenuid=7666*

Bernalillo County Planning Commission, 1992, East Mountain area plan: Albuquerque, N. Mex., Bernalillo County Planning Commission Report, June 23, 1992, 86 p.

Bexfield, L.M., and Anderholm, S.K., 2000, Predevelopment water-level map of the Santa Fe Group aquifer system in the Middle Rio Grande Basin between Cochiti Lake and San Acacia, New Mexico: U.S. Geological Survey Water-Resources Investigations Report 00-4249, 1 sheet. Available at: *http://pubs.er.usgs.gov/usgspubs/wri/wri004249*

Black, B.A., 1979, Structure and stratigraphy of the Hagan embayment-a new look, *in* Ingersoll, R.V., Woodward, L.A., and James, H.L., eds., Santa Fe County: New Mexico Geological Society Guidebook 30, p. 101-106.

Black, B.A., Cather, S.M., and Connell, S.D., 2000, Geology of the San Felipe Pueblo NE 7.5-min. quadrangle: New Mexico Bureau of Geology and Mineral Resources Open-File Geologic Map OF-GM 37, scale 1:24,000. Available online at: *http://geoinfo.nmt.edu/publications/maps/geologic/ofgm/details.cfml?Volume=37*

Blanchard, P.J., 2003, Water quality and depth to water, 2001-02, and graphs of selected constituents and depth to water, period of record through 2002, in selected wells, eastern Bernalillo County, New Mexico: U.S. Geological Survey Open-File Report 03-81, 37 p. Available online at: *http://pubs.er.usgs.gov/usgspubs/ofr/ofr0381*

Blanchard, P.J., 2004, Precipitation; groundwater age; groundwater nitrate concentrations, 1995-2002; and groundwater levels, 2002-03 in eastern Bernalillo County, New Mexico: U.S. Geological Survey Scientific Investigations Report 2004-5189, 36 p. Available online at: *http://pubs.er.usgs.gov/usgspubs/sir/sir20045189*

Blanchard, P.J., and Kues, G.E., 1999, Groundwater-quality and susceptibility of ground water to effects from domestic wastewater disposal in eastern Bernalillo County, central New Mexico, 1990-91: U.S. Geological Survey Water-Resources Investigations Report 99-4096, 109 p.

Broadhead, R.F., 1997, Subsurface geology and oil and gas potential of Estancia Basin, New Mexico: New Mexico Bureau of Mines and Mineral Resources Bulletin 157, 54 p.

Bruns, J.J., 1959, Petrology of the Tijeras greenstone: Albuquerque, University of New Mexico, M.S. thesis, 119 p.

Bryan, Kirk, 1938, Geology and ground-water conditions of the Rio Grande depression in Colorado and New Mexico in (U.S.) National Resources Committee, Regional Planning; Pt. VI, The Rio Grande Joint Investigation in the upper Rio Grande basin in Colorado, New Mexico and Texas, 1936-37: U. S. Government Printing Office, v. 1, p. 197-225.

Bullard, T.F., and Wells, S.G., 1992, Hydrology of the Middle Rio Grande from Velarde to Elephant Butte Reservoir, New Mexico: U.S. Department of Interior Fish and Wildlife Service Resource Publication 179, 51 p.

Cantor, L.W., and Knox, R.C., 1985, Septic tank system effects on ground water quality: Chelsea, Mich., Lewis Publishers, Inc., 360 p.

Caprio, E.R., 1960, Water resources of the western slopes of the Sandia Mountains, Bernalillo and Sandoval Counties, New Mexico: Albuquerque, University of New Mexico, M.S. thesis, 176 p.

Cather, S.M., 1992, Suggested revisions to the Tertiary tectonic history of north-central New Mexico, *in* Lucas, S.G. and others, eds., San Juan Basin IV: New Mexico Geological Society Annual Field Conference Guidebook, v. 43, p. 109-122.

Cather, S.M., Connell, S.D., Lucas, S.G., Picha, M.G., and Black, B.A., 2002, Geology of the Hagan 7.5-min. quadrangle, Sandoval County, New Mexico: New Mexico Bureau of Geology and Mineral Resources Open-File Geologic Map OF-GM 50, scale 1:24,000. Available online at: *http://www.geoinfo.nmt.edu/publications/maps/geologic/ofgm/details.cfml?Volume=50*

CH2M Hill, 1992a, The effect of lot sizes on potential groundwater contamination from conventional septic-tank systems-numerical modeling: Albuquerque, N. Mex., CH2M Hill.

CH2M Hill, 1992b, The delineation of crucial areas for groundwater protection in Bernalillo County: Albuquerque, N. Mex., CH2M Hill.

Clay Kilmer and Associates, Ltd., 1994, Geohydrologic report for Coyote Springs subdivision Bernalillo County, New Mexico: Albuquerque, N. Mex., Clay Kilmer and Associates, Ltd., 24 p.

Clay Kilmer and Associates, Ltd., 1995, Pinon Development Corporation Coyote Springs well nos. 1, 2 and 3 completion and testing report: Albuquerque, N. Mex., Clay Kilmer and Associates, Ltd., 16 p.

Clay Kilmer and Associates, Ltd., 1996a, Firstmark Homes Corporation geohydrologic support document for Prairie Hills subdivision, Santa Fe County, New Mexico: Albuquerque, N. Mex., Clay Kilmer and Associates, Ltd., 12 p., 1 pl. in pocket.

Clay Kilmer and Associates, Ltd., 1996b, Geohydrologic report for Caballo Grande Subdivision, Santa Fe County, New Mexico: Albuquerque, N. Mex., Clay Kilmer and Associates, Ltd.

Clay Kilmer and Associates, Ltd., 1997a, Associated Development Inc. water availability assessment for Ventana de la Sierra land division Bernalillo County, New Mexico: Albuquerque, N. Mex., Clay Kilmer and Associates, Ltd., 9 p.

Clay Kilmer and Associates, Ltd., 1997b, Geohydrologic report for Sierra Vista Subdivision (formerly Caballo Grande Subdivision) Santa Fe County, New Mexico: Albuquerque, N. Mex., Clay Kilmer and Associates, Ltd., 13 p.

Clay Kilmer and Associates, Ltd., 1997c, Water availability assessment Mountain Ranch Limited Partnership wells T. 10 N. R.8 E. and T. 11 N. R. 8 E. Santa Fe County, New Mexico: Albuquerque, N. Mex., Clay Kilmer and Associates, Ltd., 9 p.

Chudnoff, M.D., 1998a, Hydrologic evaluation of the Horton applications for permits to appropriate underground water in the Estancia Basin, New Mexico, E-2298 through E-2298-S-44 (1 and 2): New Mexico Office of the State Engineer TDHB Report 98-1, 24 p.

Chudnoff, M.D., 1998b, Hydrologic evaluation of the Entranosa Water and Wastewater Cooperative applications for permits to appropriate underground water in the Estancia Basin, New Mexico, E-6722 and E-6722-S: New Mexico Office of the State Engineer TDHB Report 98-2, 31 p., 2 plates in pocket.

Condie, C.J., Hordes, S.M., and Stout, M.K., 1987, Historic wooden water flumes in New Mexico: Quivira Research Center, 57 p.

Connell, S.D., 2001, Stratigraphy of the Albuquerque Basin, Rio Grande Rift, New Mexico-a progress report, *in* Connell, S.D., Lucas, S.G., and Love, D.W., Stratigraphy and tectonic development of the Albuquerque Basin, central Rio Grande Rift-Minipapers: New Mexico Bureau of Geology and Mineral Resources Open-File Report 454B, p. A1-A27. Available online at: *http://geoinfo.nmt.edu/publications/ openfile/downloads/OFR400-499/451-475/454/ofr_454B. pdf*

Connell, S.D., and Cather, S.M., 2001, Stratigraphy of the lower Santa Fe Group, Hagen Embayment, North Central New Mexico—Preliminary results: New Mexico Bureau of Geology and Mineral Resources Open-File Report 454B, p. H-1 to H-7.

Connell, S.D., Cather, S.M., Dunbar, N.M., McIntosh, W.C., and Peters, L., 2002, Stratigraphy of the Tanos and Blackshare Formations (lower Santa Fe Group), Hagan embayment, Rio Grande rift, New Mexico: New Mexico Geology, v. 24, no. 4, p. 107-120. Available online at: *http://geoinfo.nmt.edu/publications/periodicals/nmg/24/n4/ tanosfm.pdf*

Connell, S.D., Cather, S.M., Ilg, B., Karlstrom, K.E., Menne, B., Picha, M., Andronicus, C., Read, A.S., Bauer, P.W., and Johnson, P.S., 1995a (revised 2 July 2000), Geology of the Placitas 7.5-min. quadrangle: New Mexico Bureau of Geology and Mineral Resources, Open-File Geologic Map OF-GM 2, scale 1:24,000. Available online at: *http:// geoinfo.nmt.edu/publications/maps/geologic/ofgm/details. cfml?Volume=2*

Connell, S.D., Cather, S.M., Ilg, B., Karlstrom, K.E., Menne, B., Picha, M., Andronicus, C., Read, A.S., Bauer, P.W., and Johnson, P.S., 1995b (revised 2 July 2000), Geology of the Bernalillo 7.5-min. quadrangle: New Mexico Bureau of Geology and Mineral Resources, Open-File Geologic Map OF-GM 16, scale 1:24,000. Available online at: *http:// geoinfo.nmt.edu/publications/maps/geologic/ofgm/details. cfml?Volume=16*

Connell, S.D., Love, D.W., Lucas, S.G., Koning, D.J., Derrick, N.N., Maynard, S.R., Morgan, G.S., Jackson-Paul, P.B., and Chamberlin, Richard, 2001, Stratigraphy and tectonic development of the Albuquerque Basin, central Rio Grande Rift: New Mexico Bureau of Geology and Mineral Resources Open-File Report 454A, Field-trip guidebook for the Geological Society of America Rocky Mountain-South Central Section Meeting, Albuquerque, pre-meeting field trip, 53 p. Available online at: *http://geoinfo.nmt.edu/ publications/openfile/downloads/OFR400-499/451-475/454/ ofr_454A.pdf*

Connell, S.D., Pazzaglia, F.J., and Lucas, S.G., 1999, Albuquerque geology-Cenozoic stratigraphy, *in* Pazzaglia, F.J., Lucas, S.G., and Austin, G.S., eds., Albuquerque geology: New Mexico Geological Society Guidebook 50, p. 448.

Connell, S.D., and Wells, S.G., 1999, Pliocene and Quaternary stratigraphy, soils, and tectonic geomorphology of the northern flank of the Sandia Mountains, Albuquerque Basin, New Mexico, *in* Pazzaglia, F.J., Lucas, S.G., and Austin, G.S., eds., 1999, Albuquerque geology: New Mexico Geological Society Guidebook 50, p. 379-392.

Connolly, J.R., 1981, Geology of the Precambrian rocks of Tijeras Canyon, Bernalillo County, New Mexico: Albuquerque, University of New Mexico, M.S. thesis, 147 p.

Connolly, J.R., 1982, Structure and metamorphism in the Precambrian Cibola Gneiss and Tijeras Greenstone, Bernalillo County, New Mexico, *in* Grambling, J.A., Wells, S.G., eds., Albuquerque Country II: New Mexico Geological Society Guidebook 33, p. 197-202.

Coplen, T.B., 1993, Uses of environmental isotopes, *in* Alley, W.M., ed., Regional groundwater quality: New York, Nan Nostrand Reinhold, p. 227-254.

Corbin Consulting, Inc., 2001, Geohydrology report Shelton well (E08002) San Pedro area-North Mountain (section 34, T12N, R7E) Santa Fe County, New Mexico: Santa Fe, N. Mex., Corbin Consulting, Inc., 12 p.

Core, A.B., 1991, Evaluation of hydrologic issues related to application S-11-A into S-1532, for permit to change location of well and place of use of underground waters: New Mexico Office of the State Engineer Report, 8 p.

Craig, Harmon, 1961, Isotopic variations in meteoric waters: Science, v. 133, No. 3465, p. 1,702-1,703.

Cravens, D.L., 1995, Geohydrology investigation/pump test section 3, T9N, R6E: Albuquerque, N. Mex., Dames and Moore, Project no. 29450-001-034, 9 p.

Cravens, D.L., 1996, Geohydrological investigation, pump test and finite difference analysis, 25 acres in section 26, T10N, R4E Bernalillo County (revised): Albuquerque, N. Mex., RE/SPEC Inc., RSI Report no. 0674, 13 p.

Cravens, D.L., and Pease, R.E., 1996, Water supply investigation for Pinon Developments production well: Albuquerque, N. Mex., RE/SPEC Inc., RSI Report no. 0760, 11 p.

Daly, Christopher, 2002, A new effort to update precipitation frequency maps for the United States: *in* 13th AMS Conference on Applied Climatology, Portland, Oregon, 2002, Proceedings: American Meteorological Society, p. 197-198. Available online at: *http://www.prism.oregonstate. edu/pub/prism/docs/appclim02-pptupdate-daly.pdf*

Daly, Christopher, Neilson, R.P., and Phillips, D.L., 1994, A statistical-topographic model for mapping climatological precipitation over mountainous terrain: Journal of Applied Meteorology, v. 33, p. 140-158. Available online at: *http:// www.prism.oregonstate.edu/pub/prism/docs/jappclim94-modeling_mountain_precip-daly.pdf*

Daly, Christopher, Taylor, G.H., and Gibson, W.P., 1997, The PRISM approach to mapping precipitation and temperature: *in* 10th Conference on Applied Climatology, Reno, Nevada: American Meteorological Society, p. 10-12. Available online at: *http://www.prism.oregonstate.edu/pub/prism/ docs/appclim97-prismapproach-daly.pdf*

Daly, Christopher, and Taylor, G.H., with the Oregon Climate Service, 1998, 1961-90 mean monthly precipitation maps for the conterminous United States: accessed November 30, 2005, at: *http://www.ocs.orst.edu/prism/state_products/ maps.phtml?id=NM*

D. B. Stephens and Associates, 2003, Sangre y Jemez regional water plan, volume 1: Albuquerque, N. Mex., D.B. Stephens and Associates report for Sangre y Jemez Water Planning Council. Available online at: *http://www.dbstephens.com/ project_plans.php?plan_id=51*

DeBrine, B.E., 1971, Quantitative hydrologic study of a closed basin with a playa (Estancia Valley, New Mexico): Socorro, New Mexico Institute of Mining and Technology, Ph.D. dissertation, 165 p.

Disbrow, A.E., and Stoll, W.C., 1957, Geology of the Cerrillos area, Santa Fe County, New Mexico: New Mexico Bureau of Mines and Mineral Resources, Bulletin 48, 73 p.

Dorman, J.H., 1956, Structure of the Priest granite, Manzano Mountains, New Mexico: Evanston, Ill., Northwestern University, MS thesis,

Drakos, P., Lazarus, J., Jetter, S., and Hodgins, M., 1999, Hydrogeologic characterization of fractured Abo and Madera Formation aquifers, hydrocarbon contamination, and transport along the Zuzax Fault, Tijeras Canyon, New Mexico, *in* Pazzaglia, F.J., Lucas, S.G., and Austin, G.S., eds., Albuquerque geology: New Mexico Geological Society Guidebook 50, p. 419-424.

Duke Engineering and Services, 2001, Water supply study, Jemez y Sangre Water Planning Region, New Mexico: Albuquerque, N. Mex., Duke Engineering and Services report prepared for the Jemez y Sangre Water Planning Council.

Elston, W.E., 1967, Summary of the mineral resources of Bernalillo, Sandoval, and Santa Fe Counties, New Mexico: New Mexico Bureau of Mines and Mineral Resources Bulletin 81, 81 p.

Emerick, W.L., 1950, Geology of the Golden area, Santa Fe County, New Mexico: Albuquerque, University of New Mexico, MS thesis, 66 p.

Erskine, D.W., and Smith, G.A., 1993, Compositional characterization of volcanic products from a primarily sedimentary record: The Oligocene Espinoso Formation, north-central New Mexico: Geological Society of America Bulletin, v. 105, p. 1,214-1,222.

Estancia Basin Planning Committee, 1999, Estancia Basin recommended regional water plan (year 2000 to year 2040), 4 volumes: Santa Fe, N. Mex., variously paged. Available online at: *http://www.ose.state.nm.us/isc_regional_plans13. html*

Fallis, J.F., Jr., 1958, Geology of the Pedernal Hills area, Torrance County, New Mexico: Albuquerque, University of New Mexico, MS thesis.

Fenneman, N.M., 1931, Physiography of Western United States: New York, McGraw-Hill, 534 p., 1 pl. in pocket.

Ferguson, C.A., Osburn, G.R., and Allen, B.D., 1999, Geology of the San Pedro 7.5-min. quadrangle, Santa Fe County, New Mexico: New Mexico Bureau of Mines and Mineral Resources, Open-File Geologic Map OF-GM 29, scale 1:24,000, 7 p. Available online *http://geoinfo.nmt.edu/ publications/maps/geologic/ofgm/details.cfml?Volume=29*

Ferguson, C.A., Timmons, J.M., Pazzaglia, F.J., Karlstrom, K.E., and Osburn, G.R., Bauer, P.W., 1996 (revised: 31 August 1999), Geology of the Sandia Park 7.5-min quadrangle, New Mexico Bureau of Mines and Mineral Resources, Open-File Geologic Map OF-GM 1, scale 1:24,000. Available online at: *http://geoinfo.nmt.edu/ publications/maps/geologic/ofgm/downloads/1/Sandia_ Park_map_final.pdf*

Finch, S.T., Peery, R.L., and Shomaker, J.W., 1995, Assessment of hydrologic impacts from post-1970 mining activities, San Pedro Mine, Santa Fe County, New Mexico: Albuquerque, N. Mex., John Shomaker and Associates, Inc.

Fisch, G.S., and Porto, A.F., 1994, Visual inspection of data-does the eyeball fit the trend? *in* Rogowitz, B.E., and Allebach, J.P., Human Vision, Visual Processing, and Digital Display V : Proceedings of SPIE-The International Society for Optical Engineering, v. 2179, p. 268-276. Available online at: *http://spiedl.aip.org/getabs/servlet/Geta bsServlet?prog=normal&id=PSISDG00217900000100026 8000001&idtype=cvips&gifs=yes*

Fontes, J.-Ch., 1980, Environmental isotopes in groundwater hydrology *in* Fitz, P., and Fontes, J.-Ch., eds., Handbook of Environmental isotope geochemistry, v.1A, the terrestrial environment: Amsterdam, Elsevier, p. 75-140.

Geohydrology Associates, Inc., 1985, Aquifer-test evaluation of well S-41-enlarged Bernalillo County, New Mexico: Albuquerque, N. Mex., Geohydrology Associates, Inc., 19 p.

Geohydrology Associates, Inc., 1986, Geohydrology of the Heatherland Hills subdivision and proposed additional acreage in eastern Bernalillo County, New Mexico (appendix G): Albuquerque, N. Mex., Geohydrology Associates, Inc., 31 p.

Geohydrology Associates, Inc., 1987, Geohydrological conditions and water supply for Lomas Lindas subdivision Bernalillo County, New Mexico: Albuquerque, N. Mex,. Geohydrology Associates, Inc., 31 p.

Geohydrology Associates, Inc., 1989, Well test and aquifer assessment-Estancia Basin, New Mexico: Albuquerque, N. Mex., Geohydrology Associates, Inc., 25 p.

Geohydrology Associates, Inc., 1994, Geohydrologic conditions and water supply for Los Manzanares subdivision Bernalillo County, New Mexico: Albuquerque, N. Mex., Geohydrology Associates, Inc., 32 p., 1 appendix.

Gibbons, J.F., 1990, Tectonic disruption of Tijeras Canyon drainage [abs.]: New Mexico Geology, v. 12, no. 4, p. 93.

Gran, G., 1950, Determination of the equivalence point in potentiometric titrations: Acta Chemica Scandinavica, v. 4, p. 559-577.

Gran, G., 1952, Determination of the equivalence point in potentiometric titrations-Part II: Acta Chemica Scandinavica, v. 77, p. 661-671.

Grant, P.R., 1999, Subsurface geology and related conditions, Santa Fe embayment and contiguous areas, New Mexico, *in* Pazzaglia, F.J., Lucas, S.G., and Austin, G.S., eds., Albuquerque geology: New Mexico Geological Society Guidebook, p. 425-435.

Hall Engineering Company, Inc., 1987, Geohydrological conditions in the area of Christian Rich subdivision Bernalillo County, New Mexico: Albuquerque, Hall Engineering Company, Inc., 9 p.

Hawley, J.W., and Hernandez, J.W., 2003, A new perspective on the hydrogeologic framework and brackish-groundwater resources of the eastern Estancia Basin, central New Mexico [abs.] *in* Second New Mexico Water Symposium on Hydrologic Modeling, New Mexico Tech, August 12, 2003: Symposium Program, p. E-25.

Hayes, P.T., 1951, Geology of the pre-Cambrian rocks of the northern end of the Sandia Mountains, Bernalillo and Sandoval Counties, New Mexico: Albuquerque, University of New Mexico, M.S. thesis, 55 p.

Helsel, D.R. and Hirsch, R.M., 1992, Statistical methods in water resources: Amsterdam, Elsevier, 529 p.

Herrick, C.L., 1898, The geology of the San Pedro and Albuquerque districts: University of New Mexico Geology Series, v. 1, no. 4, p. 93-116.

Hydrotechnics, 1976, Pump test of Sierra Vista South Estates well 1 (10-5-2-141) Bernalillo County, New Mexico: Hydrotechnics, 11 p.

Jenkins, D.N., 1979, Geohydrology and long-term capability of the Entranosa Water Corporation wells near Edgewood, Santa Fe County, New Mexico: Albuquerque, N. Mex., Geohydrology Associates, Inc., 27 p., 1 pl. in pocket.

Jenkins, D.N., 1980, Geohydrology of the Abo and Madera aquifers in the vicinity of the wells of the Entranosa Water Corporation, near Edgewood, Santa Fe County, New Mexico: Albuquerque, N. Mex., Geohydrology Associates, Inc., 40 p.

John W. Shomaker, 1984, Ground water conditions, Campbell Farming Corporation lands, San Pedro Grant, New Mexico: Albuquerque, N. Mex., John W. Shomaker, 22 p., 1 pl. in pocket.

John W. Shomaker, 1985, Pump test analysis for Campbell Ranch Subdivision: Albuquerque, N. Mex., John W. Shomaker, Inc.

John W. Shomaker Inc., 1986, Estimated drawdown effects due to pumping of wells proposed by Ameriwest Corporation in Sandia underground water basin (State Engineer Office file no. S-1065): Albuquerque, N. Mex., John W. Shomaker, Inc., 29 p., 3 pls. in pocket.

John W. Shomaker Inc., 1987a, Estimated drawdown effects due to pumping of wells proposed by Ameriwest Corporation in Sandia underground water basin (State Engineer Office file no. S-1065, as revised): Albuquerque, N. Mex., John W. Shomaker, Inc., 41 p., 2 pls. in pocket.

John W. Shomaker Inc., 1987b, Estimated drawdown effects due to pumping of wells proposed by Ameriwest Corporation in Sandia underground water basin (State Engineer Office file no. S-1065, as revised and described in Supplement to Notice of Appeal): Albuquerque, N. Mex., John W. Shomaker, Inc., 41 p., 2 pls. in pocket.

John W. Shomaker Inc., 1987c, Estimated drawdown effects due to pumping of wells proposed by Ameriwest Corporation in Sandia underground water basin (State Engineer Office file no. S-1065, as revised drawdowns, all rights plus 480 afy; 28.4 afy retired at S-11, Part 1): Albuquerque, N. Mex., John W. Shomaker, Inc., no page numbers.

John W. Shomaker Inc., 1987d, Estimated drawdown effects due to pumping of wells proposed by Ameriwest Corporation in Sandia underground water basin (State Engineer Office file no. S-1065, as revised drawdowns, all rights plus 480 acre-feet per year; 28.4 acre-feet per year retired at S-11, Part 2): Albuquerque, N. Mex., John W. Shomaker, Inc., no page numbers.

John W. Shomaker Inc., 1987e, Estimated drawdown effects due to pumping of wells proposed by Ameriwest Corporation in Sandia underground water basin (State Engineer Office file no. S-1216): Albuquerque, N. Mex., John W. Shomaker, Inc., 41 p., 2 pls. in pocket.

John W. Shomaker Inc., 1987f, Estimated drawdown effects due to pumping of wells proposed by Ameriwest Corporation in Sandia underground water basin (State Engineer Office file no. S-1216 through S-1216-S-3) appendix 2, effects of existing rights: Albuquerque, N. Mex., John W. Shomaker, Inc., no page numbers.

John W. Shomaker Inc., 1987g, Estimated drawdown effects due to pumping of wells proposed by Ameriwest Corporation in Sandia underground water basin (State Engineer Office file no. S-1216 through S-1216-S-3) appendix 3, effects of existing rights plus S-1216: Albuquerque, N. Mex., John W. Shomaker, Inc., no page numbers.

John W. Shomaker Inc., [1988], Groundwater conditions in parts of sections 25 and 26, T.13N., R.4E., Sandoval County, New Mexico: Albuquerque, N. Mex., John W. Shomaker, Inc., 6 p.

John Shomaker and Associates, Inc., 1997, Regional water plan, Estancia underground water basin, New Mexico: Albuquerque, N. Mex., John Shomaker and Associates, Inc., 543 p. Available online at: *http://www.ose.state.nm.us/ water-info/NMWaterPlanning/regions/estancia/Estancia- Plan-book2.pdf*

Johnson, D.W., 1903, The geology of the Cerrillos Hills, New Mexico: Colorado School of Mines Quarterly, v. 24, p. 173- 246, 303-350, 456-500; v. 25, p. 69-68.

Johnson, P.S., 1999, A double porosity model of groundwater flow in the Madera Formation based on spring hydrographs and aquifer test analyses from Placitas, New Mexico, *in* Pazzaglia, F.J., Lucas, S.G., and Austin, G.S., eds., Albuquerque geology: New Mexico Geological Society Guidebook 50, p. 393-400.

Johnson, P.S., 2000, Phase II hydrogeologic and water resource assessment for the Placitas Development Area, Sandoval County, New Mexico: New Mexico Bureau of Mines and Mineral Resources Final Technical Report, 57 p.

Karlstrom, K.E., 1999, Southern margin of the Sandia Pluton and the "Cibola problem": New Mexico Geological Society Guidebook 50, p. 30.

Karlstrom, K.E., Connell, S.D., Ferguson, C.A., Read, A.S., Osburn, G.R., Kirby, E., Abbott, J.C., Hitchcock, C., Kelson, K.I., Noller, J., Sawyer, T., Ralser, S., Love, D.W., Nyman, M., and Bauer, P.W., 1994 (revised: 28 February 2000), Geology of the Tijeras 7.5-min. quadrangle, Bernalillo County, New Mexico: New Mexico Bureau of Geology and Mineral Resources, Open-File Geologic Map OF-GM 4, scale 1:24,000. Available online at: *http:// geoinfo.nmt.edu/publications/maps/geologic/ofgm/details. cfml?Volume=4*

Kautz, P.F., Ingersoll, R.V., Baldridge, W.S., Damon, P.E., and Shafiqullah, Muhammad, 1981, Geology of the Espinaso Formation (Oligocene), north-central New Mexico, summary: Geological Society of America Bulletin, v. 92, no. 12, p. 2,318-2,400.

Kay, B.D., 1986, Vein and breccia gold mineralization and associated igneous rocks at the Ortiz mine, New Mexico, USA: Golden, Colorado School of Mines, MS thesis, 179 p.

Kelley, V.C., 1972, Geology of the Fort Sumner sheet, New Mexico: New Mexico Bureau of Mines and Mineral Resources Bulletin 98, 55 p.

Kelley, V.C., 1978, Geology of the Espanola Basin, New Mexico: New Mexico Bureau of Mines and Mineral Resources Geologic Map 48, scale 1:125,000.

Kelley, V.C., and Northrup, S.A., 1975, Geology of Sandia Mountains and vicinity, New Mexico: New Mexico Bureau of Mines and Mineral Resources Memoir 29, 136 p., 4 pls. in pocket.

Kelson, K.I., Hitchcock, C.S., and Harrison, J.B.J., 1999, Paleoseismology of the Tijeras Fault near Golden, New Mexico, *in* Pazzaglia, F.J., Lucas, S.G., and Austin, G.S., Albuquerque geology: New Mexico Geological Society Guidebook 50, p. 201-209.

Kernodle, J.M., McAda, D.P., and Thorn, C.R., 1995, Simulation of groundwater flow in the Albuquerque Basin, central New Mexico, 1901-1994, with projections to 2020: U.S. Geological Survey Water-Resources Investigations Report 94-4251, 114 p., 1 pl.

Keyes, Eric, 2001, The Estancia Basin groundwater flow model, OSE model design and future scenarios: New Mexico Office of the State Engineer, Technical Division Hydrology Report 01-3.

Koning, D.J., Connell, S.D., Pazzaglia, F.J., and McIntosh, W.C., 2001, Stratigraphy of the Tuerto and Ancha Formations (Upper Santa Fe Group), Hagan and Santa Fe embayments, north-central New Mexico, *in* Connell, S.D., Lucas, S.G., and Love, D.W., Stratigraphy and tectonic development of the Albuquerque Basin, central Rio Grande Rift-Minipapers: New Mexico Bureau of Geology and Mineral Resources, Open-File Report 454B.

Kues, G.E., 1990, Groundwater availability and quality in eastern Bernalillo County and vicinity, central New Mexico: U.S. Geological Survey Water-Resources Investigations Report 89-4127, 82 p. Available online at: *http://pubs. er.usgs.gov/usgspubs/wri/wri894127*

Kues, G.E., and Garcia, B.M., 1995, Groundwater-quality and groundwater-level data, Bernalillo County, central New Mexico, 1990-1993: U.S. Geological Survey Open-File Report 95-385, 76 p. Available online at: *http://pubs.er.usgs. gov/usgspubs/ofr/ofr95385*

Lambert, P.W., 1961, Petrology of the Precambrian rocks of part of the Monte Largo area, New Mexico: Albuquerque, University of New Mexico, MS thesis, 108 p., 1 pl. in pocket.

LeFevre, W.J., 1999, Geochemical characterization of geologically complex mountain front aquifers-Placitas, New Mexico: New Mexico Institute of Mining and Technology, MS thesis, 209 p.

Lewis, A.C., and West, Francis, 1995, Conceptual hydrologic systems for Santa Fe County, *in* Bauer, P.W., Kues, B.S., Dunbar, N.W., Karlstrom, K.E., and Harrison, Bruce, Geology of the Santa Fe region, New Mexico: New Mexico Geological Society Guidebook 46, p. 299-306.

Lisenbee, A.L., 1976, Shale diapirism and structural development of Galisteo syncline, Santa Fe County, New Mexico, *in* Woodward, L.A. and Northrop, S.A., eds., Tectonics and mineral resources of southwestern North America: New Mexico Bureau of Mines and Mineral Resources Special Publication No. 6, p. 88-94.

Lodewick, R.B., 1960, Geology and petrology of the Tijeras gneiss, Bernalillo County, New Mexico: Albuquerque, University of New Mexico, MS thesis.

Lucas, S.G., Cather, S.M., Abbott, J.C., and Williamson, T.E., 1997, Stratigraphy and tectonic implications of lower Tertiary strata in the Laramide Galisteo basin, north-central New Mexico: New Mexico Geology, v. 19, no. 4, p. 89-95.

Lucas, S.G., and Heckert, A.B., 1995, Triassic stratigraphy around the Sandia uplift, central New Mexico, *in* Bauer, P.W., Kues, B.S., Dunbar, N.W., Karlstrom, K.E., and Harrison, Bruce, Geology of the Santa Fe region: New Mexico Geological Society Guidebook 46, p. 233-241.

Lucas, S.G., Pazzaglia, F.J., and Connell, S.D., 1999, Albuquerque geology-Paleozoic and Mesozoic stratigraphy, *in* Pazzaglia, F.J., Lucas, S.G., and Austin, G.S., eds., Albuquerque geology: New Mexico Geological Society Guidebook 50, inside back cover.

Maxey, G.B., and Eakin, T.E., 1949, Ground water in White River Valley, White Pine, Nye, and Lincoln Counties, Nevada: Nevada State Engineer Water Resources Bulletin 8, 59 p.

Maynard, S.R., 1995, Gold mineralization associated with mid-Tertiary magmatism and tectonism, Ortiz Mountains, Santa Fe County, New Mexico, *in* Bauer, P.W., Kues, B.S., Dunbar, N.W., Karlstrom, K.E., and Harrison, Bruce, eds., Geology of the Santa Fe region: New Mexico Geological Society Guidebook 46, p. 161-166.

Maynard, S.R., 2000, Geology of the Golden 7.5-min. quadrangle, Santa Fe County, New Mexico: New Mexico Bureau of Mines and Mineral Resources Open-File Geologic Map OF-GM 36, scale 1:12,000, 26. p. Available at URL: *http://geoinfo.nmt.edu/publications/maps/geologic/ofgm/details.cfml?Volume=36*

Maynard, S.R., 2005, Laccoliths of the Ortiz Porphyry Belt, Santa Fe County, New Mexico: New Mexico Geology, v. 27, no. 1, p. 3-21. Available online at: *http://geoinfo.nmt. edu/publications/periodicals/nmg/27/n1/laccoliths.pdf*

Maynard, S.R., Nelsen, C.J., Martin, K.W., and Schutz, J.L., 1990, Geology and gold mineralization of the Ortiz Mountains, Santa Fe County, New Mexico: Mining Engineering, v. 42, no. 8, p. 1,007-1,011.

Maynard, S.R., Sawyer, D.J., and Rodgers, John, 2001, Geologic map of the Madrid quadrangle, Santa Fe and Sandoval Counties, New Mexico: New Mexico Bureau of Geology and Mineral Resources Open-file Digital Map OF-DM 40, scale 1:24,000.

Maynard, S.R., Woodward, L.A., and Giles, D.L., 1991, Tectonics, intrusive rocks, and mineralization of the San Pedro-Ortiz Porphyry Belt, north-central New Mexico, in Julian, B., and Zidek, J., Field guide to geologic excursions in New Mexico and adjacent areas of Texas and Colorado: New Mexico Bureau of Mines and Mineral Resources Bulletin 137, p. 57-69.

McAda, D.P., and Barroll, Peggy, 2002, Simulation of groundwater flow in the Middle Rio Grande Basin between Cochiti and San Acacia, New Mexico: U.S. Geological Survey Water-Resources Investigations Report 02-4200, 81 p. Available online at: http://pubs.er.usgs.gov/usgspubs/wri/wri20024200

McQuillan, Denis, Doremus, Dale, and Swanson, Baird, 1988, Hydrogeologic investigation of the Carnuel Deadman's Curve site Tijeras Canyon, Bernalillo County, New Mexico: New Mexico Health and Environment Department, Environmental Improvement Division, 22 p.

McRae, O.M., 1958, Geology of the northern part of the Ortiz Mountains, Santa Fe County, New Mexico: Albuquerque, University of New Mexico, MS thesis, 112 p.

Meinzer, O.E., 1910, Preliminary report on the ground waters of Estancia Valley, New Mexico: U.S. Geological Survey Water-Supply Paper 260, 33 p. Available online at: http://pubs.er.usgs.gov/usgspubs/wsp/wsp260

Meinzer, O.E., 1911, Geology and water resources of Estancia Valley, New Mexico, with notes on ground water conditions in adjacent parts of central New Mexico: U.S. Geological Survey Water-Supply Paper 275, 89 p. Available online at: http://pubs.er.usgs.gov/usgspubs/wsp/wsp275

Metric Corporation, 1985, Well construction and aquifer testing of well S-816: Albuquerque, N. Mex., Metric Corporation, 1 p.

Middle Rio Grande Council of Governments, 2003, Population and economic data-Torrance County: accessed January 8, 2003, at: http://www.mrgcog.org/torrco.prof.html

Middle Rio Grande Water Assembly, 2004, Middle Rio Grande Regional Water Plan, 2000-2050: Albuquerque, Middle Rio Grande Water Assembly and Mid-Region Council of Governments, variously paged, plus appendices and supporting documents. Available online at: http://www.ose.state.nm.us/isc_regional_plans12.html

Milford, H.E., 1995, Mining history of the Cunningham deposit and Ortiz Mine Grant, Santa Fe County, New Mexico, in Bauer, P.W., Kues, B.S., Dunbar, N.W., Karlstrom, K.E., and Harrison, Bruce, eds., Geology of the Santa Fe region: New Mexico Geological Society Guidebook 46, p. 65-67.

Molzen-Corbin and Associates, and Lee Wilson and Associates, 1991, Bernalillo County East Mountain Area Water Feasibility Study: Final Report: Albuquerque, N. Mex., Molzen-Corbin and Associates and Lee Wilson and Associates.

Mourant, W.A., 1980, Hydrologic maps and data for Santa Fe County, New Mexico: New Mexico State Engineer Basic Data Report, 180 p.

Mueller, D. K. and Helsel, D. R., 1996, Nutrients in the nation's waters-Too much of a good thing?: U.S. Geological Survey Circular 1136, 24 p. Available online at: http://pubs.er.usgs.gov/usgspubs/cir/cir1136

Myers, D.A., 1973, The upper Paleozoic Madera Group in the Manzano Mountains, New Mexico: U.S. Geological Survey Bulletin 1372-F, 13 p. Available online at: http://pubs.er.usgs.gov/usgspubs/b/b1372F

Myers, D.A., 1988, Stratigraphic distribution of fusulinid foraminifera from the Manzano Mountains, New Mexico: U.S. Geological Survey Professional Paper 1446, 64 p. Available online at: http://pubs.er.usgs.gov/usgspubs/pp/pp1446

Myers, D.A., and McKay, E.J., 1970, Geologic map of the Mount Washington quadrangle, Bernalillo and Valencia Counties, New Mexico: U.S. Geological Survey Geologic Quadrangle Map GQ-886, 1 sheet, scale 1:24,000.

Myers, D.A., and McKay, E.J., 1971, Geologic map of the Bosque peak quadrangle, Torrance, Valencia, and Bernalillo Counties, New Mexico: U.S. Geological Survey Geologic Quadrangle Map GQ-948, 1 sheet, scale 1:24,000.

Myers, D.A., and McKay, E.J., 1976, Geologic map of the north end of the Manzano Mountains, Tijeras and Sedillo quadrangles, Bernalillo County, New Mexico: U.S. Geological Survey Map I-968, 1 sheet.

Newcomer, R.W., Jr., and Peery, R.L., 1994, Hydrogeology of proposed San Pedro Creek Estates subdivision Sandoval County, New Mexico: Albuquerque, N. Mex., John Shomaker and Associates, Inc., 16 p., 1 pl. in pocket.

New Mexico Drought Monitoring Work Group, 2006, Report on drought conditions, October 20, 2006: Governor's Drought Task Force, accessed November 3, 2006, at: *http://www.nmdrought.state.nm.us/*

New Mexico Interstate Stream Commission, 1974a, County profile Bernalillo County—water resources assessment for planning purposes: New Mexico State Engineer Office, 37 p.

New Mexico Interstate Stream Commission, 1974b, County profile Santa Fe County—water resources assessment for planning purposes: New Mexico State Engineer Office, 35 p.

New Mexico Interstate Stream Commission, 1974c, County profile Santa Fe County—water resources assessment for planning purposes, *in* Bureau of Reclamation, 1976: Santa Fe, New Mexico State Engineer Office, water resources assessment for planning purpose Supporting data, v. IV of IV, 28 p.

New Mexico Interstate Stream Commission, 1974d, County profile Torrance County—water resources assessment for planning purposes: New Mexico State Engineer Office, 29 p.

New Mexico Interstate Stream Commission, 1974e, County profile Torrance County—water resources assessment for planning purposes, *in* Bureau of Reclamation, 1976: Santa Fe, New Mexico State Engineer Office, water resources assessment for planning purpose Supporting data, v. IV of IV, 29 p.

New Mexico SSC Proposal, 1987a, Estancia Basin New Mexico superconducting super collider, v. 4, regional resources: New Mexico Office of the Governor, 259 p.

New Mexico SSC Proposal, 1987b, Estancia Basin New Mexico superconducting super collider, v. 5, Environment: New Mexico Office of the Governor, 26 p., 1 pl. in pocket.

New Mexico SSC Proposal, 1987c, Estancia Basin New Mexico superconducting super collider, v. 6, setting: New Mexico Office of the Governor, 39 p.

New Mexico SSC Proposal, 1987d, Estancia Basin New Mexico superconducting super collider, v. 7, regional conditions: New Mexico Office of the Governor, 24 p.

New Mexico SSC Proposal, 1987e, Estancia Basin New Mexico superconducting super collider, v. 8, utilities: New Mexico Office of the Governor, 32 p.

Patterson, T.C., 1979, Geohydrological conditions and potential of existing wells Sweethart Engineering and Santa Fe Builders Supply, Inc. Entranosa Water Corporation-suppliers to the proposed Steeplechase subdivision: 19 p.

Pazzaglia, F.J., Lucas, S.G., Estep, J.W., Connell, S.D., Karlstrom, K.E., Black, B.A., Smith, G.A., Hawley, J.W., Johnson, P.S., Cather, S.M., and Stearns, C.E., 1999a, First-day road log, from Albuquerque to Placitas, Hagan Basin, and Espinaso Ridge, *in* Pazzaglia, F.J., Lucas, S.G., and Austin, G.S., Albuquerque geology: New Mexico Geological Society Guidebook 50, p. 1-46.

Pazzaglia, F.J., Woodward, L.A., Lucas, S.G., Anderson, O.J., Wegmann, K.W., Estep, J.W., 1999b, Phanerozoic geologic evolution of the Albuquerque area, *in* Pazzaglia, F.J., Lucas, S.G., and Austin, G.S., Albuquerque geology: New Mexico Geological Society Guidebook 50, p. 97-114.

Pease, R.E., and Cravens, D.L., 1996a, Review and analysis of well E-4728: Albuquerque, N. Mex., RE/SPEC Inc., RSI Report no. 0736, 7 p.

Pease, R.E., and Cravens, D.L., 1996b, Review and analysis of well E-4728: Albuquerque, N. Mex., RE/SPEC Inc., Supplement to RSI Report no. 0736, 6 p.

Pease, R.E., and Cravens, D.L., 1997, Hydrogeological study of increased diversion from well S-1: Albuquerque, N. Mex., RE/SPEC Inc., RSI Report no. 0797, 14 p.

Pease, R.E., and Cravens, D.L., 1998, Hydrogeological report for Desert Mountain Estates wells 3 and 4: Albuquerque, N. Mex., RE/SPEC Inc., Addendum to RSI Report no. 0674, 10 p.

Peery, R.L., and Newcomer, R.W., Jr., 1996, Update of hydrogeologic conditions at the Campbell Farming Corporation San Pedro Creek Estates, Sandoval County, New Mexico: Albuquerque, N. Mex., John Shomaker and Associates, Inc., 16 p.

Personius, S.F., Machette, M.N., and Kelson, K.I., 1999, Quaternary faults in the Albuquerque area—an update, *in* Pazzaglia, F.J., Lucas, S.G., and Austin, G.S., Albuquerque geology: New Mexico Geological Society Guidebook 50, p. 189-200.

Peterson, J.L., 1999, Coordinated water resource planning for the Sandia Basin-A perspective into regional water planning needs: Albuquerque, University of New Mexico Water Resources Program Professional Project Report, 77 p.

Peterson, J.W., 1958, Geology of the southern part of the Ortiz Mountains, Santa Fe County, New Mexico: Albuquerque, University of New Mexico, MS thesis, 115 p.

Phillips, F.M., 1994, Environmental tracers for water movement in desert soils of the American Southwest: Soil Science Society of America Journal, v. 58, p. 15-24.

Plummer, L.N., Bexfield, L.M., Anderholm, S.K., Sanford, W.E., and Busenberg, Eurybiades, 2004, Geochemical characterization of groundwater flow in the Santa Fe Group aquifer system, Middle Rio Grande Basin, New Mexico: U.S. Geological Survey Water-Resources Investigations Report 03-4131, 395 p., CD-ROM in pocket. Available online at: *http://pubs.er.usgs.gov/pubs/wri/wri034131*

Plummer, L.N., and Busenberg, Eurybiades, 1999, Chlorofluorocarbons, *in* Cook, Peter, and Herczeg, Andrew, eds., Environmental tracers in subsurface hydrology, Chapter 15: Amsterdam, Kluwer Academic Press, p. 441-478.

Pratt, H.R., and Zbur, R.T., 1971, Geology and material properties of the Pedernal Hills test site, New Mexico: Air Force Weapons Laboratory Technical Report AFWL-TR-69-103, 78 p.

Rankin, D.R., 1996, Water-quality and groundwater-level data, Bernalillo County, central New Mexico, 1995: U.S. Geological Survey Open-File Report 96-578, 14 p. Available online at: *http://pubs.er.usgs.gov/pubs/ofr/ofr96578*

Rankin, D.R., 1999, Plan of study to define hydrogeologic characteristics of the Madera Limestone in the East Mountain area of central New Mexico: U.S. Geological Survey Open-File Report 99-201, 44 p. Available online at: *http://pubs.er.usgs.gov/pubs/ofr/ofr99201*

Rankin, D.R., 2000, Water-quality and groundwater-level trends, 1990-99, and data collected from 1995 through 1999, East Mountain area, Bernalillo County, central New Mexico: U.S. Geological Survey Open-File Report 00-476, 41 p. Available online at: *http://pubs.er.usgs.gov/pubs/ofr/ofr00476*

Read, A.S., Allen, B.D., Osburn, G.R., Ferguson, C.A., and Chamberlin, R.M., 1998, Geology of the Sedillo 7.5-min quadrangle, Bernalillo County, New Mexico: New Mexico Bureau of Mines and Mineral Resources, Open-File Geologic Map OF-GM 20, scale 1:24,000. Available online at: *http://geoinfo.nmt.edu/publications/maps/geologic/ofgm/details.cfml?Volume=20*

Read, A.S., Karlstrom, K.E., Connell, S.D., Kirby, E., Ferguson, C.A., Ilg, B., Osburn, G.R., Van Hart, D., Pazzaglia, F.J., 1995, Geology of the Sandia Crest 7.5-min quadrangle, Bernalillo and Sandoval Counties, New Mexico: New Mexico Bureau of Mines and Mineral Resources, Open-File Geologic Map OF-GM 6, scale 1:24,000. Available online at: *http://geoinfo.nmt.edu/publications/maps/geologic/ofgm/details.cfml?Volume=6*

Read, A.S., Karlstrom, K.E., and Ilg, Brad, 1999, Mississippian Del Padre Sandstone or Proterozoic quartzite?, *in* Pazzaglia, F.J., Lucas, S.G., and Austin, G.S., Albuquerque geology: New Mexico Geological Society Guidebook 50, p. 41-45.

Reiche, Parry, 1949, Geology of the Manzanita and north Manzano Mountains, New Mexico: Geological Society of America Bulletin, v. 60, no. 7, p. 1,183-1,212.

Rocky Mountain Geotech, Inc., 1989, Geohydrologic report Sunrise communities a proposed subdivision section 35 T 11 N, R 5 E: Tijeras, N. Mex., Rocky Mountain Geotech, Inc., 20 p.

Rocky Mountain Geotech, Inc., 1990, Geohydrologic report Casa Loma a proposed subdivision section 11 T 10 N, R 5 E: Tijeras, N. Mex., Rocky Mountain Geotech, Inc., 21 p.

Rocky Mountain Geotech, Inc., 2001, Documentation and support for application to change point of diversion and place and/or purpose of use from surface to groundwater: Cedar Crest, N. Mex., Rocky Mountain Geotech, Inc., 3 p., 1 pl.

Sauer, R.R., 1999, Petrochemistry and geochronology of plutons relative to tectonics in the San Pedro-Ortiz porphyry belt, New Mexico: Boulder, Colo., University of Colorado, MS thesis, 115 p.

Scanlon, B.R., 1991, Evaluation of moisture flux from chloride data in desert soils: Journal of Hydrology, v. 128, p. 137-156.

Shafike, N.G., and Flanigan, K.G., 1999, Hydrologic modeling of the Estancia Basin, New Mexico, *in* Pazzaglia, F.J., Lucas, S.G., and Austin, G.S., eds., Albuquerque geology: New Mexico Geological Society Guidebook 50, p. 409-418.

Smith, G.A., and Kuhle, A.J., 1998, Geology of the Santo Domingo Pueblo and Santo Domingo Pueblo SW 7.5-min quadrangles, Sandoval County, New Mexico: New Mexico Bureau of Mines and Mineral Resources, Open-File Geologic Map OF-GM 15 and 26, scale 1:24,000. Available online at: *http://geoinfo.nmt.edu/publications/maps/geologic/ofgm/details.cfml?Volume=15*

Smith, R.E., 1957, Geology and groundwater resources of Torrance County, New Mexico: New Mexico Bureau of Mines and Mineral Resources Groundwater Report GW-5, 186 p.

Stark, J.T., 1956, Geology of the south Manzano Mountains, New Mexico: New Mexico Bureau of Mines and Mineral Resources Bulletin 34, 46 p.

Stark, J.T., and Dapples, E.C., 1946, Geology of the Los Pinos Mountains, New Mexico: Geological Society of America Bulletin, v. 57, no. 12, p. 1,121-1,172.

Stearns, C.E., 1943, The Galisteo Formation of north-central New Mexico: Journal of Geology, v. 51, p. 301-319.

Stearns, C.E., 1953a, Early Tertiary vulcanism in the Galisteo-Tonque area, north-central New Mexico: American Journal of Science, v. 251, p. 415-452.

Stearns, C.E., 1953b, Tertiary geology of the Galisteo-Tonque area, New Mexico: Geological Society of America Bulletin, v. 64, no. 4, p. 459-508.

Stearns, C.E., 1953c, Upper Cretaceous rocks of the Galisteo-Tonque area, north-central New Mexico: American Association of Petroleum Geologists Bulletin, v. 37, no. 5, p. 961-974.

Stearns, C.E., 1979, New K-Ar dates and the late Pliocene to Holocene geomorphic history of the central Rio Grande region, New Mexico—Discussion: Geological Society of America Bulletin, pt. 1, v. 90, p. 799-800.

Summers, W.K., 1973, Pumping test data Sept. 22-28, 1973 wells E-6 (7.8.16.142) and E-20-S (7.8.9.420) Estancia Basin, Torrance County, New Mexico: Socorro, N. Mex., W.K. Summers, 6 p.

Summers, W.K., 1978, A hydrogeologic assessment of the Malela well (11N, 6E, 22, 1411): Socorro, N. Mex., W.K. Summers and Associates, Inc., 21 p.

Summers, W.K., 1981, Water wells and springs of the Ortiz Mine area, New Mexico: Albuquerque, N. Mex., W.K. Summers and Associates, Inc.

Summers, W.K., 1982, Supplement to Water wells and springs of the Ortiz Mine area, New Mexico: Albuquerque, N. Mex., W.K. Summers and Associates, Inc., 37 p.

Summers, W.K., 1984, Groundwater conditions in the feasibility-study area, Sandia Underground Basin, Bernalillo County, New Mexico; Albuquerque, N. Mex., W.K. Summers and Associates, Inc.

Thompson, T.B., 1964, The geology of the South Mountain area, Bernalillo, Sandoval, and Santa Fe Counties, New Mexico: Albuquerque, University of New Mexico, M.S. thesis, 69 p.

Thomson, Bruce, Hall, Gwinn, Stormont, John, Van Tassell, Lisa, 2000, Evaluation of onsite wastewater treatment and disposal-Volume 1, Determination of groundwater contamination and demonstration of alternative technologies: Albuquerque, University of New Mexico Department of Civil Engineering, 161 p., 1 CD in pocket.

Timmons, J.M., Karlstrom, K.E., and Kirby, E., 1995, Geology of the Monte Largo Hills area, New Mexico—Structural and metamorphic study of the eastern aureole of the Sandia Pluton, in Bauer, P.W., Kues, B.S., Dunbar, N.W., Karlstrom, K.E., and Harrison, Bruce, eds., Geology of the Santa Fe region: New Mexico Geological Society Guidebook 46, p. 227-232.

Titus, F.B., Jr., 1969, Late Tertiary and Quaternary hydrogeology of Estancia Basin, central New Mexico: Albuquerque, University of New Mexico, Ph.D. dissertation,

Titus, F.B., Jr., 1973, Hydrogeologic evaluation of Estancia Valley, a closed basin in central New Mexico: New Mexico Bureau of Mines and Mineral Resources Open-File Report OF-69, 184 p.

Titus, F.B., Jr., 1980, Ground water in the Sandia and northern Manzano Mountains, New Mexico: New Mexico Bureau of Mines and Mineral Resources, Hydrologic Report HR-5, 66 p., map in pocket.

Trauger, F.D., 1974, Geohydrologic conditions in Bachelor Draw area near Edgewood, Santa Fe County, New Mexico: Earth Environmental Consultants Inc., 20 p.

Tuan, Yi-Fu, Everard, C.E., and Widdison, J.G., 1969, The climate of New Mexico: New Mexico State Planning Office, 169 p.

Turner Environmental Consultants, 1990, (revised 1992), The geology and hydrology of eastern Bernalillo and southern Santa Fe Counties, New Mexico: Albuquerque, N. Mex., Turner Environmental Consultants, 205 p.

Turner Environmental Consultants, 1999a, 100-year water plan for the Horton Water Company- prepared for T.C. Horton Family Interests, May 31, 1999: Turner Environmental Consultants.

Turner Environmental Consultants, 1999b, Results of aquifer performance tests for selected Horton wells before and after deepening: Albuquerque, N. Mex., Turner Environmental Consultants, 6 p.

Umari, A.M.J., Martin, P.M., Schroeder, R.A., Duell, Jr., L.F.W., and Fay, R.G., 1993, Potential for groundwater contamination from movement of wastewater through the unsaturated zone, Upper Mojave River Basin, California: U.S. Geological Survey Water-Resources Investigations Report 93-4137, 117 p. Available online at: *http://pubs.er.usgs.gov/pubs/wri/wri934137*

U.S. Census Bureau, 2005, 1990 and 2000 decennial census data sets: Accessed November 30, 2005 at: *http://factfinder.census.gov/servlet/DatasetMainPageServlet?_program=DEC&_lang=en&_ts*

U.S. Department of Commerce, 2006, National Climatic Data Center, Climate Division drought data-graphing options: accessed November 3, 2006, at: *http://www.ncdc.noaa.gov/oa/climate/onlineprod/drought/xmgrg3.html*

U.S. Environmental Protection Agency, 2005, Drinking Water Contaminants and MCLs: last updated August 12, 2005, accessed December 20, 2005 at: *http://www.epa.gov/safewater/mcl.html*

U.S. Geological Survey, variously dated, Office of Ground, Water Technical Procedures: accessed December 21, 2005, at: *http://water.usgs.gov/usgs/ogw/tech_proc/index.html*

U.S. Geological Survey, variously dated, National field manual for the collection of water-quality data: U.S. Geological Survey Techniques of Water-Resources Investigations, book 9, chaps. A1-A9. (Also available online at *http://pubs.water.usgs.gov/twri9A.*)

University of New Mexico Bureau of Business and Economic Research, 2002, Perceptions of water quality and supply in the unincorporated areas of Bernalillo County: Albuquerque, University of New Mexico Bureau of Business and Economic Research, 38 p. Available online at: *http://www.bernco.gov/upload/images/environmental_health/BCWFINAL.pdf*

Walvoord, M.A., Phillips, F.M., Stonestrom, D.A., Evans, R.D., Hartsough, P.C., Newman, B.D, and Striegh, R.G., 2003, A reservoir of nitrate beneath desert soils: Science, v. 302, p. 1,021-1,024.

Watson, J.B., 1999, Supplement to hydrogeologic report for a proposed subdivision-section 13, T.9N., R.5E., Bernalillo County, New Mexico: Albuquerque, N. Mex., John Shomaker and Associates, Inc., 12 p.

Watson, J.B., and Shomaker, J.W., 1991, Hydrogeologic report for a proposed subdivision-section 13, T.9 N., R. 5 E., Bernalillo County, New Mexico: Albuquerque, N. Mex., John Shomaker, Inc., 22 p.

Wells, S.G., Appel, J.L., Hamilton, David, Homan, D.L., Madsen, David, Mortimer, Stanley, and Young, S.A., 1980, A report on the hydrogeology of the Sandia Granite aquifer in the Three Guns Canyon, New Mexico: University of New Mexico, 12 p.

Western Regional Climate Center, 2006, New Mexico climate summaries: Western Regional Climate Center, accessed August 29, 2006, at: *http://www.wrcc.dri.edu/summary/climsmnm.html.*

White, R.R., 1994, Hydrology of the Estancia Basin, central New Mexico: U.S. Geological Survey Water-Resources Investigations Report 93-4163, 83 p., 1 pl. (Also available online at *http://pubs.er.usgs.gov/pubs/wri/wri934163.*)

Whitt, Allen,1997a, Groundwater survey of the Tijeras Basin area Sandia Mountains, New Mexico: Sedona, Water Surveys Company, variously paged.

Whitt, Allen, 1997b, Preliminary study of the South Mountain area Sandia Mountains, New Mexico: Scottsdale, Water Surveys Company, variously paged.

Williams, P.L., and Cole, J.C., comps., 2007, Geologic map of the Albuquerque 30' X 60' quadrangle north-central New Mexico: U.S. Geological Survey Scientific Investigations Map 2946, scale 1:100,000.

Wilson, B.C., and Lucero, A.A., 1997, Water use by categories in New Mexico counties and river basins, and irrigated acreage in 1995: New Mexico State Engineer Office Technical Report 49, 149 p.

Wilson, B.C., Lucero, A.A., Romero, J.T., and Romero, P.J., 2003, Water use by categories in New Mexico counties and river basins, and irrigated acreage in 2000: New Mexico Office of the State Engineer Technical Report 51, 164 p.

Woodward, L.A., 1982, Tectonic framework of Albuquerque country, *in* Grambling, J.A., and Wells, S.G., eds., Albuquerque Country II: New Mexico Geological Society Guidebook 33, p. 141-145.

Woodward, L.A., 1984, Basement control of Tertiary intrusions and associated mineral deposits along Tijeras-Canoncito fault system, New Mexico: New Mexico Geology, v. 12, no. 9, p. 531-533.

Wycherley, H., Fleet, A., and Shaw, H., 1999, Some observations on the origins of large volumes of carbon dioxide accumulations in sedimentary basins: Marine and Petroleum Geology, v.16, no. 6, p. 489-494.

Appendix 1.   Description of Map Units Used on East Mountain Study Area

Description of Map Units

Map unit descriptions are summarized from descriptions in the Albuquerque 30' x 60' quadrangle (Williams and Cole, 2007) and modified to reflect general characteristics of the unit across the East Mountain study area.

RIVER ALLUVIUM OF THE RIO GRANDE

Qroc Older river alluvium (lower Pleistocene) – Light grayish-brown coarse, heterolithic bouldery gravel, and light brown to yellowish-gray sand, cobble gravel, pebbly sand, and silt; weakly cemented, moderately sorted; coarse sand deposits typically display conspicuous planar and trough cross-bedding at meter scale. Thickness highly variable, but may exceed 400 feet in total.

STREAM ALLUVIUM OF TRIBUTARY STREAMS

Qa Tributary-stream alluvium (Holocene) – Unconsolidated light brown to yellowish-brown sand, silt, and gravel beneath tributary arroyos and small alluvial fans marginal to the Rio Grande flood plain.

Qty Young tributary-stream alluvium (upper Pleistocene) – Poorly consolidated sand, silt, and gravel deposits in low terraces that flank tributary streams. In the Galisteo Creek drainage, unit consists of three strath and fill terraces about 6 to 30 feet above creek level. Unit may locally include some Holocene deposits. Thickness variable.

ALLUVIAL DEPOSITS ON ERODED SLOPES

Qay Young slope alluvium (upper Pleistocene) – Poorly consolidated deposits of light brown to yellowish-brown sand, sandy clay, and local gravel. Deposits form low-gradient alluvial slopes adjacent to flood plains of Rio Grande and major tributary drainages, and form the youngest stream channels and terraces along minor tributary valleys.

Qam Medial-age slope alluvium (middle Pleistocene) – Poorly consolidated deposits of light yellow to brown sand, silt, and local gravel that cover extensive low-gradient alluvial slopes throughout the quadrangle. Unit may locally include some upper Pleistocene deposits. In the western part of Estancia Basin, geomorphic position allows local subdivision into:

Qam2 Younger medial-age slope alluvium

Qam1 Older medial-age slope alluvium

Qao Old slope alluvium (middle to lower Pleistocene) – Moderately consolidated deposits of light to dark brown sand, silty loam, and boulder to cobble gravel.

PIEDMONT-SLOPE ALLUVIAL DEPOSITS WEST OF SANDIA CREST

Qpy Young piedmont-slope alluvium (upper Pleistocene) – Poorly consolidated deposits of sand and gravel in low geomorphic positions; contain subangular boulder and cobble gravel near Sandia Mountain front.

Qpm Medial-age piedmont-slope alluvium (middle Pleistocene) – Poorly consolidated deposits of sand and gravel in intermediate geomorphic positions; gravels contain subangular clasts near Sandia Mountain front. Unit may locally include some upper Pleistocene deposits.

Qpo Old piedmont-slope alluvium (middle to lower Pleistocene) – Moderately consolidated deposits of sand and gravel in high geomorphic positions near the Sandia Mountain front; deposits are chiefly erosional remnants inset by younger piedmont-slope units.

QTp Older piedmont-slope alluvium (lower Pleistocene to upper Pliocene?) – Light brown, red-brown, and yellowish-brown deposits of conglomerate, conglomeratic sandstone, sandstone, and minor siltstone and mudstone eroded from Sandia Mountain uplift.

MINOR SURFICIAL UNITS

Qae Eolian sand and slope-wash alluvium, undivided (Holocene to middle? Pleistocene) – Light brown, poorly consolidated sand and silt with scattered pebbles; deposits form discontinuous mantles on upland surfaces throughout the area. Soil development weak to moderate.

Qc Colluvium (Holocene to middle? Pleistocene) – Poorly sorted, unconsolidated to partly consolidated, coarse- to fine-grained, weathering debris on steep slopes.

Qac — Colluvium and alluvium, undivided (Holocene to middle? Pleistocene) – Poorly sorted, poorly consolidated mixture of sand, silt, and angular gravel derived from mass-movement slope processes and rain-wash. Commonly mixed with eolian sand and silt.

Ql — Landslide deposits (upper to lower? Pleistocene) – Poorly consolidated, very poorly sorted fine- to very coarse-grained deposits formed by mass movement processes on steep slopes.

SEDIMENTARY UNITS

Santa Fe Group – Pliocene units

[Pliocene units of the Santa Fe Group are largely coeval but differ in clast composition because these units were transported from distinct source areas; are typically interbedded where two occur together and contacts are inherently arbitrary at map scale]

Tt — Tuerto Gravel (Pliocene) – Yellowish- to reddish-brown and light red, moderately consolidated pebble to cobble conglomerate and pebbly sandstone with scattered boulders, and some interbedded silty-muddy fine sandstone; matrix of conglomerate is mostly poorly sorted fine- to coarse-grained sandstone. Base of Tuerto is a sub-regional erosion surface (Ortiz pediment surface of Bryan, 1938; lower Ortiz surface of Stearns, 1979) that was cut across Tertiary, Mesozoic, and Paleozoic rocks in and around the Ortiz Mountains. Thickness variable, but typically 40 to 100 feet in little-eroded exposures. Unit is the Tuerto Gravel of Stearns (1953a).

Santa Fe Group – Pre-Pliocene units, Hagan Basin

Tbh — Blackshare Formation (Miocene) – Pink to light-brown, fine- to coarse-grained, massive to thin-bedded sandstone with lenticular, discontinuous beds of granule to pebble conglomerate and reddish-brown mudstone. Thickness at least 1,800 feet, although top not defined (Black and others, 2000). Description based on Connell and Cather (2001) and Connell and others (2002).

Tth — Tanos Formation (lower Miocene to upper Oligocene) – Sandstone, mudstone, and conglomerate that unconformably overlie the Espinaso Formation in the Hagan Basin. Lower conglomeratic subunit consists of hornfels and porphyry clasts eroded from Ortiz Mountains. Middle mudstone-dominated subunit contains freshwater limestone beds and probably accumulated in lake environment. Upper subunit marked by tabular fluvial sandstones, which grades into overlying Blackshare Formation. Thickness about 830 feet (250m) adjacent to Espinaso Ridge on west side of Hagan Basin; description based on Connell and Cather (2001) and Connell and others (2002).

PRE-MIOCENE SEDIMENTARY UNITS

Te — Espinaso Formation (Oligocene and upper Eocene) – Gray and light-brown, andesitic-latitic, tuffaceous sandstone, volcaniclastic conglomerate, and volcanic debris-flow deposits; includes some ash-flow tuff and ash- and pumice-flow deposits. Lower part is calc-alkaline and upper part is alkaline (Erskine and Smith, 1993). Deposited around volcanic vent complexes of the Ortiz Porphyry Belt. Thickness about 1,400 feet at Espinaso Ridge (Black and others, 2000).

Tg — Galisteo Formation (Eocene) – Variegated yellow, white, and red cross-bedded arkosic sandstone and pebbly sandstone, red and green mudstone, and channel conglomerate. Pebbles and cobbles consist of quartzite, chert, limestone, granite, and sandstone eroded from Laramide fault-block uplifts and deposited in a northeast-trending basin. Thickness highly variable, but locally greater than 4,000 feet in drillholes (Cather, 1992).

Tdt — Diamond Tail Formation (lower Eocene to upper(?) Paleocene) – Yellow, orange, and gray, medium- to coarse-grained arkose and subarkose, commonly cross-bedded; with variegated gray, purplish and maroon mudstone. Thickness about 450 feet but variable (Black and others, 2000). Unit defined by Lucas and others (1997).

MESOZOIC SEDIMENTARY UNITS

Mesaverde Group

Kmv — Mesaverde Group, undivided (Upper Cretaceous) – Dark gray and olive-gray shale and light yellow and light brown sandstone; contains coal seams in upper part. Dominantly nonmarine strata. Thickness more than 1,000 feet; locally subdivided as follows:

| Kme | Menefee Formation – Gray, light brown and orange-brown sandstone with gray and olive-gray shale and coal. Thickness about 1,250 feet. |

Kmch   Medial sandstone member – Light gray and light brown medium-grained, well sorted, cross-bedded fluvial sandstone. Designated as the "Cliff House Tongue" in the Hagan Basin (Cather and others, 2002) and as "Harmon Sandstone" in the Madrid area (Maynard and others, 2001). Thickness about 330 feet.

Kpl   Point Lookout Sandstone – Light gray, light brown, and drab yellow, fine- to medium-grained sandstone with thin interbeds of gray shale. Thickness 125 to 300 feet.

Khd   Hosta Tongue of Point Lookout Sandstone and Dalton Sandstone Member, undivided – Yellow-gray and yellowish-brown, fine- to medium-grained moderately cemented sandstone with minor olive-brown shale lenses. Thickness 220 to 370 feet.

Mancos Shale

| Km | Mancos Shale, undivided (Upper Cretaceous) – Marine shale and littoral sandstones; dominantly gray to olive-gray sandy shale, yellowish sandstone, and argillaceous limestone. Major marine unit that reflects the youngest (last) marine deposition in the region. Subdivided as follows: |

| Kps | Point Lookout Sandstone (Mesaverde Group) and Satan Tongue of the Mancos Shale, undivided. |

Kmn   Niobrara Shale Member – Yellowish-brown to gray, thin-bedded sandy marine shale containing brown calcareous concretions as large as 2 feet in diameter. Total thickness of Niobrara is variable, 280 to 1,350 feet.

| Kml | Mancos Shale, lower part, undivided (Upper Cretaceous). |

| Kmd | Mancos Shale and Dakota Sandstone, undivided. |

| Kd | Dakota Sandstone, undivided (Upper Cretaceous) – yellowish-gray to yellowish-orange, fine- to medium-grained sandstone and silty sandstone with local pebble conglomerate lenses. Littoral-sand body, interbedded with variable amounts of marine Mancos Shale. Total thickness variable from 25 to 270 feet; locally subdivided as: |

| Jm | Morrison Formation, undivided (Upper Jurassic) – Gray, white, and light brown quartz-rich and arkosic sandstone with gray, green, maroon, and light brown mudstone, and minor conglomerate. Thickness about 850 feet. |

| Jmb | Brushy Basin Member – Gray, green, and maroon mudstone with minor gray and light-brown, fine- to medium-grained sandstone. Thickness about 450 feet. |

| Jms | Salt Wash(?) Member – Gray to light yellowish-brown, coarse-grained, cross-bedded fluvial sandstone with minor grayish-green and light brown mudstone, and sparse conglomerate lenses. Thickness about 200 feet. |

| Jw | Wanakah Formation (Middle Jurassic) – Light-red, fine-grained sandstone and red to greenish-gray mudstone with minor thin beds and nodules of limestone. Where possible, compiled as separate unit from Morrison Formation. Thickness about 160 feet. The Todilto member of the Wanakah Formation is white to gray gypsum and limestone about 235 feet thick. |

| Jte | Todilto Member of Wanakah Formation and Entrada Sandstone, undivided. |

| TRc | Chinle Formation (Upper Triassic) – Reddish-brown, nonmarine mudstone, reddish-brown, medium-grained sandstone with minor mudstone beds, and reddish-brown, purple, and greenish-gray mudstone with minor silty sandstone and limestone-pebble conglomerate lenses, with pervasive gypsum. Includes variegated mudstone unit correlated with Petrified Forest Member. Total thickness of Chinle is 1,200 to 1,650 feet. |

| TRs | Santa Rosa Formation (Upper Triassic) – Light gray, light brown, and reddish-brown, cross-bedded nonmarine sandstone and variegated mudstone. Equivalent to Agua Zarca Formation of Lucas and Heckert (1995). Thickness 100 to 220 feet. |

| TRcm | Chinle and Moenkopi Formations, undivided. Moenkopi Formation (Middle? and Lower Triassic) – Maroon and brown, thin- to thick-bedded, fine-grained, nonmarine, micaceous sandstone and siltstone, with minor interbedded reddish-brown mudstone. Thickness 45 to 100 feet. |

PALEOZOIC SEDIMENTARY UNITS

| Psg | San Andres Limestone and Glorieta Sandstone, undivided (Lower Permian). San Andres Limestone – Light gray and light brown, thin- to medium-bedded limestone interbedded with light gray quartz sandstone interbeds near the base. Thickness 80 to 130 feet. Glorieta Sandstone – White to light gray, thick-bedded, well indurated, medium-grained quartz sandstone. Locally includes a thin greenish-yellow silty mudstone near the top, about 3 feet thick. Total thickness 35 to 50 feet.

| Py | Yeso Formation (Lower Permian) – Light brown, very fine-grained silty gypsiferous sandstone and light-brown, light-red and gray ripple-laminated sandstone. Thickness about 175 feet.

| Pa | Abo Formation (Lower Permian) – Reddish-brown mudstone alternating with grayish-white and light-orange lenticular beds of coarse-grained conglomeratic sandstone. Thickness about 1,000 feet.

| Pya | Yeso and Abo Formations, undivided (Lower Permian).

| PPm | Madera Formation (Upper and Middle Pennsylvanian) – Gray arkosic limestone, subarkosic sandstone, and dense limestone. Thickness about 1,260 feet. Locally subdivided as:

| PPmu | Upper arkosic limestone member – Gray, greenish-gray, olive-gray, and brown limestone interbedded with layers of variegated subarkosic sandstone and mudstone. Thickness about 600 feet.

| PPml | Lower gray limestone member – Gray ledge-forming cherty limestone with thin interbeds of variegated shale. Thickness about 650 feet.

| PPs | Sandia Formation (Middle Pennsylvanian) – Interbedded brown claystone, gray limestone, and olive-brown and gray subarkosic sandstone. Thickness about 190 feet.

| Ma | Espiritu Santo Formation of the Arroyo Penasco Group (Lower Mississippian) – Green and purplish-brown sandstone and stromatolitic limestone and dolomite. Discontinuously preserved in the Sandia Mountains. Maximum total thickness about 73 feet.

PROTEROZOIC METAMORPHIC UNITS

| Xms | Metasedimentary rocks (Early Proterozoic) – Red-brown, strongly crenulated mica schist, quartz-muscovite schist, metaquartzite (some cross-bedded), and quartz-chlorite schist.

| Xmv | Metavolcanic rocks (Early Proterozoic) – Greenish-gray chlorite-amphibole phyllite and schist, gray and light green metadacite tuff, greenschist derived from basalt and andesite, and reddish-orange, banded metarhyolite.

IGNEOUS UNITS

Intrusive rocks of Ortiz porphyry belt

| Tvt | Vent breccia and tuff (Oligocene) – Lithic tuff containing abundant chips and blocks of Tertiary and Cretaceous sedimentary rocks and some igneous porphyries; location probably marks one of the sources of the Espinaso Formation volcanic rocks.

| Tl | Latite porphyry (Oligocene) – Light-gray to light-brown, feldspar-phyric latite with trachytic groundmass. Alkali feldspar phenocrysts 2 to 3 mm (2 to 3 cm in stock at Cunningham Gulch in Ortiz Mountains); groundmass contains hornblende and aegirine-augite. Typically forms stocks, plugs, and thick dikes.

| Tam | Augite monzonite (Oligocene) – Gray to dark-gray, medium-grained, equigranular to slightly porphyritic monzonite. Rock appears spotted because of orthoclase rims on andesine phenocrysts and disseminated augite, in matrix of orthoclase and minor biotite. Forms stocks in San Pedro Mountains and South Mountain.

| Tqmd | Quartz-hornblende monzodiorite (Oligocene) – Medium-gray to light-gray, hypidiomorphic-granular monzodiorite with plagioclase phenocrysts and interstitial quartz and hornblende. Forms a stock at Candelaria Mountain in San Pedro Mountains; similar bodies throughout the Ortiz Porphyry Belt.

| Tap | Andesite porphyry (Oligocene) – Grayish-green and gray intrusive rock that weathers olive- to brownish-green. Contains phenocrysts of plagioclase, hornblende, and rare quartz in aphanitic groundmass. Forms laccoliths, dikes, sills, and irregular bodies throughout the Ortiz porphyry belt.

| Tr | Rhyolite (Oligocene) – White to light-brown, aphanitic to porphyritic rhyolite; phenocrysts consist of subhedral quartz and rare biotite. Forms sills and dikes in the eastern San Pedro Mountains.

Proterozoic intrusive rocks

| Ys | Sandia Granite (Middle Proterozoic) – Pink and grayish-pink, very coarse-grained biotite monzogranite to granodiorite porphyry. Microcline phenocrysts show igneous flow-alignment. Rock contains elongate inclusions of microdiorite, fine-grained granite, and blocks of gabbro, as well as irregular xenoliths of metasedimentary and metavolcanic country rock. |

Ys — Sandia Granite (Middle Proterozoic) – Pink and grayish-pink, very coarse-grained biotite monzogranite to granodiorite porphyry. Microcline phenocrysts show igneous flow-alignment. Rock contains elongate inclusions of microdiorite, fine-grained granite, and blocks of gabbro, as well as irregular xenoliths of metasedimentary and metavolcanic country rock.

Yss — Sandia Granite, sheared – Rock within broad northeast-trending zone shows protomylonitic fabric and rounded phenocrysts.

Yfg — Fine-grained granite (Middle Proterozoic) – Pale leucogranite, probably related to Sandia Granite. Discordantly intrudes metavolcanic rocks in fault block near Monte Largo.

Xg — Granite (Early Proterozoic) – Gray and pinkish-gray, massive to foliated, leucogranite, biotite granite, and biotite monzogranite. Includes granite in the Manzanita pluton (Karlstrom and others, 1994) and foliated granite (the Cibola Gneiss of Kelly and Northrup, 1975).

Appendix 2.   Selected Data for Wells and Springs in and Adjacent to the East Mountain Study Area

Appendix 3.   Selected Groundwater-Quality Data for Wells and Springs in the East Mountain Study Area